An Introduction to Advanced Academic Argumentative Writing Approach for High School and Undergraduate Students

Dr Julius Nang Kum

Ukiyoto Publishing

All global publishing rights are held by

Ukiyoto Publishing

Published in 2024

Content Copyright © Dr Julius Nang Kum

ISBN 9789362692450

All rights reserved.
No part of this publication may be reproduced, transmitted, or stored in a retrieval system, in any form by any means, electronic, mechanical, photocopying, recording or otherwise, without the prior permission of the publisher.

The moral rights of the author have been asserted.

This is a work of fiction. Names, characters, businesses, places, events, locales, and incidents are either the products of the author's imagination or used in a fictitious manner. Any resemblance to actual persons, living or dead, or actual events is purely coincidental.

This book is sold subject to the condition that it shall not by way of trade or otherwise, be lent, resold, hired out or otherwise circulated, without the publisher's prior consent, in any form of binding or cover other than that in which it is published.

www.ukiyoto.com

Dedication

This book is dedicated to my lovely wife and children, who keep pushing me forward to bring out the best in me everyday.

Contents

Chapter One - Pragmatic knowledge for an Advanced Writer and Beyond   1

Chapter Two - Background Knowledge To The Writing Skill   46

Chapter Three - Background Knowledge To Academic Argumentative Essay   73

Chapter Four - The Introduction Part Of An Essay   98

Chapter Five - The Body Part Of An Argumentative Essay   136

Chapter Six - The Conclusion Of The Long Essay   214

References   232

Appendix 1   239

Appendix 2   248

Appendix 3   249

About the Author   *251*

Chapter One - Pragmatic knowledge for an Advanced Writer and Beyond

1.0   Introduction

After the brilliant performances at the ordinary level, some students often feel as to rest, others are often imbued with excessive confidence, excessive self satisfaction or pride to the detriment of their real capacities. These faulty self-destructive ideologies often lead to poor performances at the lower–sixth, at the upper sixth and even beyond. Using this chapter, we intend to remind our students that on the contrary more is expected from them and so they have to get up from that short period of relaxation or momentary confusion. As a student, your outstanding victory at the ordinary level suggests that you are becoming a reliable member of your family. As a future reliable member of your family in particular and the world in general, you must defend that hope till success embraces you at the end of your academic ladder. This chapter serves as a re-awakening chapter. It is a re-awakening chapter because it suggests some important characteristics of advanced writers which you may find very interesting and of great help to you and then may inspire you to get up from your slumber. As soon as you realize their realities and their importance, the chapter may motivate you to embark on real academic works to the detriment of your pride, your over self- confidence, your relaxation, and other self-destructive ideas. In fact, if you read this chapter with seriousness and hope, then you may look at things in a different way firstly at your level and secondly for the rest of your academic world. Some of the characteristics handled in this chapter include: the influence of time in your success, the differences between the real world and the academic world, the differences between practical problems and research problems, the importance of curiosity, critical thinking, tones in writing, the need for a sound knowledge of language, and computer, the negative results of plagiarism and collusion and the world of work for hardworking students. In order to facilitate understanding, these important characteristics of an advanced writer are discussed under sections in this chapter.

1.1 The Influence of Time on Students' Success

Throughout your academic ladder, you have been taught many things which have helped you to succeed at the ordinary level. However, it should be noted that amongst those most important things that helped you to succeed at the ordinary level was time. Time is so important that it determines whether a students should succeed or not, whether a student should have good grades or not, whether a student should write or not, and so on. In fact, before this lesson, many students of your age and level do not yet know in which time group they belong. However, pragmatics under chronemics teaches us that there are two time groups-monochronic and polychronic. Monochronic people, or cultures, or countries, or societies, and so on are people who do one thing at a particular time. This means that in a monochronic culture, each activity has its given or its particular time to be done. For example, people in this group have time to eat, time to sleep, time to read, time to work, time to speak, time to rest, and so on. Meanwhile in a polychronic society, or culture, people do many activities at a single moment. This suggests that people in a polychronic culture or society will want to use a single moment, to talk, to eat, to laugh, to read, to sleep, to drive and so on. As you can see, you may be in the monochronic culture or in the polychronic one. But now that you know them, it is your duty to judge which culture can easily invite success as a student. In my opinion success may easily follow a monochromic student because he or she is organized. Organized in the sense that a monochromic student knows when to read, when to play, when to talk, when to pray, where to be, how to study, and so on rather than a polychronic student who is disorganized in many aspects. Looking again at these two groups of students; one may also think that a monochronic student might be further better than the polychronic one because a monochromic student seems to respect the Holy Bible which recognizes the value of time for everything, in the book of Ecclesiastes 3:1-8. In this sense, a polychronic student seems not to know the Bible and is therefore "a Jack of all trades but master of none", which is not what this world needs for it development.

The discussion above suggests that as a student at the high school and beyond, you should be organized in order to succeed. In fact, you may be living in a polychronic culture in which many things are done at the same time. This suggests that you are a polychronic student. Now that you know these differences, we suggest that you select the better side because success in the academic world hinges on organization. An organized students means you know when to play, when to work at home, when to keep your dresses clean, when to pray, when to talk, how to talk or how to write, and so on. In other words, you have to be a monochronic person because you are living in the academic world that demands you to read a lot. We cannot remember the number of our students, friends or relatives who were very intelligent but failed in their academic career because of their inability to manage time. In fact the time for them to read was the very same time they had to attend students' meetings, it was the same time they had to sleep, the very same time they had to learn how to sing in social meetings and so on. In fact they ended up knowing many people and places to the detriment of their studies. As you will observe in the next section below, you are operating in an academic world, which is very different from the real world. The ability to manage your time very well is very importance because it orientates you toward a sense of direction, it open doors for specialization, it instills humility in you and it drives away regrets in the nearest future. Now that you are orientated toward the academic world, it is very necessary for you to know the difference between the real world and the academic world in which you belong for you to see the necessity to be organized for a genuine victory in life.

1.2 The Real World and the Academic World

At the outset, it is worth mentioning that many people in general and students in particular have misfired because they do not know that two worlds exist - the Real World and the Academic World. This state of ignorance compels students to operate with the same energy in both worlds, which often leads to devastating consequences. The main difference between the real world and the academic world can be read from Levin (2004) quoted by Macgibbon () thus:

The real world is where we experience our lives we live and works, raise children, play or watch sport, spend time with family and friends and interact with the natural world. A lot of what we know about the real world is from our experiences.

The academic world on the other hand is one of theories, explanations, ideas and critiques. We can't experience them the same way as we experience the real world, through seeing, hearing, touching, tasting, smelling. In the academic world we learn from what is spoken, or more often written, about the world. This means that in the academic world you learn at second hand, from what other people have written, rather than from your own experience.

The scholar above tells us that in the real world; we know things through our experiences, which include seeing, hearing, touching, tasting and smelling. As you can observe, the real world is common to every human being irrespective of age, sex, religion, color, nationality etc. because illiterates, literates, children, girls, boys, whites, blacks etc. can hear, see, touch, taste and smell. In fact, all human beings including animals, plants and minerals live in the real world. Talking about the academic world, the writer above explains that it is reserve for a special people because those special people or students in the academic world know things "at second hand". This means that in the academic world, the special people rely more on what other people saw, heard, tasted, touched and smelt billions of years before they were born. As a student, you are aspiring to be a member of the special group found in the academic world. This means you have to be initiated into the nature of the academic world by others intellectuals in general and this study in particular. As already suggested above, people in the academic world are the owners of the world because they know the world from the experiences of their ancestors in different parts of the world to the present and can even predict the future. In the academic world you read how the world was formed, how early man lived, how the generation that followed early man lived, what they saw, what they ate, how they felt, what they heard etc. With these experiences, the people of the academic world can now compare the past world or past experiences with their present world or present experiences, in order to understand better the changes that have occurred and how the future can be predicted. The knowledge we acquire in the academic world comes to us through two ways- through what other people spoke (spoken form) and in most cases through what they wrote (written form). In this light, an educated person must live in the academic world in which he or she acquires knowledge by listening or by reading a lot. For example, for us to truly know what happened during the periods of the Early man, the Egyptian, the Mesopotamian, the Greek, the Roman, the Chinese civilizations, the Empires of Ghana, Mali, Songhai, or what Socrates, Plato, Aristotle and so on, did, saw, felt, touched and so on, we must read a lot because in those days, the tape recorders were not yet invented to record their voices, but the act of writing was already invented before then and they wrote down many things.

To our students, as we have already mentioned above, the academic world enables us to learn "at second hand". This phenomenon of educated people learning at second hand was well articulated by Sir Isaac Newton (1642-1727). In one of his writings, Sir Isaac Newton made the world to know that his success in academic or research stemmed from the fact that he had been "standing on the shoulders of Giants". McKay, Hull and Buckler, (1983:635) report:

With a charming combination of modesty and self-congratulation, Newton once wrote: "If I have seen further (than others), it is by standing on the shoulders of Giants". Surely the path from Copernicus to Newton confirms the "internal" view of the scientific revolution as first of all, a product of towering individual genius.

In the citation above, Sir Isaac Newton attests to the fact that his greatness in academics comes from the reading of previous works of great scientists such as Copernicus, in other words he was standing on the works of intellectuals. This characteristic of the academic world is so important that very few persons if not, none succeeds in academics without second hand learning. For example we know of the Atomic theories because Newton experienced it, which means Newton was the first person or one of the earliest intellectuals to experience the atomic nature and then he proposed a theory for it. We are learning it at the second position to either perfect or condemn what Newton experienced. By drawing a lot of inspiration from Newton and even from other scientists before him, we in the academic world now have an idea of the existence of an atom, and better still we now have a complete or detailed nature of the atom. We can now add our experiences on the experiences of the other scientists before or after

Newton on the atomic nature and have a complete life of the atom in our hands. But if we were to rely only on our experiences like those in the real world then we might not even know if something exists like an atom. This reminds us that the real world is momentary and limited whereas the academic world is broad and progressive. As you can see there are many examples in different fields of studies. For example in Chemistry, we know about chlorine because Aston invented a machine for this, in History we know of the Reformation because Martin Luther criticized the church, etc. In fact we learn these things "at second hand" because the first persons who experienced them have died but made us to know these things because they wrote them down, so we are just second people to know or learn them. That is the nature of the academic world.

The main difference between you who is an educated person and your illiterate grandfather in the village is that you depend a lot on other people's knowledge, skills, theories that were experienced many years before you were born, which has increased your knowledge of the world through reading (Academic World), and your illiterate grandfather depends much on his personal experiences that are very limited because his experiences depends on what he sees, feels, do, smells, touches and hears (Real World). Another good example of the life of the academic world was illustrated by an illustrious citizen of this world, Abraham Lincoln. According to Naija Book Club, Abraham Lincoln once said "All I have learned, I learned from books". If we can imagine the greatness of President Abraham Lincoln in the History of USA in particular and that of the world in general then the academic world is an exceptional world that harbors or transform great and educated person. Since great or educated persons live mostly in the academic world, great or educated persons must develop the skills to read, to write, to listen, and to speak fluently for them to understand better the experiences of their ancestors, then their own experiences, and later the experiences of their future generations. It is only through broad reading that great or educated person can know or learn much about the world, and then add their own experiences through research or other ways. In order to add to their knowledge, educated persons evaluate, analyze, synthesize, judge, argue, compare, discuss, carry out research, and so on. All these demand a sound knowledge of critical thinking and the argumentative skills. In addition to the main difference stated above between the real world and the academic world, Raita () highlights some other differences thus;

Objective not subjective

Intellectual not emotional

Serious not conversational

Impersonal not personal

Formal rather than colloquial.

From the above illustrations, we suggest that the qualities found on the left side remind us of an academic world and those on the right stand for the real world. As an educated person you might use the tool of curiosity to investigate the real differences between each pair above in order to deepen your understanding. In fact we are suggesting that the academic world belongs to educated persons and demands a lot of reading. So if you think you might be looked upon as an educated person one day, then you must read broadly in order to gain much knowledge at the second hand in your field of study. Now that we have highlighted the world of an educated person, the discussion below focuses on the world of problem solving.

1.3 The World of Practical Problems and the World of Research Problems

In the discussion above, we have observed that students are supposed to live in the academic world that demands them to learn more at second hand. This means students are compelled to read broadly in whatever fields they are found and even beyond. Intensive and broad reading suggests that students are researchers. At this level, students should know that there are two types of problems: a practical problem and a research problem. Talking about the nature of each of the problems, Booth et al. (1995, 2003) say:

• A practical problem is caused by some condition in the world, from e-mail spam to terrorism, that makes us unhappy because it costs us time, money, respect, security, pain, even our lives. You solve a practical problem by doing something that changes the world by eliminating the causes that lead to its costs, or by encouraging others to do so.

• A research problem is motivated not by palpable unhappiness, but by incomplete knowledge or flawed understanding. You solve it not by changing the world but by understanding it better.

Looking at the citation above, we realize that a practical problem is that problem which makes us to be unhappy, to be traumatized, to be afraid, to be angry, to be ashamed, and so on. In normal life, many decent people, if not all, truly hate practical problems because these problems can bring death, can bring disgrace, can cost much money, can reduce our dignity, can cause people to be exiled, or killed, can put us into prison, can bring pains and suffering, can bring our schooling to an end, and so on. Due to the negative consequences of practical problems, most people avoid them with vigor. So as a student, you must run away from these types of problems because they may distort your prospects to a dignified life.

The second type of problems mentioned in the citation above is research problems. Unlike the practical problems that are hated by most or everybody, research problems are admired by scholars or educated people. In fact, the academic world appreciates and promotes those scholars, those educated persons or those researchers who are capable of identifying many research problems, even if they solve them or not. Research problems are caused by limited knowledge about a thing, ignorance about its existence, or inability to solve a problem or to cure an illness. Research problems enable intellectuals to promote knowledge, to increase knowledge, to add knowledge, to discover knowledge, and so on. As you can see, because students are in the academic world, they must be trained to know the nature of a research problem, its definition, where to find it, how to solve it, its origin, and so on. In order to attain these stages, students are demanded to be curious, to be critical, to read intensively, to read to understand, to attend certain conferences, to be honest, to avoid practical problems, to respect everything, let alone everybody they meet, and so on. These values are very important because they are sources of wisdom and success. Due to the importance of the values cited above for the identification of research problems the next section examines curiosity, which is an important tool for the identification of a research problem and for a successful student at your level.

1.4 Curiosity

Curiosity has two concepts- a negative concept and the positive one. In the negative sense, there is this popular notion that curiosity pushed the ever first human being to sin against God. In fact, Adam and Eve were pushed by curiosity to know why and what God was hiding from them in a fruit or a tree in the Garden of Eden (see the book of Genesis in the Bible). Considering the fact that curiosity caused Adam and Eve to disobey God by touching, let alone by tasting the forbidden fruit in the Garden of Eden, many religious authorities such as Saint Augustine condemned curiosity as an evil or an illness (Bineth, 2020). However, on the positive notion, many intellectuals think that whatever God created was meant for man to understand it, because man is God's image on earth. For example Robert Boyle (1772:13) in Bineth (2020:9) says: "whatever God himself has been pleased to think worthy of his making, its fellow-creature man should not think unworthy of his knowing". So some scholars think that curiosity was created by God to enable mankind to understand him. If curiosity was the first concept to anger God and that our suffering on earth is due to curiosity, then we must handle curiosity with proper understanding. Talking from an intellectual perspective and not from a religious angle, we may say that curiosity is the most powerful tool for knowledge awareness because God, who created mankind in his own image, who controls and determines everything for an ignorant mankind, who is the Alpha and the Omega, used curiosity to cause mankind to sin against him, and to be driven out of the Garden of Paradise into this suffering world. From the suffering on earth, the same Almighty God uses the same curiosity again to empowered mankind to improve on the life on earth for them to reduce the suffering through scientific observations and inventions. For example mankind has invented cars, ships, planes to reduce or solve the suffering of trekking or swimming for long distances on earth before reaching other people. In order to achieve his goals, the Almighty God sent sound intelligent minds like the Socrates, Plato, and Aristotle etc. to initiate the idea of inadequacy of this world thereby provoking the spirit of critical thinking for a constant change or improvement on earth. God uses curiosity to push mankind to work constantly because curiosity demands constant desire for knowledge. In view of the importance of curiosity, much is needed to understand this treasure. Again much cannot be said about curiosity in this study due to its nature, but we suggest that our students dedicate some vital moments in their lives to know what curiosity is all about for their intellectual greatness. At our level, curiosity is therefore defined as a need, thirst or desire for knowledge. Curiosity was identified and defined since the periods of the ancient Greek philosophers. Loewenstein (1994:76) states:

Since the identification of curiosity by ancient philosophers, intellectuals in many generations have worked a lot to understand in details the nature of curiosity. However, talking about the definition of curiosity, Whitecomb (2010:6) explains:

Curiosity is a desire for knowledge, not in that its contents always involve some concept of knowledge, but instead in that it comes to be satisfied iff you come to know the answer to the question that is its content. Curiosity is thus satisfied by knowledge alone, in the same way hunger is satisfied by nourishment alone. In each case there is a state and a desire, such that the desire comes to be satisfied iff you come to be in the state. When states are in this way related to desires, I'll call those states the "unique satisfiers" of those desires. Nourishment is the unique satisfier of hunger, and knowledge is the unique satisfier of curiosity.

First, curiosity was seen as an intrinsically motivated desire for information. Aristotle, for example, commented that men study science for intrinsic reasons and "not for any utilitarian end" (Posnock, 1991, p. 40), and Cicero referred to curiosity as an "innate love of learning and of knowledge . . . *without the lure of any profit* [italics added]" (1914, p. 48). Although they acknowledged that information was also desired for extrinsic reasons, these early thinkers drew a sharp distinction between such an extrinsically motivated desire for information and curiosity.[3]

The most important message we learn from the citation above is "Nourishment is the unique satisfier of hunger, and knowledge is the unique satisfier of curiosity". The importance of hunger on earth cannot be explained because even foetus that are still in mothers' wombs feel and know what hunger is all about. So if anything can be likened to hunger then we must know the important position it occupies in our society. For example, in the discussion above, curiosity is likened to hunger. We learn that food is to hunger just as knowledge is to curiosity. This suggests that hunger and curiosity are some of the most important feelings that rule the world. We must eat in other to survive and we must search for knowledge in order to improve for the best. Beside the knowledge we have acquired above on curiosity, there is another explanation from Sarukkai (2009:760) thus:

Curiosity is seen to be the catalyst that creates knowledge. Because we are curious, we think. Because we are dissatisfied with the answers we get, we come up with new ways of thinking. Because we are curious, we discover methods. We discover science. We can distinguish – loosely – different types of curiosity. We may be curious about what something is – for example, I see an object I have not seen before and I am curious to know 'what' the object is. We are curious to know why something is the case – why is the sky blue? Why the neighbour's door is locked all the time? We are curious about how something works. Experimental science is based so much on the character of curiosity – our first engagement with tools and technological objects is often one of curiosity.

You don't need to be a psychologist or a philosopher or a linguist, etc. to understand the meaning of curiosity as stated above. Curiosity is found in all active human beings irrespective of sex, age, color, religion, race, country, tribe, ethnic group and so on. The fact that curiosity is found in everybody including animals does not mean that curiosity is seen in everybody or in all animals. www.posproject.org | ©2016 The Positivity Project explains:

Curiosity is a crucial component of one's character. Our innate urge for discovery and exploration is a key element of our human desire for wisdom and knowledge. It's what keeps us intrigued in the plotlines of movies and books. It's what pushes us to try new activities or travel to different places. All individuals experience curiosity, but differ in their willingness to experience it – behaviorally, intellectually, and emotionally.

The citation above is very important because it suggests the manner in which curiosity manifest itself in different individuals. In the citation above we learn that "All individuals experience curiosity, but differ in their willingness to experience it – behaviorally, intellectually, and emotionally". As we have seen so far, everybody has curiosity, but it is the willingness to develop it in us that differentiate one individual from another. Some individuals due to religious inclinations might not want to look into other people's joy, problems, activities, beliefs, sexual orientations, speeches, dressings or the dangerous scientific inventions of this earth because these things are against their religion. People of this way of life might develop low curiosity towards all these contradictory things. Others because of culture might tend to hate certain things and develop no curiosity in them. Many, due to ignorance, laziness, up-bringing, health, occupation, etc. might never develop curiosity in one thing or the other. Most girls or women think that they can use some parts of their body to arouse emotional curiosity in men. For example, some expose their thighs, other expose their breasts, many expose their hair, their legs, etc., yet some men due to religion, fear, self-control, culture, color are not moved by any of these exposures. In fact they develop very low curiosity towards them. These are some of the complex and unpredictable characteristics of curiosity. The treasure, the unpredictable, and the complex nature of curiosity have caused many scholars to misinterpret it. For example, many years ago Aristotle condemned curiosity as an erratic nosiness, whereas Saint Augustine likened curiosity to an illness because it caused Adam and Eve to sin against God. Bineth (2020:8-9) reports:

If the capability to create knowledge is what makes us human, then curiosity – this carnal desire to know – must be a characteristic equally central to our identity. However, this perspective of curiosity is quite recent considering the records of history. In fact, for the greater part of recorded history, at least until the 17th century, curiosity was not a trait held in high regard (Daston and Park 1998). Often curiositas (from the Latin cura to care) was understood as something close to prying into matters one had no business with. Contrary what his oft-cited quote suggests, Aristotle thought that curiosity (periergia) has a negligible role to play in philosophy, as he understood it as an erratic nosiness, rather, he thought it was the sense of wonder (thauma) which inspired one to seek knowledge consistently. The influential Christian philosopher, Saint Augustine saw curiosity as a "malady" (morbo) which drove the folly off the path of faith and into the ungodly matters of magical arts (Saint Augustine [ca. 400]1982:55).

Based on the citation above, we observe that Aristotle condemned curiosity as a way of poking or sticking our noses into people's lives. , Saint Augustine saw curiosity as a "malady", nowadays, some genders especially the female gender looks upon curiosity as interest, but majority of educated persons in the academic society look upon curiosity as a desire or thirst for knowledge. All these opinions only demonstrate the misinterpretations given to curiosity by mankind. Aristotle looked upon wonder as the appropriate inspiration for knowledge acquisition instead of curiosity. Due to the confusion between curiosity and other feelings as seen above, the discussion below highlights some differences between curiosity and wonder, curiosity and doubt, and curiosity and interest.

Curiosity versus Wonder

From the explanations given so far, we have seen the complex nature of curiosity in relationship to other feelings. In our search to isolate curiosity, we now turn to the distinction between curiosity and wonder. Torbjörn (2021) gives the distinction between curiosity and wonder thus:

Whereas wonder is a mode of attention that ultimately seeks repose in the object itself as an image of beauty and truth or as a haven from worldly distress, curiosity is a mode in which we search out concrete, earthly matters, always in search for the next novelty. Restless and insatiable, it exemplifies humankind's desolate isolation from its divine origins as well as its self-divinization. This is obvious from the complex history of curiosity in modernity, where it has been denigrated as a sinful poking into others' business, and a dangerous search for the secrets of creation, and hailed as the primary mode of attention of modern sciences. Just like wonder, curiosity is associated with transgressions of borders, and the upsetting of established identities and categories (Benedict 2001, 4, 254). As such, this mode of attention has become intrinsic to explorations of the world; children's first encounter with nature's marvels is a conventional image of curiosity that both scientists and artists refer to (Fuller 2012

Based on the citation above, wonder is a feeling that comes from anything that might be extremely beautiful, interesting, ugly, hard, easy, colored, short, tall, long, fat etc. But as we can see, wonder is not curiosity because, for example, after the feelings of wonder on that extremely beautiful lady or so, many men might not develop the desire to know more about the magnificent lady. In other words, this group of men though marveled by the lady's beauty has no desire to know more about the extremely beautiful lady. In this case, there is only wonder and no desire in that extremely beautiful lady. On the contrary, the other group of men who might be carried away by the lady's beauty and then develops that mind to investigate more about the beautiful lady are been driven by curiosity. We can then suggest that wonders can cause curiosity or not. So wonder is just a part of curiosity. The next feeling to discuss below is doubt.

Curiosity versus Doubt

Considering the fact that the distinction between curiosity and wonder has been established above, we now focus our attention to the distinction between the feeling of curiosity and the one of doubt. This is very important because many students encounter some difficulties to distinguish the feeling of curiosity from the feelings of doubt. According to Sarukkai (2009:760) the distinction between curiosity and doubts go thus:

Curiosity is often seen as being synonymous with the questioning attitude. Here it is worthwhile to distinguish between curiosity and doubt. Doubt is an epistemological term – it is derivative to something more basic such as perception11. I see an object which looks like a man but because it is some distance away I am not sure whether it is a tree or whether it could be a tall man. This creates doubt in me and I have a question concerning that doubt. Doubt also can be classified into types of doubt – like curiosity, we have doubt about what something is, why something is the case, how something works and so on. But doubt is not a human trait that is basic in the way curiosity is seen to be. It is not because we doubt that we ask these questions –

doubt is based on some judgements we make about our perception and inference. But doubt, like curiosity, is what leads us to questions and also to knowledge. However, curiosity is a psychological act and not an epistemological one. That is, curiosity is 'biological' – the fact that some people are more curious than others is like saying some people have better eyesight than others. But all have eyesight and all of us have the capacity for curiosity. Doubt is a higher order term in this sense.

The explanation above has revealed a detailed distinction between curiosity and doubt. The key thing we learn is that doubt is linked to knowledge, and curiosity has much to do with feeling or psychology. In their different positions, doubt can influence curiosity or not because when you doubt somebody or something, you either abandon him, her or it or you develop much desire to know more about that person or thing. But when you are curious about a person or thing you must develop a lot of doubt on the person or that thing by asking many questioning about the character, level of education etc. As we can see so far, doubt is still parts of curiosity. With the relation between curiosity and doubt already highlighted, we now look at curiosity and interest.

Curiosity and Interest

In the discussion above, curiosity has been examined in relation to doubt and wonder. This section contrast curiosity with interest. Interest is closely linked to curiosity in meaning so much so that some students think curiosity is synonymous to interest. Their differences are highlighted by Xin Tang[1], K. Ann Renninger[2], Suzanne E. Hidi[3], Kou Murayama[4], Jari Lavonen[1], Katariina Salmela-Aro[1] thus:

Across the studies, we found consistent differences between the feelings associated with curiosity and those associated with interest. While the feelings of curiosity reflected feelings of inquisitiveness and eagerness to know more, the feelings of interest were aligned with positive affect such as enjoyment and happiness. Importantly, an asymmetrical pattern was found in curiosity-interest co-occurrences: when the feelings of curiosity occurred, the co-occurrence of the feelings of interest was highly likely, but not so vice versa. That is, when the feelings of interest occurred, the feelings of curiosity did not always co-occur.

From the discussion above, we observe that interest has much to do with the feeling of joy, happiness, excitement etc. This suggests that Interest is a subset of curiosity. In other words, like the feeling of wonder and doubt discussed above, interest is just part of curiosity. Curiosity as we have examined above is that powerful tool that urges us to go for more knowledge. It can be provoked by the feeling of wonder, by doubt, by interest, and so on. Curiosity is that tool used by our Creator to push us out of the Garden of Paradise ,he uses the same tool to enable us to overcome the problems of this earth through constant hardwork or a longing to perfect our lives or relations, before we come back to him in paradise. In the subsequent discussions below we will examine the types of curiosities and their causes.

Types of Curiosity

Much has been said on curiosity above. This section highlights the various curiosities known by researchers. RSA SOCIAL BRAIN CENTRE (2012: 35-36) says:

On one axis lies **Epistemic curiosity**, which is the desire for information and knowledge, and **Perceptual curiosity**, which describes one's attention to novel objects in their immediate environment. The other axis runs from **Specific curiosity**, which is the desire for a particular piece of knowledge such as the final piece of a puzzle, to **Diversive curiosity**, which is less directed and would describe seeking stimulation to escape boredom or when ready to grow. It is important to grasp that these contrasts are not zero-sum, and one can grow in epistemic curiosity without losing perceptual curiosity, and, as we will show, it is possible, indeed desirable to have both convergent (specific curiosity) and divergent (diversive curiosity) thinking for innovative solutions to emerge.

The citation above has highlighted some basic kinds of curiosities- epistemic curiosity, perceptual curiosity, specific curiosity and diversive curiosity, Besides the discussion above,let read To et al ()

Empirical work on curiosity has further shown that curiosity is not unitary, but can in fact be conceived of in the following five key types: (1) perceptual curiosity, categorized by increased attention to novel stimuli, (2) manipulatory curiosity, categorized by the feeling experienced while encountering a manually explorable object, (3) curiosity about the complex or ambiguous, categorized by the preference for interacting with more intricate stimuli (4) conceptual curiosity, categorized by active information seeking about concepts behind things and (5) adjustive-reactive curiosity, that just describes how people explore novel environments. In the following section we will review empirical work on

As already mentioned above, much about curiosity cannot be handle in this work and at this level. The citation above has identified some five types of curiosities. The great importance of the tool of curiosity might push many of you to verify in greater details the types and even add more. The next section below highlights causes of curiosity.

Causes of curiosity

There is no single stimulus for curiosity. The need, thirst or desire for knowledge can be stimulated by different things in different people. However, the various causes below can be read in Dubey et al. thus:

Curiosity based on novelty.

New and unusual things, ideas, people, situations, phenomena, inventions etc. can arouse curiosity. For example a new teacher in a class or a new toy to a child can arouse the curiosity of a child. Talking about Curiosity based on novelty, Dubey et al say:

Several psychological theories have linked curiosity with novelty by hypothesizing that gaining information about novel stimuli is intrinsically rewarding (Berlyne, 1950). Berlyne described this as a driving force that motivates an organism to seek out novel stimuli which diminishes with an increase in exposure.

The first cause of curiosity in this study is novelty or simply known as newness. Many things, people, ideas, feelings, stories, etc. that are new always arouse curiosity. You can list everything that newly appeared to you and the feelings of wonder, interest, excitement etc. that you experienced. That desire which pushed you to look at the new thing or idea etc. for some time because of its newness is what we might call curiosity. The next idea that causes curiosity is known as Information-gap hypothesis.

Information-gap hypothesis

This type of curiosity is cause by Suspense. This is a situation in which people start listening to a story or an event and in the middle of the story, the story stops without reaching the end. The urge to know the end or the final stage of an event, a situation is known as information-gap hypothesis which causes curiosity. In explaining Information-gap hypothesis Dubey et al say:

One such theory is Loewenstein's information-gap hypothesis (Loewenstein, 1994) which proposes that curiosity arises whenever an individual has a gap in information prompting it to complete its knowledge and resolve the uncertainty.

Many intellectuals have exploited this cause of curiosity in films or movies, in stories, in speeches etc. To promote, initiate or understand the level of curiosity people have in films, stories, speeches, lectures, activities, and so on, intellectuals always start the project and at the middle of the project, they deliberately stop it without reaching the natural end of the story or project. That feeling in people to see or listen or know the end of the project or the film or story is known as information-gap and it is an important cause of curiosity. Besides the novelty and information-gap that can cause curiosity, moderately difficult tasks can also cause curiosity.

Curiosity is highest for moderately difficult tasks.

There are many people whose curiosities are aroused by difficult tasks. These persons find it very rewarding to solve problems that are beyond the reach of the common man. They know that by so doing, they will earn more internal satisfaction or achievement and more respect, more admiration, more love, and so on, from their fellow human beings. Dubey et al explain:

In recent years, researchers have also studied the influence of task difficulty on curiosity (Baranes et al., 2014; Geana et al., 2016). Similar to the effect of uncertainty, these studies demonstrate that in the absence of any external rewards, people prefer to spend most time exploring tasks that are moderately difficult. This finding is in accordance with complexity-based theories such as the learning-progress hypothesis but not novelty-based theories.

As you have read above, many students sometimes are pushed to study things that are very complex to understand by the common man on street. They might want to solve the difficult task to help other people or to satisfy their desire. This then suggests that tasks that are difficult can instead arouse the curiosities of some strong people and instead scare away those people that are weak. This means that difficult tasks can arouse curiosity. The last cause of curiosity in this study is the learning-progress hypothesis.

The learning-progress hypothesis

Success in learning has aroused curiosity in many people. In fact, students as well as teachers have attested to the fact that their success in learning has helped them to develop much curiosity in certain fields. This type of stimulant has been explained by Dubey et al thus:

Another recent theory based on the idea of stimulus complexity is the learning-progress hypothesis which proposes to model optimal incongruity via prediction errors. According to the learning progress hypothesis, curiosity is guided by the hypothesis that learning progress generates intrinsic reward (Schmidhuber, 1991, 2010; Oudeyer et al., 2007). This hypothesis proposes that the brain is intrinsically motivated to pursue tasks in which one's predictions are always improving. Thus, an individual will not be interested in tasks that are too easy or too difficult to predict but will rather focus on tasks that are learnable

We do not need to be specialists in the study of curiosity to know that the more we are succeeding in whatever thing we do, the more interest, the more love, the more desire we develop in that thing. This suggests that more success in anything that we do can cause curiosity. Talking about the causes of curiosity, we have illustrated four from books we read. As we have highlighted above, there are many causes of curiosity such as surprise, contradictions, uncertainty, and so on. It is your duty to read more books or examine yourself and identify some of the things that cause you to be curious. To still highlight the importance of curiosity, the discussion below focuses on some few citations on curiosity.

Quotations on Curiosity

The importance of curiosity in the creation of an intellectual can be seen from the citation of highly respected intellectuals like Einstein. Some citations on the importance of curiosity can be read from Donald Latumahina, thus:

Intellectual curiosity is so important! We see that most clearly in how it manifests itself in geniuses. Intellectual giant are always curious persons. For example, Thomas Edison, Leonardo da Vinci, Albert Einstein, Richard Feynman are all curious characters. Richard Feynman was especially known for his adventures which came from his curiosity. Curiosity is not only important for those with high IQs. Successful students (and people who are successful after college) often display a good measure of intellectual curiosity.

The important thing is not to stop questioning... Never lose a holy curiosity. Albert Einstein

"Curiosity is the very basis of education and if you tell me that curiosity killed the cat, I say only the cat died nobly." MonaR119 Arnold Edinborough

"When you're curious, you find lots of interesting things to do." Walt Disney

"We keep moving forward, opening new doors, and doing new things, because we're curious and curiosity keeps leading us down new paths." Walt Disney

"Curiosity is as much the parent of attention, as attention is of memory." Richard Whately

Besides the discussion above, there are other citations on the importance of curiosity that can be read from Rsa Social Brain Centre (2012) thus:

"Curiosity is not an only child; it is part of a family of terms used by writers, scientists, and everyday people making conversation to capture the essence of recognising, seeking out, and showing a preference for the new." Todd Kashdan6

"If we were encouraged to be curious, we would stand a better chance of survival" Mark Haw41

"When people feel curious, they devote more attention to an activity, process information more deeply, remember information better, and are more likely to persist on tasks until goals are met."80

Another source of the importance of curiosity comes from by Pete Moorhouse thus:

Albert Einstein famously quoted: "I am neither clever nor especially gifted, I am only very, very curious". Probably a little modest too!

JL Cropley (Author, leading thinker on creativity)

'Curiosity is about the openness to experience' –

Curiosity - the spark of exploration

Curiosity - the catalyst of engagement

Curiosity - the fuel of creativity

Our intention above has been to highlight the various notions that outstanding intellectuals have said or experienced of curiosity. More can be read from other books especially by curious and then would be successful citizens of this world. The next discussion below is dedicated to critical thinking which is another important tool in the academic world.

1.5 Critical Thinking

Critical thinking is one of the most important skills needed in the academic world. Many scholars have talked about this important skill in the world of academics and its benefits. Talking about critical skills, Facione, and Paul, organized by the American Philosophical Association (APA), in Abrami et al (2015) explain:

We understand critical thinking to be purposeful, self-regulatory judgment which results in interpretation, analysis, evaluation, and inference, as well as explanation of the evidential, conceptual, methodological, criteriological, or contextual considerations upon which that judgment is based. . . . The ideal critical thinker is habitually inquisitive, well-informed, trustful of reason, open-minded, flexible, fair-minded in evaluation, honest in facing personal biases, prudent in making judgments, willing to reconsider, clear about issues, orderly in complex matters, diligent in seeking relevant information, reasonable in the selection of criteria, focused in inquiry, and persistent in seeking results which are as precise as the subject and the circumstances of inquiry permit. (Facione, 1990b, p. 2)

From the citation above, we learn that critical thinking has to do with values such as purposeful, self-regulatory judgment, inquisitive, well-informed, trustful of reason, open-minded, flexible, fair-minded in evaluation, honest in facing personal biases, prudent in making judgments, willing to reconsider, clear about issues, orderly in complex matters, diligent in seeking relevant information, reasonable in the selection of criteria, focused in inquiry, and persistent in seeking results which are as precise as the subject and the circumstances of inquiry permit. Based on this explanation, we observe that critical thinking is a skill. Skills are processes, procedures and strategies that enable human beings to perform any activity at their disposal. We can have teaching skills, playing skills, singing skills, driving skills, governing skills etc. Skill is knowledge in action. Skills have been classified by many intellectuals. For example, Peterson et al. (1997) in Pellegrino and Hilton (2012:31) state:

TABLE 2-1 Skills in the O*NET Content Model

Basic Skills	
Content Skills	**Process Skills**
Active listening	Active learning
Reading comprehension	Learning strategies
Writing	Monitoring
Speaking	Critical thinking
Mathematics	
Science	

Cross-Functional Skills	
Complex Problem Solving	**Social Skills**
Complex problem solving	Social perceptiveness
	Coordination
	Persuasion
	Negotiation
	Instruction
	Service orientation
Technical Skills	**Systems Skills**
Operations analysis	Systems analysis
Technology design	Judgment and decision
Equipment selection	making
Installation	Systems evaluation
Programming	
Quality control analysis	
Operation monitoring	
Equipment maintenance	
Troubleshooting	
Repairing	
Resource Management Skills	
Time management	
Management of financial resources	
Managing material resources	
Managing personnel resources	

SOURCE: Adapted from Peterson et al. (1997). Copyright 1999 by the American Psychological Association. Reproduced with permission. The use of APA information does not imply endorsement by APA.

The classification of skills above enables us to know that there are two main skills- Basic skills and Cross- functional skills. Basic skills are made up of two sub- skills- Content skills and Process skills.

1) BASIC SKILLS

Basic skills are made up of two main skills:

A) Content Skills

Under Content Skills we have sub-skills such as:

-Active listening,

-Reading comprehension,

-Writing,

-Speaking,

-Mathematics

- Science

B) Process Skills

Under Process Skills there is:

-Active learning,

-Learning strategies,

-Monitoring and

-Critical thinking.

2. CROSS-FUNCTIONAL SKILLS.

The second main skill is cross-functional skills. Cross-functional skills is made up of five sub skills-

A) Complex problem solving skills,

B) Technical skills,

C) Resource management skills,

D) Social skills, and

E) System skills.

A) Complex problem solving skills

Complex problem solving skills, has one sub skill

-complex problem solving.

B) Technical skills,

-operational analysis,

- Technological design,

-equipment selection

- Installation,

-programming,

-quality control analysis,

-operational monitoring,

-equipment maintenance,

-troubleshooting and

- repairing.

C) Resource Management Skills-

Under resource management Skills-

-time management,

- Management of financial resources,

- managing material resources,

-managing personal resources.

D) Social skills-

Under social skills-

-social perceptiveness,

-coordination, persuasion,

- Negotiation,

-instruction,

- Service orientation.

System skills

Under system skills-

-system analysis,

-judgment and decision making,

-systems evaluation.

As it has been mentioned above, we are interested in critical thinking. This is very important because most educated persons have often shown this special quality in many domains. Besides the definition and classification done above, more details of a critical student can be read from The Ontario Curriculum Grades 11 and 12(2018) thus:

Critical thinking is the process of thinking about ideas or situations in order to understand them fully, identify their implications, make a judgement, and/or guide decision making. Critical thinking includes skills such as questioning, predicting, analysing, synthesizing, examining opinions, identifying values and issues, detecting bias, distinguishing between alternatives, and reflecting on their learning. Students who are taught these skills become critical thinkers who can move beyond superficial conclusions to a deeper understanding of the issues they are examining. They are able to engage in an inquiry process in which they explore complex and multifaceted issues, and questions for which there may be no clear-cut answers. Students use critical-thinking skills when they assess, analyse, and/or evaluate the impact of something and when they form an opinion and support that opinion with a rationale. In order to think critically, students need to ask themselves effective questions in order to: interpret information; detect bias in their sources; determine why a source might express a particular bias; examine the opinions, perspectives, and values of various groups and individuals; look for implied meaning; and use the information gathered to form a personal opinion or stance, or a personal plan of action with regard to their education and career/ life planning. Students approach critical thinking in various ways. Some students find it helpful to discuss their thinking, asking questions and exploring ideas. Other students may take time to observe a situation or consider a text carefully before commenting; they may prefer not to ask questions or express their thoughts orally while they are thinking.

Talking about the citation above, we learn that critical thinkers often ask questions, predict, analyze, synthesize, examine opinions, identify values and issues, detect bias, distinguish between alternatives, and reflect on their learning. We also learn that student approach critical thinking in many ways-some students find it helpful to discuss their thinking, asking questions and exploring ideas. Other students may take time to observe a situation or consider a text carefully before commenting; they may prefer not to ask questions or express their thoughts orally while they are thinking (The Ontario Curriculum Grades 11 and 12;2018). Teachers and students should work hard to domesticate critical thinking because it is very important for our success in life. A solid base in critical thinking might enable students to know that there are two main skills in a human being: the soft skills and the hard skills. The discussion below examines these two main skills that must be found in a human being for a successful life.

The Notion of Soft Skills

As an advanced level or an undergraduate university student, you have already schooled but you are not really educated because much is still expected from you. The society wants to know you better. So, "soft skills" or "who you are" are those skills in an individual that reveal who that individual is. Talking about soft skills or who you are, Sandi Melkonian in Kum (2023) says:

Investopedia defines them this way, "Soft skills have more to do with who we are than what we know. As such, soft skills encompass the character traits that decide how well one interacts with others, and are usually a definite part of one's personality

From the citation above we learn that soft skills or who we are count much on our individual characters. Soft skills are inherited, others get them through experience, some through reading, and other people acquire soft skills through religion, and so on. Many writers such as Wibowo et al (2020) think that soft skills are very important for employment. Since much has been highlighted on soft skills in Kum (2023) we hint you that soft skills are linked to types of values which are seen in Gündüz (2016- 217) such as:

National values

Patriot

National spirit

Country- nation

Tied to customs and traditions

Knowing where you come from

Knowledge –based values.

Logical

Questioning

Creative

Educated

Successful

Curious

Humanistic values

Endearment

Benevolent

Caring

Respect for human rights

Mature

Being a decent person

Communal values

Obeying the rules

Being useful for the society

Sharing

Being a leader

Political tolerance

Not harming others

Universal values

Honesty

Love

Sacrifice

Kindness

Mercy

Trust

Leader's values

Happiness

Health

Salvation

Family
Personal success
Recognition
Ethical –social values
Peace
Planet ecology
Social justice
c Ethical moral values
Honesty
Sincerity
Responsibility
Loyalty
Solidarity
Values of competition
Money
Imagination
Logic
Beauty
Intelligence
Religious values
Belief
Morality
Honor
Spirituality
Religionist
Chastity
9. PERSONAL VALUES

The list below gives you a wider range of some common values you might have been ignoring

Acceptance	Fast pace action	Power
Achievement	Financial rewards	Privacy
Adventure	Focus	Productivity
Altruism	Freedom	Promotion prospects
Ambition	Friendship	Reaching potential
Appreciation	Fun	Recognition
Authenticity	Happiness	Respect
Authority	Harmony	Responsibility
Autonomy	Health	Results
Balance	Helping others	Risk taking
Beauty	Honesty	Romance
Belonging	Humor	Routine
Challenge	Imagination	Security
Choice	Independence	Self-expression
Collaboration	Influence	Service
Commitment	Intellect	Sharing
Community	Intuition	Solitude
Compassion	Justice	Spirituality

Competition	Kindness	Status
Connection	Leadership	Success
Contribution	Learning	Teaching
Creativity	Love	Team work
Equality	Loyalty	Tolerance
Excellence	Making a difference	Tradition
Excitement	Nature	Travel
Expertise	Nurturing	Trust
Fairness	Order	Variety
Faith	Passion	Winning
Fame	Peace	Wisdom
Family	Personal growth	Zest for life

The Notion of Hard Skills

Unlike "soft skills" that reveal "who you are", "hard skills" reveal "what you know". Much about hard skills can be read in Wibowo et al (2020:557) thus:

According to Bahrumsyah (2010) hard skills are the mastery of science, technology and technical skills related to their field of knowledge. According to Syawal (2010) hard skills are more oriented towards developing the intelligence quotient (IQ). From these two opinions, it can be concluded that hard skills are the ability to master technological knowledge and technical skills in developing intelligence quotient related to their fields.

Hard skills from the citation above are the different branches of knowledge you acquire in whatever field of study or training that mankind knows. Hard skills come from writing, reading, communication, mechanics, carpentry, building, engineering, medicines, teaching, secretariat, hunting, sciences (Chemistry, Physics, Mathematics, Geology, Biology, Geography, etc.,) military, and administration. Arts (History, Literature, Languages, Geography, etc.) cultural studies, women studies, hair caring, barbing, tapping, typing, and so on. These are some of the basic skills that enable a human being to be looked upon as a reasonable person in the society and then his or her comportment might reveal the rest of the tools. Besides being a curious and a critical thinker, a sound knowledge of language is also important for your ability to identify and solve research problems in the academic world. The next discussion focuses on language.

1.6 Language

The importance of knowing a language cannot be handled in a work of this magnitude because language is the tool you must use in order to communicate your ideas, the organization of your ideas, your argument and so on. However, some basic notions of English language can be highlighted here. In fact, traditional grammar has taught us that a language is made up of word classes- nouns, pronouns, adjectives, verbs, adverbs, articles, prepositions, conjunctions, exclamation marks. At the level nouns we must know their types and their plural forms, at the level of pronouns we must know their types and how they replace nouns, at the level of adjectives, we must know their types and how we can compare them right up to the superlative forms, at the level of verbs, we must know their types and the tenses in which they are used, at the level of adverbs we must know their types and how they modify verbs, adjectives and even adverbs, at the level of articles we must know their types and how they qualify nouns, at the level of preposition we must know their types and how they link nouns, phrases and clauses, at the level of conjunctions we must know their types and how the link words or phrases. After words we move to the next structure which is the phrase, we must know types of phrases (noun phrases, appositive phrases, gerund phrases, verb phrases, infinitive phrases, adverbial phrases, adjectival phrases, participial phrases, absolute phrases, prepositional phrases, and so on) and their functions. After the phrasal level language moves to the next higher structures- clauses, sentences, semantic, pragmatics, discourse, and so on. Knowing these structures of a language may help in many domains in the academia. Closely associated with language is the concept of tone which is the attitude of a writer in certain contexts. Due to its importance in the academic world, the section below examines tones.

1.7 Tones in writing

Many scholars of the academic writings (essay, dissertation, thesis articles, and so on) look upon an essay as an academic genre which should be written with a lot of caution. This means that in the course of writing an essay, the writer should have a sincere and a tentative attitude toward the reader. This is so because if the attitude of the writer is authoritative, the writer may discourage many readers who might had loved to join the writer in the domain, if the attitude of the writer is sarcastic, many readers might not also admire or appreciate the essay. Tone is therefore the attitude of the writer in the essay. Considering the importance of tone in any academic writing, the discussion below focuses on the description of tone and its various types according to Jean- Wyrick thus:

Tone is a general word that describes writers' attitudes toward their subject matter and audience. There are as many different kinds of tones as there are emotions. Depending on how the writer feels, an essay's "voice" may sound light-hearted, indignant, or solemn, to name but a few of the possible choices. In addition to presenting a specific attitude, a good writer gains

Credibility by maintaining a tone that is generally reasonable, sincere, and authentic.

Although it is impossible to analyze all the various kinds of tones one finds in essays, it is nevertheless beneficial to discuss some of those that repeatedly give writers trouble. Here are some tones that should be used carefully or avoided altogether:

Invective

Invective is unrestrained anger, usually expressed in the form of violent accusation or denunciation. Let's suppose, for example, you hear a friend argue, "Anyone who votes for Joe Smith is a Fascist pig." If you are considering Smith, you are probably offended by your friend's abusive tone. Raging emotion, after all, does not sway the opinions of intelligent people; they need to hear the facts presented in a calm, clear discussion. Therefore, in your own writing, aim for a reasonable tone. You want your readers to think, "Now here is someone with a good understanding of the situation, who has evaluated it with an unbiased, analytical mind." Keeping a controlled tone doesn't mean you shouldn't feel strongly about your subject—on the contrary,

you certainly should—but you should realize that a hysterical or outraged tone defeats your purpose by causing you to sound irrational and therefore untrustworthy. For this reason, you should probably avoid using profanity in your essays; the shock value of an obscenity may not be worth what you might lose in credibility. (Besides, is anyone other than your Great-Aunt Fanny really amazed by profanity these days?). The most effective way to make your point is by persuading, not offending, your reader.

Sarcasm

In most of your writing you'll discover that a little sarcasm—bitter, derisive remarks—goes a long way. Like invective, too much sarcasm can damage the reasonable tone your essay should present. Instead of saying, "You can recognize the supporters of the new tax law by the points on the tops of their heads," give your readers some reasons why you believe the tax bill is flawed

Sarcasm can be effective, but realize that it often backfires by causing the writer to sound like a childish name-caller rather than a judicious commentator.

Irony

Irony is a figure of speech whereby the writer or speaker says the opposite of what is meant; for the irony to be successful, however, the audience must understand the writer's true intent. For example, if you have slopped to school in a rainstorm and your drenched teacher enters the classroom saying, "Ah, nothing like this beautiful, sunny weather," you know that your teacher is being ironic. Perhaps one of the most famous cases of irony occurred in 1938, when Sigmund Freud, the famous Viennese psychiatrist, was arrested by the Nazis. After being harassed by the Gestapo, he was released on the condition that he sign a statement swearing he had been treated well by the secret police. Freud signed it, but he added a few words after his signature: "I can

heartily recommend the Gestapo to anyone." Looking back, we easily recognize Freud's jab at his captors; the Gestapo, however, apparently overlooked the irony and let him go.

Although irony is often an effective device, it can also cause great confusion, especially when it is written rather than spoken. Unless your readers thoroughly understand your position in the first place, they may become confused by what appears to be a sudden contradiction. Irony that is too subtle, too private, or simply out of context merely complicates the issue. Therefore,

you must make certain that your reader has no trouble realizing when your tongue is firmly embedded in your cheek. And unless you are assigned to write an ironic essay (in the same vein, for instance, as Swift's "A Modest Proposal"), don't overuse irony. Like any rhetorical device, its effectiveness is reduced with overkill.

Flippancy or Cuteness

If you sound too flip, hip, or bored in your essay ("People with IQs lower than their sunscreen number will object . . ."), your readers will not take you seriously and, consequently, will disregard whatever you have to say. Writers suffering from cuteness will also antagonize their readers. For example, let's assume you're assigned the topic "Which Person Did the Most to Arouse the Laboring Class in Twentieth-Century England?" and you begin your essay with a discussion of the man who invented the alarm clock. Although that joke might be funny in an appropriate situation, it's not likely to impress your reader, who's looking for serious commentary. How much cuteness is too much is often a matter of taste, but if you have any doubts about the quality of your humor, leave it out. Also, omit personal messages or comic

asides to your reader (such as "Ha, ha, just kidding!" or "I knew you'd love this part"). Humor is often effective, but remember that the point of any essay is to persuade an audience to accept your thesis, not merely to entertain with freestanding jokes. In other words, if you use humor, make sure it is appropriate for your subject matter and that it works to help you make your point.

Sentimentality

Sentimentality is the excessive show of cheap emotions—"cheap" because they are not deeply felt but evoked by cliches and stock, tear-jerking situations. In the nineteenth century, for example, a typical melodrama played on the sentimentality of the audience by presenting a black-hatted, cold-hearted, mustache-twirling villain tying a golden-haired, pure-hearted "Little Nell" to the railroad tracks after driving her ancient, sickly mother out into a snowdrift.

Today, politicians (among others) often appeal to our sentimentality by conjuring up vague images they feel will move us emotionally rather than rationally to take their side: "My friends," says Senator Stereotype, "this fine nation of ours was founded by men like myself, dedicated to the principles of family, flag, and freedom. Vote for me, and let's get back to those precious basics that make life in America so grand." Such gush is hardly convincing; good writers and speakers use evidence and logical reason to persuade their audience. For example, don't allow yourself to become too carried away with emotion, as did this student: "My dog, Cuddles, is the sweetest, cutest, most precious little puppy dog in the whole wide world, and she will always be my best friend because she is so adorable." In addition to sending the reader into sugar shock, this passage fails to present any specific reasons why anyone should appreciate Cuddles. In other words, be sincere in your writing, but don't lose so much control of your emotions that you become mushy or maudlin.

Preachiness

Even if you are so convinced of the rightness of your position that a burning bush couldn't change your mind, try not to sound smug about it. No one likes to be lectured by someone perched atop the mountain of morality. Instead of preaching, adopt a tone that says, "I believe my position is correct, and I am glad to have this opportunity to explain why." Then give your reasons and meet objections in a positive but not holier-than-thou manner.

Pomposity

The "voice" of your essay should sound as natural as possible; don't strain to sound scholarly, scientific, or sophisticated. If you write "My summer sojourn through the Western states of this grand country was immensely pleasurable" instead of "My vacation last summer in the Rockies was fun," you sound merely phony, not dignified and learned. Select only words you know and can use easily. Never write anything you wouldn't say in an ordinary conversation.

As you have observed so far the tone of a writer must be known for us to determine the nature of knowledge in which he or she wants to highlight. A sound knowledge of tones in writing will enable us to identify many research problems especially for language students. The next important tool for the academic world is intellectual honesty. The section below highlights the importance of intellectual honesty in the success of any student.

1.8 Intellectual Honesty

Besides all the meanings and types of honesty you know at your age and level, there also exists intellectual honest. Many students may be amazed to know that in the academia, there is a type of honesty which must be respected by all scholars, and that whenever any scholar goes against this honesty, he or she is demoted or sent out of the academic family. In fact, many dishonest intellectuals have been demoted or dismissed in their jobs because they committed academic crimes that stand against intellectual honesty. Some two major crimes against intellectual honesty are plagiarism and collusion. Due to the vital importance of intellectual honesty in the academia, the discussion below dedicates itself to what it is all about under the two major academic crimes of plagiarism and collusion.

Plagiarism and Collusion

History has taught us that knowledge no matter its popularity, no matter its strength, no matter its necessity, no matter its importance, no matter its richness, no matter its strategic position, no matter its less importance to mankind must have a source. The academic world respects and appreciates any intellectual who starts by acknowledging the source of his or her knowledge or idea before presenting his or her new knowledge, new Idea, new invention, new theory, new dream etc. This goes back to justify the basic phenomenon of the academic world which we highlighted in section 1.1 of this chapter. As a reminder, we have seen above how in the academic world, people learn at second hand. This suggests that every scholar should be honest to acknowledge the use of someone's word, someone's phrase, someone's clause, someone's sentence, someone's text, and so on in his or her work. That intellectual who fails to acknowledge his source of inspiration is accused of plagiarism. Many intellectuals even suggest that it is not the truth of your knowledge that matters but the background or history or society from where the knowledge comes that is of higher interest. For example, Bineth (2020:13) says:

Arguably, a more fruitful attempt of studying the social aspects of knowledge production came from the sociology of scientific knowledge which started in the 1970s by a group of academics at the University of Edinburgh. This interdisciplinary Science Studies Unit inaugurated the 'strong programme' which adhered to the maxim that no piece of scientific knowledge becomes accepted simply because it is true. Rather scientific knowledge is contingent on socio-historical context, dependent on the negotiation processes of the local context, and it demands constant work to keep knowledge legitimized (Daston 2009:804).

The citation above reminds us that the source of any knowledge is very important to the reality of the knowledge. The section below handles plagiarism and collusion which are the most hated concepts in an educated person because they lead to disgrace, insincerity, and so on in the academy. They come as a result of not acknowledging the source of any knowledge. In defining plagiarism, Essay writing from the English for Uni website states: "Plagiarism means using someone else's words, ideas or diagrams without acknowledgement". As we have seen above, we plagiarize when we do the followings without acknowledgement:

-use someone else's words,

-use someone else's ideas

-use someone else's diagrams

-use someone else's clause

-rearrange someone else's clause

-substitute a few words or phrases in someone else's clause

-Insert someone else's clause or clauses in your paragraph

Everything being equal, we must learn to acknowledge any external voice that we use in our writings. The advantages of acknowledging external voices below are from the English for Uni website and Bowker (2007). They include:

-To show respect for other people's ideas and work

-To clearly identify information coming from another source

-To distinguish an external source from your interpretation or your own findings

-To support your own arguments, thus giving you more credibility

-To show evidence of wide (and understood) reading

-You make your argument convincing for the marker.

-You show the marker you understand the literature.

-You follow the conventions of academia.

-You avoid being accused of plagiarism.

-You motivate and encourage other people by citing their works.

Apart from the academic crime of plagiarism discussed above, there is the academic crime of collusion. Collusion is very common among lazy students. It is a situation where two or more students write the same essay, or the same writing but with their different names written on each copy. In a detailed discussion on collusion, Essay writing from the English for Uni website states:

Collusion means that you work with someone else and submit the same or very similar assignments without your lecturer's permission. For example, if you and a friend work together on an essay and then submit identical or very similar versions of the essay, one under your name and one under your friend's name, that is collusion. However, if you are doing a group work assignment and your lecturer has asked you to work together and submit the assignment jointly, that is **not** **collusion***. Collusion, like plagiarism, has an element of dishonesty in it. People who collude do so secretly, as they know that the lecturer would not be happy.*

From the discussion above, we learn that there are two important things that the academic family hates to see from you now: plagiarism and collusion. We now know that plagiarism is the act of using another person's ideas, words or diagrams without recognizing the source or the person. Collusion on its own part is the act of summiting the same ideas, words or diagrams under two or more names without the authority of the teacher or the marker. Other crimes are:

a.   Fabrication
It is making up data or results and recording or reporting them.

b.   Falsification
It is manipulating research materials, equipment, or processes, or changing or omitting data or results such that the research is not accurately represented in the research record.

c.   Self-plagiarism
The verbation copying or reuse of one's own research or essays (IEEE policy statements) (see Kum 2023).

These suggest that in order to succeed in the academic world, students should avoid plagiarism fabrication, falsification, self-plagiarism and collusion. These vices are not acceptable especially in advanced or long essays that await us in the nearest future. In addition to the items discussion above, much success in the academic world also depends on your computer knowledge. So the next section reminds you of the importance of your knowledge in the computer world.

1.9 Computer knowledge

Everybody knows the importance of a computer, a cell phone etc. in this digital world. For example, learning, teaching, research and so on has been greatly facilitated by these ICT tools. If you wish to succeed in this age, you must master the use of a computer. Like the language, the computer is so vast that more knowledge is not yet known but you must know some basic skills about the computer in order to communicate with other worlds.

Although there are other vital qualities of an advanced writer that are not discussed above, such as self-discipline, orderliness, a prayerful life, and so on, we suggest that the ones mentioned above should be implemented for a successful life. A successful life can be interpreted from many angles by sound minds. However, in this study, we are more interested in the world of work as the final goal of a successful life. This may be so because we just think that a well-trained human being must be useful in his or her community through a well-recognized and a challenging work. This does not mean that only educated persons have the rights to work in our economy, no, because even the less educated people have contributed immensely to the growth of any economy. In other words, the world of work belongs to everybody be you educated or not, however, it should be noted that there are many differences at all levels in the world of work which has been discussed below. The aim of the section below is to inform our students and others of the various grading of skill levels in the world of work on earth. This is deemed necessary because a sound knowledge of these skills levels can motivate some of our ignorance but dynamic students to implements the qualities examined above and work very hard in order to attain some of these prestigious and highly specialized jobs in the nearer future.

1.10 The World of Work

The world is made in a way that everybody must produce and consume at a certain age. In other words, everybody is expected to work in a family, in a village, in a town, in a city, in a country and in the world as a whole. In order to meet up with this, our educational systems are fashioned to prepare citizens of the world to be productive at all levels. Boyer, E. (1995) states:

We all participate, for much of our lives, in the commonality of work. As Thoreau reminds us, we both "live" and "get a living." Regardless of differences, all people on the planet produce and consume. A quality education will help students understand and prepare for the world of work. Unfortunately, our own culture has become too preoccupied with consuming, too little with the tools for producing

As a High school or university student, you must know that you are being prepared for a prestigious job market in whatever field you are studying. It might be of great importance to hint you on how the International Labor Office at Geneva classifies skills for the job market. Based on the International Standard Classification of Occupations, ISCO-08(2008:12-13), the following four skill levels, their occupations, their tools and their educational levels read thus:

Skill Level 1

50. Occupations at Skill Level 1 typically involve the performance of simple and routine physical or manual tasks. They may require the use of hand-held tools, such as shovels, or of simple electrical equipment, such as vacuum cleaners. They involve tasks such as cleaning; digging; lifting and carrying materials by hand; sorting, storing or assembling goods by hand (sometimes in the context of mechanized operations); operating non-motorized vehicles; and picking fruit and vegetables.

51. Many occupations at Skill Level 1 may require physical strength and/or endurance. For some jobs basic skills in literacy and numeracy may be required. If required these skills would not be a major part of the work.

52. For competent performance in some occupations at Skill Level 1, completion of primary education or the first stage of basic education (ISCED-97 Level 1) may be required. A short period of on-the-job training may be required for some jobs.

53. Occupations classified at Skill Level 1 include office cleaners, freight handlers, garden labourers and kitchen assistants.

Skill Level 2

54. Occupations at Skill Level 2 typically involve the performance of tasks such as operating machinery and electronic equipment; driving vehicles; maintenance and repair of electrical and mechanical equipment; and manipulation, ordering and storage of information.

55. For almost all occupations at Skill Level 2 the ability to read information such as safety instructions, to make written records of work completed, and to accurately perform simple arithmetical calculations is essential. Many occupations at this skill level require relatively advanced literacy and numeracy skills and good interpersonal communication skills. In some occupations these skills are required for a major part of the work. Many occupations at this skill level require a high level of manual dexterity.

56. The knowledge and skills required for competent performance in occupations at Skill Level 2 are generally obtained through completion of the first stage of secondary education (ISCED-97 Level 2). Some occupations require the completion of the second stage of secondary education (ISCED-97 Level 3), which may include a significant component of specialized vocational education and on-the-job training. Some occupations require completion of vocation-specific education undertaken after completion of secondary education (ISCED-97 Level 4). In some cases experience and on-the-job training may substitute for the formal education.

57. Occupations classified at Skill Level 2 include butchers, bus drivers, secretaries, accounts clerks, sewing machinists, dressmakers, shop sales assistants, police officers, hairdressers, building electricians and motor vehicle mechanics.

Skill Level 3

58. Occupations at Skill Level 3 typically involve the performance of complex technical and practical tasks that require an extensive body of factual, technical and procedural knowledge in a specialized field. Examples of specific tasks performed include: ensuring compliance with health, safety and related regulations; preparing detailed estimates of quantities and costs of materials and labour required for specific projects; coordinating, supervising, controlling and scheduling the activities of other workers; and performing technical functions in support of professionals.

59. Occupations at this skill level generally require a high level of literacy and numeracy and well-developed interpersonal communication skills. These skills may include the ability to understand complex written material, prepare factual reports and communicate verbally in difficult circumstances.

60. The knowledge and skills required for competent performance in occupations at Skill Level 3 are usually obtained as the result of study at a higher educational institution for a period of 1–3 years following completion of secondary education (ISCED-97 Level 5b). In some cases extensive relevant work experience and prolonged on-the-job training may substitute for the formal education.

61. Occupations classified at Skill Level 3 include shop managers, medical laboratory technicians, legal secretaries, commercial sales representatives, diagnostic medical radiographers, computer support technicians, and broadcasting and recording technicians.

Skill Level 4

62. Occupations at Skill Level 4 typically involve the performance of tasks that require complex problem-solving, decision-making and creativity based on an extensive body of theoretical and factual knowledge in a specialized field. The tasks performed typically include analysis and research to extend the body of human knowledge in a particular field, diagnosis and treatment of disease, imparting knowledge to others, and design of structures or machinery and of processes for construction and production.

63. Occupations at this skill level generally require extended levels of literacy and numeracy, sometimes at a very high level, and excellent interpersonal communication skills. These skills usually include the ability to understand complex written material and communicate complex ideas in media such as books, images, performances, reports and oral presentations.

64. The knowledge and skills required for competent performance in occupations at Skill Level 4 are usually obtained as the result of study at a higher educational institution for a period of 3–6 years leading to the award of a first degree or higher qualification (ISCED-97 Level 5a or higher). In some cases extensive experience and on-the-job training may substitute for the formal education, or may be required in addition to formal education. In many cases appropriate formal qualifications are an essential requirement for entry to the occupation.

65. Occupations classified at Skill Level 4 include sales and marketing managers, civil engineers, secondary school teachers, medical practitioners, musicians, operating theatre nurses and computer systems analysts.

We can summarize the classification above thus:

Skill level one is about doing common manual works such as sweeping, tapping, digging, working on the farm with a cutlass, a hoe, a spade etc., fishing, pushing, taking care of people, goods, services etc. The tools here are very simple to be used such as cutlasses, hoes, spades, nets, sticks, ropes, brooms, dishes etc. The tools can be used by anybody (illiterates, literates, children, adults etc.)

Skill level two is more advanced than skill level one. Unlike skill level one that demands you to use your physical energy a lot, skill level two wants you to use the energy from your head to operate a tool and so you must be literate or trained to operate at this level. Some of the works in skill level two include driving, building, mechanics, secretariat, typing, trading, etc

Skill level three is too advanced because it does not only rely on performance; it demands additional calculation, management, critical thinking, directing, supervising, planning, deep reasoning etc. The power of the brain is needed here more than the physical energy. Some of the positions at this level include managers, directors, captains, principles, barristers, etc.

Skill level four is the highest of human training and educational levels. At this level people take decisions, they create new things or ideas, they solve complex problems, they govern, they criticize; they carry out risky operations of all natures, etc. Some positions at this level include Professors, Doctors, Engineers, Generals, Commissioners, etc.

The purpose of the discussion on skill levels above is to remind our High school and university students that their levels demand the energy of the brain because they belong to the level 3 and the level 4 skills above. This means they must inculcate the habits of critical thinking, deeper reasoning, logical speaking and writing, high sense of calculation, a high level of socialization, etc. All these qualities can be attained through literacy.

1.11 Conclusion

This chapter has highlighted the following characteristics of an advanced writer: the differences between the real world and the academic world, the world of work, the importance of curiosity, the importance of critical thinking, the bad-sides of academics (plagiarism and collusion), tones in writings, the need for a sound knowledge of language, and computer. As you will soon discover, these are only the tip of an iceberg, because there are many more aspects of a decent advanced level writer that we have not identified. The most important thing we have done in this chapter is to initiate you to the wonderful tool of curiosity. As you might imagine, curiosity is a weapon just like the knife you use at home. If you use the knife badly, it must cause havoc and if you use it very well then you will enjoy it functions. So if you develop curiosity in a positive direction then the sky is your limit in the domain of success because it will push you to do much research in reading, in writing, in listening, in speaking, in typing, and so on. Play your part to develop yourself through hard work.

Chapter Two - Background Knowledge To The Writing Skill

2.0 Introduction

As a student, more is expected from you. One of those important things that people may use to measure your capacity for training, for employment, and so on is writing. Intellectuals may evaluate your writing skills based on some pertinent questions such as: Is your writing coherence?, what about your spellings?, what about your vocabulary, is it broad or limited in English or even in your domain of study?, do you master the content of your subject?, what about your knowledge of punctuations?, do you use persuasive language in order to persuade other people to admire and then join you in your field of study?, can you convince people with a sound argument?, what about the logical presentation in your work?, and so on. From the number of questions raised above, you can now imagine what is expected of you in any of your future writings. The great importance of writing cannot be handled in a chapter like this one. However, as you might have observed so far in your life, many public examinations start with the writing phase before any other phases such as the spoken part, for example an interview if necessary. In fact, in many examinations, candidates often write first and if successful in the written phase, the examination authorities may then programme an interview if necessary or not. In view of the vital importance of the written form of discourse, this chapter identifies some common features of writing such as, the definition of writing, the origin of writing, aspects of writing, purposes of writing, stages of writings, the origin of essay, strategic classification of essays, the classification of an essay as a genre, the ordinary- level essay genre, a brief description of the five-paragraph essay, functions of the five-paragraph essay, and at what level, we abandon the five- paragraph essay?. Just like the previous introduction, we use sections to structure these items linked to writing in this study.

2.1 The Definition of Writing

In the course of reading through this study so far, a keen student might have understood up to this point that the academic world demands people or intellectuals to learn in the second position. In other words, people in the academic world do a lot of reading. This phenomenon of learning at the second hand enables intellectuals to chase away limitations that are too common in the real world. The knowledge intellectuals acquire in the academic world must be shared through definitions, citations, paraphrasing, and so on. Talking about definitions, it should be noted that there are many types of definitions in the academic world. At your level, you should know at least two essential types of definitions-the formal and the operational. A formal definition is the one that we get from the dictionary. It is meant for everybody to have a common or the basic idea of the concept. It can be written by a specialist in the field or by common people who master the language. For example, in the course of defining "writing", the Oxford English Dictionary tells us: "The action of one who writes, in various senses; the penning or forming of letters or words; the using of written characters for purposes of record, transmission of ideas, etc."(Mary By water, (),). This is a good example of a formal definition. It is often very general and simple to facilitate understanding for most people or to give the basic meaning of a concept, for example the concept of writing in our case. However specialists or intellectuals who have exhausted the most parts of their lives to the study of Writing can give us a better and a detailed definition of writing. This definition that we read from experts in a field is known as an operational definition. Based on operational definition which is found in By water (), writing can be defined thus:

"Writing is defined as a system of more or less permanent marks used to represent an utterance in such a way that it can be recovered more or less exactly without the intervention of the utterer."

Or:

"[writing's] essential service is to objectify speech, to provide language with a material correlative, a set of visible signs"

Or:

"a system of human intercommunications by mean of conventional visible marks17"

(Ignace Gelb, *A Study of Writing*, in Mary Bywater,...p 12)

The discussion above is aimed at initiating you into the meaning or the concept of "writing". It should be noted that each approach above has its focus. For example, this definition "writing is defined as a system of more or less permanent marks used to represent an utterance in such a way that it can be recovered more or less exactly without the intervention of the utterer." is focused on the relationship writing has with the spoken form. However, whether you understand writing from the formal definition approach or the operational approach, the essential goal here is to enable you have a better knowledge of the meaning of writing. Now that you have understood some meanings of writing, the next discussion below focuses on the origin of writing.

2.2 The Origin of Writing

Talking about the origin of literacy, we all know that literacy started in two geographical areas on earth: Mesopotamia and Egypt. Mary Bywater reports: page 64

Which region was the first to invent writing, Egypt or Mesopotamia? This question has caused serious debate between Sumerologists and Egyptologists for almost as long as the disciplines have existed. From 1928, with the discovery of the first Uruk IV tablets2 08, the earliest known cuneiform documents, it seemed for a long time as if the evidence pointed towards Mesopotamia as the birthplace of writing. However, since 19772 09 discoveries at Abydos in Egypt have pushed back the date of the earliest attested writing in Egypt so that it is almost contemporary with Mesopotamia. In this section we will look at the earliest evidence of writing from both regions and the main interpretations that have been put on them.

From the citation above, we read that literacy either started in Egypt or Mesopotamia. This knowledge is very important because any form of knowledge no matter its importance or truth must have a source. So the source of literacy is either Egypt or Mesopotamia. Literacy is one of the greatest achievements of mankind on this planet, because the ability to transcribe sounds to letters for other people to read and understand at any given time they want (literacy) must have taken mankind much time, much energy, many resources and many generations. In fact, it was a miracle. Abraham Lincoln in an unknown source once said:

When we remember that words are sounds merely, we shall conclude that the idea of representing those sounds by marks, so that whoever should, at any time after see the marks would understand what sounds they meant, was a bold and ingenious conception not likely to occur to one man of a million in the run of a thousand years. That it was difficult of conception and execution is apparent, as well by foregoing reflections as by the fact so many tribes of men have come down from Adam's time to ours without ever having possessed it.

Abraham Lincoln like any educated person today only expresses his admiration and gratitude to our ancestors who worked extremely hard to change sounds into marks so that you and I can use these marks today to read and write. In fact it was a wonderful initiative. However, we must know that literacy or writing has different forms. Mary Bywater reports: page 23) once more reports:

Recent studies by the grammatologist Peter Daniels have pointed out that the alphabet has only developed once, in Phoenicia with later refinements in Greece, so it cannot be said to be a necessary development as Gelb argued. Daniels has also argued that the tripartite system of logographic, syllabic and alphabetic scripts does not in fact cover every type of writing system. He suggests two further types of system, the abjad and the abugida. The abjad are 'alphabetic' systems that only note consonants; this term particularly relates to West Semitic scripts such as Hebrew and Arabic. The abugida are systems that are based on consonants with vowel notation obligatory but secondary so vowels do not have equal status to consonants, for example in the Indic and Ethiopic scripts

The discussion above tells us that literacy started in different places- Egypt or Mesopotamia and that there are different forms of writings- logographic, syllabic, alphabetic, abjad and abugida. This suggests that if you and I are using the alphabetic form of writing now, other human beings are using either the logographic, or the syllabic form of literacy to keep their records elsewhere. Based on the citation above, we further learn that besides the three main forms of writing- logographic, syllabic, alphabetic there are other forms- , abjad and abugida. As an educated person, you might want to know more about the other forms in order to deepen your understanding. However, it should be noted that as there are different forms of writing, there are also different ways of reasoning. Talking about different ways of reasoning, Mercier and Sperber (2013:100) state:

> The target article focused its review on experiments carried out in the laboratory, mostly with Western college students. **Narvaez** rightly points out the limitations of such a narrow focus. In their review of cross-cultural psychology work, Henrich et al. (2010) have shown that in many domains WEIRD people – people from *western educated industrialized rich democratic countries* – behave in ways that are different from the rest of the world (para. 9). In the case of reasoning and argumentation, scholars have hypothesized that such skills are a mostly Western tradition, born in classical Greece and nurtured in the Enlightenment. It would indeed by a deadly blow to the theory if some cultures were unwilling to argue or unable to reason. Happily for us (and for these cultures), the available data do not point in that direction. While there certainly are differences in reasoning and argumentative style (e.g., see Norenzayan et al. 2002), there is no report of a culture that would be deprived of these skills. The two most frequently alleged cases are illiterate societies – which are supposed to be unable to reason – and Eastern cultures – which are supposed to be unwilling to argue. Yet members

The citation above suggests that WEIRD people-people from western educated industrialized rich democratic countries inherited critical reasoning from the Greek civilization, illiterate societies seemingly were unable to reason and Eastern cultures were unwilling to argue.

This might sound very embarrassing to some students but other findings have highlighted some of the differences between the western and the eastern cultures of writings. Mary Bywater page 36 once more states:

But of course writing does not necessarily lead to 'history' as we understand it. For example China has a long tradition of written literature, but not of scientific method in the western sense of rationality, skepticism and analysis. Although it does have a tradition of compiling detailed chronological records98 it does not have the same tradition of historical research found in literate western societies99.

We now observe that despite the fact that literacy is found in many cultures, the manners of reasoning are different. For example, China has a long history of literacy but it did not think in a critical and analytical manner like the Western people. So what might be the reason behind these differences in reasoning? We cannot determine the real cause but we suggest that cultural differences play a significant part in the ways people reason despite the fact that they are all literate.

2.3 Aspects of Writing

Any good writing irrespective of its type is made up of some important aspects. These important components of writing were identified by Jacob et al. (1981). These aspects are content, organization, vocabulary, language and mechanics. Tasya (2022: 8-9) narrates:

Writing requires several aspects that should be considered being able to deliver a well-written form. According to Jacob et al. (1981), there are five aspects of writing (Yuliana et al., 2016):

Content : How the writer develops their ideas into their writing is best described as content (Roza et al., 2011). Material refers to writing stuff, the core concept experience (unity), i.e., groups of similar statements presented by the writer in creating a topic. Content paragraph conveys ideas rather than serving a special purpose of change, restatement, and emphasis.

Organization: It refers to the logical material organization (coherence). It's scarcely more than an effort to gather all the facts and jumble ideas. And in early drafts, it can still seek order, find trends in its content and work to put subject information consistent with what is indeed just half-formed with the intended notion. The organization also can be inferred as the way the writer does communication with the reader (Harris, 1979).

Vocabulary: This refers to selecting words that fit the content. It starts by assuming the writer wants to convey ideas as clearly, simply as the writer may. Overall, clarification should be the primary goal. Words that express their meaning are chosen rather than distort or blur words. By providing various vocabularies, it can help the reader in exploring the meaning of what is the writer intended to deliver (Roza et al., 2011).

Language: Use It refers to the right grammatical and syntactic pattern by separating, combining ideas into sentences, phrases, clauses, and create logical relationships in paragraph writing. In language use, the writer needs to make a coherent sentence into paragraphs.

Mechanic: It refers to the traditional graphic usage of the language, i.e., the steps of arranging letters, words, sentences, paragraphs using structural information, and some other related steps. The mechanic also describes the way the writer arranging and choosing words for their writing.

Many scholars of writing use these aspects of writing above as a stepping stone to higher levels. However, many advanced findings have been carried out in the domain of writing that a work of this nature cannot handle. It should be noted that basic aspects of writing include: content, context, the genre, spellings, vocabulary, punctuation, the purpose, the audience, organization, the use of hedges, the use of metadiscourse, and so on. More on this will be examined in subsequent studies. However, the purpose of writing is an important aspect of writing that many students often neglect. Based on this assertion, the next section highlights some key purposes of writing.

2.4 Purposes of Writing

Many scholars of writing such as Prananda have highlighted reasons that might push people to write in one moment or the other. However, it should be noted that no reason is unique because in order to entertain, a writer might also have the purpose to inform, or to reveal, to appreciate and so on. In this section, we state some important purposes and suggest some genres that are most used in each purpose.

To Inform

Many people write just to inform other human beings of certain experiences, some wonderful sights, discoveries, inventions, other people, cultures, and so on. Writers under this purpose are often clear, precise, simple, logical, they use plain language, etc. Genres good for Informative purposes are newspapers, flyers, research articles, scientific or business reports, some essays, some books, and so on.

To Entertain

Some people write to entertain or to amuse others. Writers under the influence of entertainment are often armed with certain tactics such as humor, suspense; broken language, dialogue, monologue, rhetorical devices, and so on. Since the goal hear is to entertain the readers, genres common under this influence are usually novels, love books, stories, drama, poetry, song lyrics, short stories, screenplays and so on.

To Persuade

Under the influence of persuasion, a writer neither writes to inform nor to entertain, but to change our attitude either negatively or positively. In fact, persuasion is to influence the mind of the reader towards a thing, an animal, an idea, a person, a concept, and so on. The influence can be to be positive, to be negative or to be neutral. Persuasive writers are armed with facts, evidence, reasons, credibility, and so on. Much on persuasion will be discussed later in this study. Genres that are common in persuasive writing are advertisement, some essays, some newspapers, some research articles, business reports, applications for jobs, formal letters, and so on.

To Argue

To argue means to go beyond persuasion. Writers who write under the spirit of argument often have a difficult, a hard, a complex or a controversial problem or topic that needs a sound solution. In this situation, the writer does not only persuade. He or she does research for facts, pieces of evidence, warrants, reasons, to disprove the opposite view points and facts, pieces of evidence, warrants, reasons, to support his or her point of view. Since this study is based on argumentative writing, more will be discussed later.

To Criticize

To criticize means to bring out the weaknesses or the negative side of anything or a person. Writers under this influence are focused more on highlighting negative points of a project, an idea, etc. They might persuade the public or not but their aim is always to reveal the bad sides, the moderate sides or even the good side, and so on of things or persons. They are often armed with facts. Good genres here include dissertations, theses, conference papers, and so on.

To Analyze

To analyze means to examine in greater details every parts of a whole. Writers under the spirit to analyze are often meticulous, they respect time, they are honest, and they deal with facts and not opinion. For the fact that analysis examines every small detail in a whole, it is used in many genres such as essays, stories, books, theses and so on.

To Evaluate

Writers under the aim to evaluate often look for the weaknesses and the strengths of anything or any person. They are not aimed at persuading people but only to reveal the good and the bad sides of anything as the situation is presented to them. People evaluate textbooks, speeches, and so on.

To Play with Words

During some periods in history when public speaking was restricted, or banned, some writers decided to examine how certain words could rhyme with others, how certain words had synonyms, antonyms, allophones, and so on. This actually influenced the growth of poetry and language structures. The best genre under this purpose is poetry.

As you can imagine, there are many reasons that push people to write. The reasons are so many that they cannot be exhausted in a study of this nature. However, we think that those highlighted above can influence you in one way or the other. The next important feature of writing to be examined below is the various stages of writing.

2.5 Stages of Writings

Many good works on writing remind us of the various stages of writing which must be inserted in any writing programme in an educational system. Talking about the importance and the nature of such a programme, this unknown scholar writes:

Ideally, there should be a programme to develop writing skills which works all the way through the educational system. Such a programme would list the main types of writing which it felt students should be able to master by the end of their education, and would offer guidelines to teachers on ways of achieving success with each of these...In fact, any teacher who has had to try and assess the free writing of inexperienced foreign learners of English will appreciate the need for some kind of controlled or guided writing, at least at the early stages.

The citation above reminds us that writing programmes in any educational system should be well established, the stages of writing well defined too and then taught to students. Although the above speaker highlights some of the main stages of writing, more can be read in the paragraph below thus:

It seems convenient, then, to structure a writing course through three main stages. These will be: (i) controlled writing, (ii) guided writing, and free writing. These terms have been fairly loosely used in the past, and the first two are often used as if they are interchangeable. However, it seems sensible to distinguish between writing exercises in which the final product is linguistically determined by the teacher or materials writer, and exercises in which the final content is determined. Thus a paragraph with blanks to be filled may be a legitimate early part of a writing programme, and can be considered a *controlled* composition, as is one in which, for example , picture prompt, or memory of a model presented by the teacher, leads to the students reproducing more or less exactly the same final product as each other. On the other hand a composition in which the teacher provides the situation and helps the class to prepare the written work, either through written or oral assistance is a *guided* composition, because each piece of work is different in the language used, even if the content and organization are basically the same throughout the class. A *free* composition usually means a composition in which only the title is provided, and everything else is done by the student.

As an advanced-level writer, you might have passed through the stages highlighted above without knowing. Prior to any detailed discussion, it should be noted that the approach used in the citation above is known as the product approach. It is the product approach to writing and not the process approach because it is the final product that is very important and not the various steps that must be followed in order to attain the product. So in an educational system, writing might start at the primary level. At this level, pupils might be drilled in controlled writing. As already explained in the citation above, controlled writing in most schools takes the form of writing in which pupils are asked to fill empty spaces with appropriates words for the passage to be well understood, The ideas or content of the given passage are developed by an experienced writer and pupils are only asked to fill in the missing words in the spaces provided. This therefore suggests that in a controlled writing stage, the product or the passage or picture does not change.

The next stage of writing is the guided stage. The guided stage of writing is common at the upper primary right to the High school of the educational system. Guided or directed writing has many formats. However, what makes it unique is that a situation is often presented in a distorted or incomplete way. Students are therefore demanded to arrange the ideas using their own language to form a complete situation. Sometimes, students are demanded to bring in their own ideas in a given situation and use their own language for a complete passage or write-up. For example, a student might be asked to write an application for a job opportunity using some guide-lines or not. At the higher levels of an educational system, guided writings form a part of functional writing or might be another name for functional writing. As the name suggests, functional writing are those writings that have certain immediate targets or obligations to be fulfilled. Some writers call them business writing because of the urgent needs they have to be accomplished. At your level, you must have written a letter, an e-mail, an application, a cover letter, an invitation, a cv, you might have taken minutes in meetings and so on. These are some good examples of functional writings. Many writers have examined functional or business writings but we will focus on Maggio (2001) because of her detailed classifications, her identification of the situations in which each functional genre can be used, and so on. The examples below illustrate some business writings and their sub genres drawn from on Maggio (2001) thus:

-Acknowledge or Confirm

- anniversary/birthday greetings
- apologies
- complaints
- condolences
- congratulations

-Kinds of Adjustment Letters

- billing/invoice errors
- credit
- damages
- exchanges

-Cover Letters Accompany

- application forms
- brochures/booklets/catalogs/pamphlets (see SALES)
- checks unaccompanied by statements or invoices
- contracts/agreements
- contributions to charitable causes
- documents

-Kinds of Letters Dealing with Advice

-Occasions That Call for Apologies

-Write Letters of Appreciation

-Write Letters of Complaint About

-E-mail When Your Message Is

-Fundraising Letters

"-Get Well" Letters

-Invitations

-Love Letters

-Employment Letters Deal with

Talking about the third stage of writing, it is known as free writing. In a free writing, students are only provided with the title or a topic and everything else is done by the students. Since this study is focused on the argumentative essay, we can now conclude that we are at the free writing stage. As many of us know, the argumentative essay is a kind of essay that exists amongst other forms of essays such as the narrative, the descriptive, the persuasive, the analytical, and so on. Because more on these other forms of essays will be highlighted below, we cannot examine them at this level. However, due to the fact that the argumentative essay is only a member of the genre essay, the discussion below therefore highlights the origin and the definition of an essay.

2.6 The Origin of Essay

More about the causes and the origin of the genre essay can be read on chapter one of our book under the title, "The Rhetorical Analysis of the Five Paragraph Essay"(Kum, 2023). However, talking about the origin of the genre essay, it was Michel de Montaigne from France who introduced it. McKay et al (1983:544) explain:

At the age of thirty-eight, Montaigne resigned his judicial post, retired to his estate, and devoted the rest of his life to study, contemplation and the effort to understand himself. Like the Greek, he believed that the object of life was "to know they self" for self-knowledge teaches men and women, how to live in accordance with nature and God. Montaigne developed a new literary genre, the essay- from the French "essayer" meaning to test or try- to express his thoughts and ideas.

Based on the narration above, it is evident that Michel de Montaigne introduced the genre essay into the literature of the world. He aimed at correcting the stereotyped beliefs and superstitions that were common during his period, through his personal brief writings, which he called essayer- "to try". Nowadays, scholars of the genre of essay define it as a relatively brief prose composition expressing personal ideas, or personal thoughts. Essays by nature are personal and from that personal brief prose, other people can judge your ideas, your organization of ideas, your language, your mood your persuasive or convincing skills and so on.

2.7 Strategic Classification of Essays

In the course of describing an essay above, we have highlighted that "Nowadays, scholars of the genre of essay defines it as a relatively brief prose composition expressing personal ideas, or personal thoughts". People express personal ideas, personal feelings, personal wishes, and personal deeds in different ways. These various ways of writing an essay have given rise to various kinds of essays. Though more on essay types will be handled in many sections of this study, the strategic classification of essays according to their approach in writing has been done by an unknown scholar. The document was written under the title ESSAY TYPES. Based on ESSAY TYPES, some thirteen different essay types and their various thesis sentences go thus:

Persuasive:

Convinces readers to take the student's point of view about a given subject. Differs from an argument essay in that the goal is to persuade the reader, not just explain the point of view; often, personal pronouns are acceptable. Sample thesis: Fish are the best pets because they are easy to take care of, fun to watch, and inexpensive.

Argument:

Presents the student's point of view on a controversial topic, using research and logical arguments to prove a point. Not an opinion or an editorial piece (no personal pronouns). Sample thesis: Americans should eliminate the regular consumption of fast food because a fast food diet leads to preventable and expensive health issues, such as diabetes, obesity, and heart disease. Variation: Epideictic argument: Argues that a person, organization, theory, etc. is better than all others by using praise/acknowledgement in the evaluation (eg. accomplishments, awards, selfless acts, etc). Sample thesis: Mother Theresa is the most benevolent woman in history because of her admirable selfless acts, overwhelming generosity, and capacity for love that eclipses that of all others.

Expository:

Takes a stance on an issue and explains it. This is similar to an argument essay but simpler and requires less research. When a student says "it's supposed to be an argument, but we didn't need to do research," this is usually what he/she means. Sample thesis: Though it has many opponents, Instagram is in fact a useful program because it helps people develop their creativity and learn about culture.

Narrative:

Describes something that the student has personally experienced and is told from the student's point of view, using 'I, me, my', in the past-tense. Tells a story, usually about an event that happened within the span of a few hours or one day, that has a moral or a lesson to be learned.

Sample thesis: When I met her for the first time, I had no idea that my whole idea of love was about to change for the better.

Descriptive:

Describes something – object, person, place, experience, emotion, situation. Paints a picture for the reader to visualize, using descriptive language that covers all five senses. Can be presented from the first- or third-person narrative, but not the second. Sample thesis: Colorado is my favorite place to visit because of the beautiful scenery, delicious food, and exciting activities.

Exemplification/Illustration:

Describes something using examples. This means that examples should be used, not descriptive phrases (despite the fact that 'illustration' is in the title). Typically, an exemplification essay focuses on one main topic and then uses examples to describe this one topic. Sample thesis: Although most students know that plagiarism is wrong, laziness leads them to plagiarize their work. The body paragraphs would then be made up of examples of student laziness (procrastination, not wanting to read, hating to write, etc.) and show how these lead to plagiarism. Examples should include specific personal anecdotes, generalizations, or hypothetical situations.

Cause and Effect:

Identifies either the causes OR the effects of a situation (eg. the effects of second-hand smoke OR the causes of childhood obesity). Then, the essay uses research to identify patterns and explain why things turned out the way they did. Sample thesis: Air pollution is caused by exhaust gases from cars, uncontrolled factory releases, and burning of low-quality coal for heating Variation: Some teachers will ask the students to identify the causes AND effects, but this is unusual. Sample thesis: Air pollution is caused by exhaust gases from cars, uncontrolled factory releases, and burning of low-quality coal for heating; this then leads to acid rain, eutrophication, and worsening medical conditions.

Compare and Contrast:

Identifies the similarities and/or differences between two or more things (eg. online classes vs. in-person classes). There are two methods of organizing this type of essay. First, there might be two body paragraphs, one devoted to each main topic. Or, there might be three body paragraphs, each devoted to different similarity/difference, using examples from each main topic within the paragraph. Sample thesis: While Dennys and IHOP serve similar food, they are different in their customer service, atmosphere, and quality. Variation: Some teachers will want the students to include their opinions/evaluations in the conclusion (eg. "Because of the superior customer service, atmosphere, and quality, IHOP is superior to Dennys.").

Rhetorical Analysis:

This essay focuses on any type of medium: article, film, television, commercial, magazine ad, etc. This type of essay should not discuss the topic of the medium, but should focus on how the author/creator made his/her points (tone, word choice, authority, etc.). Typically, students will discuss ethos, pathos, and logos when developing this type of essay. Sample thesis: The Gucci ad's use of ethos, pathos, and logos contributes to its overall message, which is to show women that beauty equals strength.

Literary Analysis:

Focuses on analyzing a chosen/given literary text. Reviews and further evaluates the text and its meaning, value, and implications. The essay should not be a summary, but an analysis of characterization, plot, symbols, themes, etc. Sample thesis: In The Secret Agent, Conrad uses beast and cannibal imagery to describe the characters and their relationships to each other. Variation: Character Analysis in a literary text: Similar to literary essay but focuses on a particular character. Typically, the essay will track the character's growth, development, or change without summarizing the action. Sample thesis: The character Hamlet proves to be exceedingly existential as he explores deep questions, seeks truth and understanding, and tries to come to grips with his father's death.

Evaluation essay:

Establishes a judging criteria (eg. what makes a movie good or bad? Or what makes one idea more valid than another?) and then makes a judgment on a thing, theory, action, etc. Each body paragraph will focus on a specific criterion, upon which the topic will be evaluated. Sample thesis: The Twilight movies are terrible adaptations of the books because the filmmakers have deleted necessary plot points, revised some main characters, and changed the ending.

Classification essay:

Separates things in specific categories and discusses each of them. The purpose may be to make a complex idea easier to understand by sorting its parts into logical sections. Sample thesis: Teachers usually fall into one of three categories: explainers, involvers, and enablers.

2.8 Definition essay:

Defines a term or phrase. It's usually best to use a complex idea (like 'love' or 'friendship' or 'evil') rather than a concrete object (like 'a tree' or 'television'). Sample thesis: Success is defined in terms of monetary wealth, fame, and happiness. Process essay/How-to essay: Describes the steps in a process. Usually written in chronological order and tells the reader 'how to' do something. Second-person narrative is often acceptable, here. Sample thesis: If you want to make the best cup of coffee, you should follow these steps exactly.

Despite the fact that we appreciate the exhaustive nature of ESSAY TYPES above, it should be noted that there are still many types of essays that have not been highlighted in the discussion above. It should also be noted that many experts of the genre of essay always limit themselves to the first five essay types mention above- persuasive, argumentative, expository, narrative and descriptive. However, we think that this endeavor will push you to read more about essay types. In the next section below, the discussion focuses on the classification of essay as a genre because the word genre has been us in many cases above.

2.9 The Classification of an Essay as a Genre

At the outset, it is of prime importance to remind ourselves that an essay is a genre. The term genre here does not correspond with the three genres in literature: prose, drama and poetry. Genre is beyond that; it is more of any special text written in a particular way for a particular audience. A deeper understanding of the word genre and its development is explained in Ren (2010:6) in Kum (2016: 71) thus:

The concept of genre is currently a widely discussed research area in linguistics as well as in literature. In literature, there is a long tradition of the study of genres, which can be traced back to the ancient Greek philosopher Aristotle. It is generally accepted that Aristotle was the first scholar to propose the three naturals of poetry: epic, lyric and drama. Among the literary genres, the most well developed and well –studied genre would most probably be narrative ones, especially the genres of fairy tales and parables. The concept of genre, a word of French origin which means kind of type, was generally restricted to literary works, such as poetry, novels and dramas.Russian Scholar Brahmin was the first researcher who greatly extended the denotation of the concept so as to include non-literary works under its heading, such as classified advertisements, news reports, and scientific essays or papers.

A quick glance at the explanation above reveals the word essay in the last line. Based on this, we can now observe that an essay is a genre and should be handled with caution at the level of its structure and ideas organization. More explanation on the concert of genre which means a type of or kind of a text is being discussed by Brazil (1988:21) in Bazerman et al. (2009:x) thus:

Every text is organized within a specific genre according to its communicative purposes, as part of the condition of discourse production, which generate social uses that determine any and every text.

We are very conscious of the fact that many pupils and students do not know the concept of genre. However, the discussion above has suggested that genre means a type of writing that has a particular structure, a particular purpose, for a particular audience. More knowledge about the concept of genre will be known at the higher levels, but for your level, we think that the concept has been highlighted. Now that the essay has been illustrated as a genre, the discussion below examines the essay genre that you were taught at the ordinary level of your academic ladder.

2.10 The Ordinary- Level Essay Genre

The discussion above has suggested that a genre is a type of writing that is unique. Unique in the sense that it has a particular structure, a particular way of presenting knowledge, a particular purpose, a particular audience etc. Learners from the primary levels right up to the secondary levels have been taught a particular essay structure. This structure comprises of an introduction, body and conclusion. The introduction is made up of a paragraph, the body is made up of three paragraphs and the conclusion comprises of a single paragraph. This is the famous Five-Paragraph Essay. In other words, the Five-Paragraph Essay is a particular writing that has a structure: one paragraph that serves as an introduction, three paragraphs that serve as a body and a paragraph that serves as a conclusion, it has a particular purpose which might be to inform or to persuade. It is written for various audiences- students, teachers, workers and so on. Due to the importance of the Five-Paragraph Essay at the primary and secondary writing, it must be handled with care and seriousness. So the discussion below dedicates itself to some highlights of the Five-Paragraph Essay for a quick revision.

2.11 A Brief Description of the Five-Paragraph Essay

Many scholars have talked about the Five-Paragraph Essay. Some have highlighted the structure of the Five-Paragraph Essay; others have described its functions. Some have looked at it as an academic genre, and so on (Vieregge in Ball and Loewe, 2017:209; Kum. 2023).

. Considering the importance of the Five- Paragraph Essay, we suggest that hardworking students should endeavor to have a sound knowledge of it. Very few people can argue the fact that it is the Five-Paragraph Essay that initiates us into the academic world or into individual writings. The Five - Paragraph Essay begins from the basic level of education until when we are mature in our methods of reasoning. In this section, we will look at some descriptions made by some writers on the Five-Paragraph essay. In a move to describe its nature, Vieregge in Ball and Loewe (2017:209), say:

The 5PE may sound familiar. In its most basic form, it is an introduction, three points, and a conclusion. Students are often given a topic to discuss, a passage to respond to, or a questions to answer. The introduction and body paragraphs typically follow prescribed conventions regardless of content. For instance, the introduction has an attention-gotten and explains what others have said about the topic, and the thesis usually comes close to the end of the paragraph. Each of the body paragraphs has a topic sentence that makes a claim that can be backed up with evidence and that refers back to the thesis. Each topic sentence is followed by sentences that provide evidence and reinforce the thesis. The body paragraphs end with a wrap-up sentence. The conclusion reminds the reader of the main idea, summarizes the main points, and might even leave the reader with one lasting impression.

In addition to the detailed description of the Five-Paragraph Essay given above, we also learn about how ideas should be mentioned in each paragraph. Bernstein and Lowry in Ball and Loewe (2017:214) give a sketched description below:

In your first paragraph, warn your audience that you are planning to make no more (or less) than three points which they will know to look for in paragraphs two, three and four respectively. After that, use the fifth paragraph to remind your audience of the three points you just made

Besides the two scholars mentioned above, Bowles in Ball and Loewe (2017:220) summarizes the Five - Paragraph Essay thus:

Traditionally the FPT (five paragraph theme) contains an introductory paragraph that moves from a general overview of a topic to an explicit thesis statement that highlights three main points. The three supporting paragraphs each take up one of these three main points, beginning with a topic sentence and then moving into more detailed description. Finally, the FPT ends with a standard conclusion that is often times merely a restatement of the thesis statement and reiteration of the three main points.

Judging from the three descriptions above, it might be noted that the Five- Paragraph Essay can have different descriptions, different names, but the same outcome or the same structure. Due to its standardized form, many scholars of writing think that the Five-Paragraph Essay should be modified, that is adding more paragraphs or even reducing them. Others feel that the five paragraph essay limits writer' horizons, others even suggest that the five paragraph essay should be suppressed completely from the curricula. In this line of criticisms of the Five-paragraph essay, Vieregge in Ball and Loewe (217:209) narrates:

The five-paragraph essay (5PE) doesn't have many vocal defenders in Departments of English in higher education, --- Most college writing instructors have eschewed the 5PE, contending that it limits what writing can be, constricts writers' roles, and even arbitrarily shapes writers' thoughts.

From the citation above, we can see that at the higher level, the Five-Paragraph essay has limited chances of recognition. For more on the criticisms of the five paragraph essay, see Ball and Loewe (2017). However, in view of the important position the five paragraph essay occupies in the academic life of undergraduate students and even pupils who learn English as a second or foreign language, the discussion below dedicates itself to the functions of the Five-Paragraph essay.

1.12 Functions of the Five-Paragraph Essay

The importance of the Five-Paragraph Essay is widely known. However, many students still find it very difficult to understand why this particular type of essay is often used to measure the level of students' writing at many levels of the writing process. It is for this reason that some of the important functions of the five paragraph essay are demonstrated below. The approach might not be exhaustive to some big students but we think it can create certain awareness.

The first function of the Five-Paragraph Essay is that, it serves as a tool to evaluate students' at the level of a topic, at the level of grammar and at the level of arranging ideas in a coherent manner in many public and private examinations. Talking of why the Five-paragraph essay is used in public examinations, the Foundation Programme (19:76) states:

An important component of most professional examination is the writing of an essay. The purpose for including it is three-fold:

- *The first is to test the familiarity of the candidate with the topical issues. The development in the world of trade, commerce and technology take place at a fast pace. A candidate will only be able to present facts if he knows them.*

- *An essay also tests the ability of candidates to think in a coherent manner. It is said that Clear language is the product of a clear mind. A confused writer will only produce a haphazard collection of half-truths.*
- *The third is to see whether the candidate can express his/ her views in a fluent language, which is free from errors and grammatically acceptable.*

The quotation above highlights three important things that the essay contains- facts, organization of these facts or ideas in a coherent manner, and the knowledge of the language by the candidates. These are qualities you must know when writing an essay in any domain as has already been discussed above.

The second function of the Five - Paragraph Essay is that it initiates students into academic writings. As will be highlighted later in this study, academic writing is different from ordinary writing. For instance, academic writing is that writing which deals with facts. Genres under academic writing include essays, research reports, dissertations, theses, research articles, conference papers, and so on. The essay therefore initiates students into the world of academic, and so should be studied in a careful manner.

Besides the fact that the five paragraph essay initiates students into academic writings, the five paragraph essay plays the role of a scaffold. In this light, Vieregge in Ball and Loewe (2017:210) states:

Susan L. Benko describes the five paragraphs as scaffolding that can either enhance or hinder student learning. A scaffolding can be useful as construction workers move about when working on a building, but it should be removed when the building can stand on its own.

In the quotation above, Benko in Ball and Loewe (2017:210) tells us that the Five - Paragraph Essay only serves as a scaffold in a house. This means that the essay serves as a supporter to your growth in the academic field. A good knowledge of an essay will enable you to reach higher heights because its initiates you into the skills of writing, the skills of organization and so on. But from what we will observe in the discussion below, this scaffold should be removed when students moved into the University or other higher levels.

Apart from the idea that the five paragraph essay serves as a training wheel, it also enables us to organize our ideas in a logical whole as has been suggested above. In this vein, Naomi and Lowry in Ball and Loewe (2017:215) reveal:

The role of the five paragraph essay in the move from high school to college is analogous to using training wheels when learning to ride a bike. Useful maybe even necessary at first but, as the rider becomes more proficient and broaches more complex terrain, those little wheels will collect debris, or become snagged on rocks. Thus these once useful training wheels become a liability. They may slow the rider down or, when they catch on obstacles, may throw her from the bike. At best they are a nuisance, while at worst they are a danger. Without training wheels, it may be tough to get started at the beginning of a ride, but eventually we figure out how to do it. Bumpy rides may pose a challenge, but they make us resilient.

As a training wheel the five paragraph essay has to be handled with care. This is important because when the training is inadequate or poorly done, the rest of the project or carrier cannot be effective.. In fact, naturally, training to ride a bicycle always starts from small wheels and when your legs are longer, you need bigger bikes for more proficiency.

Besides the idea that the five paragraph essay serves as a training wheel, it also enables us to organize our ideas in a logical whole as has been suggested above. In this vein, Naomi and Lowry in Ball and Loewe (2017:215) reveal:

The five paragraph essay is widely believed to be useful in terms of making students assimilate, absorbs, store, categorize, and organize new knowledge.

In fact, one of the characteristics of an English discourse is that it is linear. This means a paragraph starts with a topic sentence; this topic sentence is followed by supporting sentences in order to justify the thesis statement. The Five- Paragraph Essay therefore encourages these organizations and so must be known especially by students who want to use English Discourse as their medium of communication to the world.

Another function of the five paragraph essay is that it facilitates evaluation. This suggests that the Five-Paragraph Essay is not only used as a tool for evaluation, it also facilitate evaluation. For instance, with the help of the Five-Paragraph Essay, it is easy for experts to know if a student has stated the thesis statement, the topic sentences or the supporting sentences. The usefulness of the five paragraph essay in evaluation is highlighted by Bowles in Ball and Loewe (2017:222):

"As a general rule, the more rigid and precise the criteria for evaluation of a piece of writing, the more likely a high inter-rater reliability will be achieved. This is why the FPT (five paragraph Theme) is so efficient in scoring standardized writing assessment, with its prescriptive formula and distinct features, raters can be normed (ie trained to agree) on the presence and quality of these rather specific features. Is there a clear and concise theses statement with three main points? Check. Does each supporting paragraph have a topic sentence and move into a more detailed description? Check. Did the conclusion effectively restate the argument? Check?

The citation above ends in pertinent qualities of the five paragraph essay, thesis statement, three points, and topic sentences and supporting sentences. A good knowledge of these basic features enables the rater to know with relative ease whether a student knows how to organize his or her ideas or not.

Furthermore, the five paragraph essay brings success to many people. Success here can be in an examination or gaining a job. For instance, in a job opportunity exercise, Susan recounts the importance of knowing the paragraph essay. Bernstein and Lowry in Ball and Loewe (2017:216) *narrate:*

Susan recounts this story of a time when the five paragraph essay formula seemed helpful- at least at first. She had applied to teach in an emergency teaching-certification program in a large Northeastern city. She met with other applications in a school cafeteria to complete a series of tests including an essay-writing test. The applicants were to respond to the question, "what are the three must important skills that teachers need in our city's classroom?" Of course, this topic easily lent itself to a five paragraph essay: An introduction (including a thesis listing the three main skills), one skill per paragraph and a conclusion that repeated the most important points.

Based on the citation above, we can conclude that without a sound knowledge of the Five- Paragraph Essay, many applicants in the essay writing test above could not produce a convincing essay that would have enabled them to acquire the job to teach in that city. From the discussion in this chapter, we can see the important position the Five - Paragraph Essay occupies in our academic lives. Despite the importance functions of the Five- Paragraph essay, students at the higher level must abandoned it for more complex, persuasive, longer essays and so on. It is for this reason that the section below reminds us when to abandon the Five- Paragraph essay.

1.13 At what level, do we abandon the five- paragraph essay?

We cannot say that there is a particular level that the Five-paragraph essay should be forgotten in our academic lives. However, as we go higher and higher in our educational career, there might be moments that the Five-paragraph essay will not be appropriate as a tool to solve our writing problems. Many scholars have attempted to suggest instances that the five-paragraph essay cannot be used. For example, Berstein and Lowry in Ball and Loewe (2017:216) write:

... at what point is it time to move away from the five paragraph essay? We believe that the time comes to move away when one is focusing on a problem that defies pat answers. That is, when working on piece of writing that is designed with a purpose beyond simply organizing information by reporting on uncontroversial facts (e.g." smoking is bad for you"). As soon as a student is in a position to enter a process of inquiring to explore (and perhaps offer solutions to) an issue that may provoke more question and yield myriad answers, the five paragraph format should be thrown to the wind"

At this juncture, we can conclude that the five paragraph essay has a limit, because as we grow deeper in academics, other complicated and longer writings appear which demand us now to analyze, evaluate, synthesize and so on. However, with a good and solid base in the Five-paragraph essay, nothing will hinder our success in those advanced writings that await us in the future.

The chapter above has reminded us of our Five paragraph essay. This particular genre is very important in our academic lives because it trains us on how to organize our ideas in a coherent way. It should be noted that after a brilliant victory with the five paragraph essay, your status has changed. You are now a High School or a University student. This means that you are now an advanced member of the academic world. Talking of the transition from the Five Paragraph Essay to the long essay, Guptill (2016:19) states:

...The skills that go into a very basic kind of essay—often called <u>*the five-paragraph theme*</u>—*are indispensable. If you're good at the five-paragraph theme, then you're*

good at identifying a clear and consistent thesis, arranging cohesive paragraphs, organizing evidence for key points, and situating an argument within a broader context through the intro and conclusion.

In college you need to build on those essential skills. The five-paragraph theme, as such, is bland and formulaic; it doesn't compel deep thinking. Your professors are looking for a more ambitious and arguable thesis, a nuanced and compelling argument, and real-life evidence for all key points, all in an organically1 structured paper.

In the citation above, we observe that the knowledge we acquire from the Five Paragraph Essay include identifying a clear and consistent thesis, arranging cohesive paragraphs, organizing evidence for key points. This formulaic way of doing things in the Five Paragraph Essay is different from the high reasoning speaking or writing that is expected of you at the High school and then at the university. For example, speaking or writing at the High school or at the university demands you to be critical or persuasive and not only being informative or narrative.

1.14 Conclusion

Some of the items about the writing skill which are highlighted in this chapter include: the definition of writing, the origin of writing, aspects of writing, purposes of writing, stages of writings, the origin of essay, strategic classification of essays, the classification of an essay as a genre, the ordinary- level essay genre, a brief description of the five-paragraph essay, functions of the five-paragraph essay, and at what level, do we abandon the five- paragraph essay?. Many teachers have observed that some students carry forward the skills they acquired in the five paragraph essay to their advanced writings such as the skills of narration, description, recounting events and so on. In fact an advanced writer should be able to analyze, to evaluate, and to argue out facts and so on. This high level of reasoning offers you good grades and prepares you for the higher education. This chapter on writing skills has highlighted some purposes that can push someone to write. At your level, you must know that you do not write just to inform people on facts or opinions that you have read. Most often you write to convince people on mixed up facts that need a bid of argument and insightful brain. We hope curiosity pushes you to find out more on some good qualities of writing in general that are necessary at your level.

Chapter Three - Background Knowledge To Academic Argumentative Essay

3.0 Introduction

As a good advanced level student, you might have observed that at this point in this study we are moving from a general perspective to a specific one. This may sound convincing because chapter one talks about the general characteristics of an advanced writer, chapter two focuses on the writing skills in particular and chapter three now looks at an argumentative essay which is a genre within the writing skills. This logical ordering of knowledge from the general to the specific perspectives fosters understanding and is often used in the structure of the introduction section of an English discourse. Experience has revealed that many students shy away from the argumentative genre which on the contrary is the most needed genre for their knowledge building and then their success. In fact, the argumentative genre is about knowledge construction and not just writing about knowledge like in the other genres such as the narrative, the description, the expository, the analytical, and so on. In the discussion above, it has been observed that literacy does not necessarily mean knowing how to read and write. In fact, it goes beyond that nature. For example, Mercier and Sperber (2013:100) reminds us that WEIRD people, that is people from western educated industrialized rich democratic countries inherited critical and logical thinking from the Greek civilization and then the period of skepticism. This way of doing things is not the same as the Chinese people who started literacy many years also. As we will see later, critical and logical thinking is highly based on the argumentative writing. The argumentative genre is very important for several reasons. Firstly, it is through this genre that knowledge is constructed, and negotiated for people to either accept or to reject. Secondly, many high levels of reasoning examinations use the argumentative genre to judge the reasoning power of their candidates, which means candidates who cannot build a good argument have no place in their institutions. Thirdly many highly competitive entrance examinations into professional schools use the argumentative genre to select their future trainees. In fact the reasons are endless. This chapter therefore examines some basic concepts that may help us to understand the argumentative writing in a greater detail. Items discussed below include: the difference between a debate and an academic argument, the definition of an argumentative writing, the differences between argumentative and persuasive discourse, the importance of argumentative essay, types of argumentative writings, and elements of an argumentative writing. In order to examine these concepts, we still maintain the point by point structure as used in the previous two chapters above.

3.1 The Difference between Debate and an Academic Argument

When the concept of an argumentative writing was introduced into our classroom, most of my students made it clear to me that they hated quarrelling amongst themselves because they were not politicians in a parliamentary session. In fact, students almost abandoned the class for fear that an unnecessary aggressive debate was awaiting them. It took some time to enlighten them on the real nature of an academic argument. It seems the misinterpretation of an academic argument as a lousy and an aggressive debate, or a conflict that demands a winner and a loser depicted by my students above is a common phenomenon amongst students or people all over the world. For example, Booth, W. C.; Colomb, G. G. & Williams, J. M., (2003:113) state:

People usually think of arguments as disputes: children argue over a toy; roommates over the stereo; drivers about who had the right-of-way. Such arguments can be polite or heated, but they all involve conflict, with winners and losers. To be sure, researchers sometimes wrangle over evidence and occasionally erupt into charges of carelessness, incompetence, and even fraud. But that is not the kind of argument that made them researchers in the first place.

Based on the citation above, we observe that many people often look upon the academic argument as a conflict or a heated debate. But as we will realize later below, argumentative writing is just a form of a debate. Talking about the differences between an academic argument and a debate, Fahy (2008:2) writes:

> A scientific argument is a form of debate. A debate is a formal method of taking a position and arguing for what you want the audience to believe. Debating involves both logical argument and emotional persuasion. For example, lawyers arguing in a court room or politicians arguing in parliament are forms of debating. In that form of argument there are two sides that argue two different positions about the topic of debate. A scientific argument, like a debate, is based upon a clearly defined topic. As only one side is being presented in a paper for publication it is important to think of your paper as one 'side' of an academic argument. Authors must also be ready to have their ideas criticised by other scientific writers; that is what makes it an argument. The advancement of scientific knowledge depends upon open, clear and direct argument and evidence.

The citation above suggests that a debate comprises of two parts-a logical argument and an emotional persuasion. As you will observe, our academic argument is the logical argument in a debate and it has little or nothing to do with emotions or emotional persuasion. Intellectuals know that the advancement of knowledge is based on logic, facts, evidence, and so on, and not emotions or in emotions. Now that we have deleted the idea of emotions in knowledge advancement or construction genre, the discussion below focuses on the real definition of an academic argument for knowledge advancement.

3.2 Definition of an Argumentative writing

Due to the complex nature of the argumentative writing, it would be of great importance to remind ourselves of the origin of the word argument. Talking about the origin of the word argument, Rene (2007:269) states: *The word argument comes from the Latin 'arguere', meaning 'to make clear'.* This suggests that when writing an argumentative essay, you must be clear at the level of language, at the level of organization of ideas, at the level of logic with little or no emotions. As you can see, the academic argument has nothing to do with emotions. On the contrary, scientists write to evoke criticisms from other intellectuals in order to advance knowledge. As a future intellectual, your goal is to construct and to advance knowledge and not yourself. This is so because you will one day die but the knowledge, the ideas and so on, you leave behind will never die especially if they are real. So an emotional persuasion has no place in a scientific argument or in a scientific world. So never you use words such as extremely, very, best, no contradiction, axiomatic, etc. in a scientific work. Although many scholars have given the definitions of an academic argumentative, we are going to highlights some few definitions below from some authorities that are very common. The definitions of an academic argument in this study have been given by Maharani (2019: 300) thus:

Besides, Alvarez (2001) as stated in Chala and Chapeton(2012) defined argumentative essay writing as the set of strategies of an orator who addresses an audience looking to modify their judgment, get their adhesion, or make them admit a given situation or an idea. It is complemented by Díaz (2002) who claimed that predominantly argumentative essays deal with controversial topics, and in them an author defends a point of view that he/she considers valid. Their purpose is to convince, get an adhesion, justify a way to see facts, refute interpretations about an event, or persuade the reader to change an opinion about a subject.

Based on the citation above, we have observed certain words such as strategies, orators, ideas, controversial topics, convince, and so on. These are some qualities of an academic argumentative essay. Besides the definitions of an argumentative essay given by Maharani (2019) above, Booth, W. C.; Colomb, G. G. & Williams, J. M., (2003) explain an academic argumentative writing thus:

...a thoughtful conversation with amiable colleagues, a conversation in which you cooperatively explore a contestable issue that you all think is important to resolve, a conversation that aims not at coercing each other into agreement, but at cooperatively finding and agreeing on the best answer to a hard question.

Talking about the explanation above, we can now observe that an argumentative essay is more of a critical friendly conversation amongst friends, colleagues, brothers, sisters, and so on over a problem or a hard question that needs to be solved in the best way. In fact, in most cases, whenever there is a controversial topic or an issue, friendly people ignite a thoughtful conversation over the issue in order to jointly attain the best answer which might solve that very difficult problem. Argumentative writing or a "thoughtful conversation "might not even need an audience. Sometimes educated people might observe a controversial issue and they decide to solve it by enlightening the general public with a convincing argument. As you can see, such a conversation, or a talk over a controversial problem, that needs the best answer demands people of sound thinking, people of convincing skills, people of good characters, people who have read broadly, people who are curious, people who have carried out research in the area, and so on. The advanced level and other levels beyond, train people to acquire these skills so as to transform their worlds in particular and the rest of the world in general. The notion of informing people through narrative essays, descriptive essays are over at your level. You have to develop the skills of persuasion, explanation, convincing, etc. which will offer you good grades in your examinations, and then a successful life. Those are the ways of an educated person. However, in the discussion above, we have realized that argument and persuasion are mentioned in a debate. These concepts often confuse our students because in the course of arguing out the truth, many people think that it is all about persuasion. This suggests that many people always have some misunderstandings between the argumentative writing and the persuasive writing. Since these two strategies are often mistaken for the other, the discussion below gives the differences between an argumentative writing and a persuasive one.

3.3 Differences between an Argumentative and a Persuasive Discourse

In a class lecture on argument and persuasion, our best female student suggested that the two concepts- argument and persuasion should be separated because they have different approaches and focuses. To back up her point, this student argued that when a boy wants a girl for a friend or a wife, the male persuades the female for the relationship and not argues with her. I appreciated this hardworking student for her critical mind but her line of thought reminded me of the quotation from Monterey peninsula College, which goes thus: "Community service activities develop social and emotional skills of students while academic classes develop intellectual skill". Judging from the thinking of the student, it is but normal to think that the student is exposed to the "community service activities" or a real world approach to argument which is often very loud, aggressive, and even violent. Intellectual or academic approach to argument is different. The difference between a community service activities or real world argument and an intellectual argument has been explained by "The Academic Resource center" from http://www.wju.edu/arc thus:

The good news about offering an argument in your writing is that, unless you've been living by yourself in a cave for the past 18 years, you probably already know how to argue. The bad news is that here in college, you'll need to be persuasive, not loud. The point is not to beat an idea to death, but to invite the reader to look squarely at opposing points of view and conclude that the side you've chosen to argue is, after all, the most reasonable argument. Argument, then, is writing that takes a position on an issue and gives supporting evidence to persuade someone else to accept, or at least consider the position or even to take (or not take) an action.

Among many important things highlighted in the citation above, is the definition of an argument. In the citation above we learn that an argument, 'is writing that takes a position on an issue and gives supporting evidence to persuade someone else to accept, or at least consider the position or even to take (or not take) an action". Accordingly, an academic argument is not loud, not aggressive, not violent, and not abusive. Instead, it should be persuasive, which means it should be a way to invite readers to look at an issue and appreciate your point of view, which is often backed by supporting sentences and plenty of evidence.

As you have already read above, many students think that argumentative writing is the same as persuasive writing. This confusion is not common only amongst students. In fact, it has been a difficult task to make out the differences between a persuasive writing and an argumentative one. This phenomenon has been highlighted in Rene (2007:270) thus:

It has been rather difficult for the researcher to make the difference between the terms 'persuasion' and 'argument' because in much of the considerable empirical research to date, these two terms are used interchangeably (Connor and Lauer, 1985). To the researcher's relief, however, Kinneavy (1971:21) notes that 'persuasion' is '...that kind of discourse which is primarily focused on the reader and attempts to elicit from him a specific action or emotion or conviction'.

The citation above reveals some of the difficulties writers themselves face at the level of differentiating the persuasive essay from the argumentative one. However, Rene (2007:270) still suggests:

For the purposes of this study, 'persuasion' and 'argument' have been understood as defined by the Writer's Workshop from the University of British Columbia, in Canada:

Persuasive writing is writing that sets out to influence or change an audience's thoughts or actions, while an argument is an appeal to a person's sense of reason, emotion and good character.

In van Eemeren, F.H. and Houtlosser, P.'s view (2000):

There is also a rhetorical aspect to argumentative discourse in a more specific or strong sense: people who take part in argumentative discourse try to resolve the difference of opinion in their own favor, and their use of language and other aspects of their behavior are designed to achieve precisely this effect. This does, of course, not mean that the participants are exclusively interested in getting things their way. As a rule, they will at least pretend to be primarily interested in having the difference of opinion resolved. People who engage in argumentative discourse may be considered committed to what they have said or implicated.

In the citation above, the author reminds us of some differences between persuasive and argumentative writings. For example, we are told that persuasive has much to do with influencing peoples' emotions in their way to act, to think or to see in another way. Argumentative discourse has to do with changing people's opinions at the level of reasoning. This means that using a strong argument, you can change people's opinion toward a thing, an idea, and so on without necessarily influencing them to act or think too deeply. This might be true to an extent. However, real experts of argumentative and persuasive writings, suggest that there are some differences which are good to know. Besides the differences highlighted above, this study further focuses on more differences between argumentative and persuasive essays as published by the Academic Centers for Enrichment (2011). Our choice of these findings is grounded on the fact that the differences are many, they are also detailed, and they are orderly elaborated for a novice deeper understanding. The table below presents the differences between argumentative writing and persuasive writing according to Academic Centers for Enrichment (2011).

Argumentative vs. Persuasive Writing
Subtle, but Significant, Differences

Goal of ARGUMENTATIVE WRITING: To get reader to acknowledge that your side is valid and deserves consideration as another point of view.	**Goal** of PERSUASIVE WRITING: To get reader to agree with you/your point of view on a particular topic.
General technique of argumentative writing: Offers the reader relevant reasons, credible facts, and sufficient evidence to support that the writer has a valid and worthy perspective.	**General technique** of persuasive writing: Blends facts and emotion in attempt to convince the reader that the writer is "right." (Often relies heavily on opinion.)
Starting point of argumentative writing: *Research* a topic and *then* align with one side.	**Starting point** of persuasive writing: *Identify* a topic *and* your side.

Viewpoint used in argumentative writing: Acknowledge that opposing views exist, not only to hint at what a fair-minded person you are, but to give you the opportunity to counter these views tactfully in order to show why you feel that your own view is the more worthy one to hold. Writer presents multiple perspectives, although is clearly for one side.	Viewpoint used in persuasive writing: Persuasion has a single-minded goal. It is based on a personal conviction that a particular way of thinking is the only sensible way to think. Writer presents one side— his side. (Persuasive writing *may* include ONE opposing point, it is then quickly dismissed/refuted.)
Audience of argumentative writing: Doesn't need an audience to convince. The writer is content with simply putting it out there.	**Audience** of persuasive writing: Needs intended audience. Knowing what they think and believe, the writer "attacks" attempting to persuade them to his side.
Attitude of argumentative writing: Simply to get the reader to consider you have an idea worthy of listening to. The writer is sharing a conviction, whether the audience ends up agreeing or not.	**Attitude** of persuasive writing: Persuasive writers want to gain another "vote" so they "go after" readers more aggressively. Persuasive writing is more personal, more passionate, more emotional.

Excerpted from 2011 Smekens Education Solutions, Inc. *www.SmekensEducation.com*

Lowell Writing Center: LC-406B, 978-656-3365   Bedford Writing Center: LIB 7A, 781-280-3727

The table above summarizes the differences between argumentative and persuasive essays. Argumentative writings demand us to do research, it does not need a particular audience, ideas are proposed whether they are accepted or not, we need reasons, facts, convincing evidence, and so on. Despite the differences established above, we must still remind ourselves that it is one basic quality of persuasive writing which is not found or found in the smallest proportion in argumentative writing. This is emotion. Persuasive writing relies on emotions which are not needed in argumentative writing. Based on the table above, it might be highlighted that an argumentative writing is a deeper form of persuasive writing because persuasion may always appear in argumentative writing even in a small scale. However, you should read other works for a deeper understanding of their differences. For example look at these more differences below. They are adapted from Alamo Colleges Districts Writing Center San Antonio College (2012).

Argumentative and Persuasive Essay

This handout aims to distinguish argumentative from persuasive essays, as well as give some guidelines for writing them. In both types of essays, a strong coherence between introductions, thesis statements, body paragraphs, and conclusions drive the essay and deliver its point(s) to its readers clearly and directly. However, the difference between the two is in their appeal. Argumentative essays appeal to reason, while persuasive essay appeal to emotion. The following is a chart that explains both kinds of essays more specifically:

	PERSUASIVE WRITING	ARGUMENTATIVE WRITING
PURPOSE	The writer aims to get the reader to agree with his / her personal perspective.	The writer aims to get the reader to accept his / her perspective as truth.
GENERAL TECHNIQUE	Opinions are blended with facts, all in an attempt to convince the reader that the writer is "right."	Relevant reasons and credible data are blended to demonstrate the writer's argument as valid.
AUDIENCE	The writer has an intended audience to address his request or need. Who can give him what he wants?	To write an argument, the writer doesn't need an intended audience. The writer is satisfied with simply "putting the truth out there."
POINT OF VIEW	Since the writer is communicating directly to a person, group, or organization, it's common to use first-person (i.e., I) and second-person (i.e., you) point of view.	With no specific audience in mind, this more formal writing addresses the multiple sides of an issue using the more objective third-person point of view.
ATTITUDE	Persuasive writers "go after" their readers more aggressively. They consider the emotional strategy that will work best on their audience (e.g., manipulation, motivation, inspiration, etc.). Persuasive writing is personal, passionate, and emotional.	Argumentative writers maintain a tone of fairness and reasonableness. Their attitude is respectful, tactful, and formal.
PERSPECTIVES PRESENTED	Persuasion has a single-minded goal— Get what the writer wants. It is based on the writer's personal conviction that his way of thinking is the best. Consequently, the writer's viewpoint is typically the only one presented. (See the lopsided scales above.)	Argumentative writing acknowledges opposing views within a pro/con piece. (See the more balanced scales above.) This demonstrates the writer as a fair-minded person and gives him the opportunity to counter these perspectives with more logic, reasoning, and proof.
STARTING POINT	1. Pick a topic of interest. (What do you want?) 2. Choose a side to "fight" for. 3. Start writing.	1. Conduct initial research on a debatable topic. 2. Align with the strongest side. 3. Continue gathering facts and research.
SUPPORT	Persuasive pieces rely on opinions and feelings. The writer uses his own passion and/or plays off reader emotions to get what he wants. The audience agrees with the writer because of strong emotional appeals.	Arguments rely on logical reasons that are all substantiated by facts, data, expert quotes, and evidence. The audience agrees with the writer because of the strong logical appeals.

Now that the distinction between an argumentative and persuasive writing has been highlighted, the next section below focuses on the importance of an argumentative Essay.

3.4 The Importance of Argumentative Essay

The importance of an argumentative writing in the academic world is too great to be handled in a study of this magnitude. However, argumentative writing or thinking is used in our day- to- day interactions to create knowledge, to promote knowledge, to solve problems, to enlighten others, for international competitive examinations, to convince others, and so on. Though many scholars have highlighted the importance of the argumentative writing, some writers such as Maharani (2019: 300) explain:

One particular essay which represents English academic writing is argumentative essay. Based on Zhu (2001,p.34),"Argumentative writing as a mode of academic writing constitutes an important part of foreign language learners 'academic experience". Argumentative writing appears to be the most important task for the students as they need to use it in exams and papers. Argument is considered to be the key rhetorical purpose of much academic writing, indeed is seen as an essential aspect of intellectual activity within higher education (Coffin, et. al., 2003, p.14

The scholar in the citation above looks at the importance of the argumentative writing in the domain of academics. We are told that at the higher education, argumentative writing is an intellectual activity, it trains intellectual to communicate in a convincing way and so on. Besides the importance of the argumentative essay given above, Stab (2015: 619) writes:

Argumentation aims at increasing or decreasing the acceptability of a controversial standpoint (van Eemeren, Grootendorst, and Snoeck Henkemans 1996, page 5). It is a routine that is omnipresent in our daily verbal communication and thinking. Well-reasoned arguments are not only important for decision making and learning but also play a crucial role in drawing widely accepted conclusions.

In the citation above, we observe that many decision makings, many important conclusions, and so on in courts, in offices, in parliaments, in organizations, governments, etc. rely much on argumentation. These actually show how the skills to argue must be developed by students at the advanced and higher institutes of studies. The last voice to remind us of the importance of argumentation is drawn from Vu Le Ho (2011:2) thus:

Secondly, argumentation constitutes the core text type in academic writing, and hence, is frequently tested by standardized English tests, such as TOEFL and IELTS. However, this genre proves to be difficult both technically and culturally to second language (L2) students (Bliss, 2001). Results of the pilot study for this project suggest that ESL Vietnamese learners are no exception. My pilot Vietnamese subjects encountered numerous issues in their ESL argumentative essays that made their writing appear problematic to native speakers of English (Ho, 2009). And yet, in order to study abroad, many Vietnamese students need to achieve a good score on either TOEFL or IELTS tests, both of which require an argumentative essay. A study that focuses on this genre offers the potential of more direct assistance to Vietnamese learners of English than narrative genres.

Last but not least, in regard to methodological feasibility, the argumentative genre, being a more technically constrained writing style, facilitates both quantitative and qualitative analyses. Moreover, since texts in this genre tend to be of dialogic nature and associated with a high level of interaction (Thompson, 2001; Wenzel, 1980), investigation of argumentative essays helps highlight the interactive view of text adopted by my study.

Since this study is aimed at initiating students into the argumentative writing, it is of prime importance to read the difficulties some students encounter in writing this genre in other areas such as Vietnam. Vietnam in the citation above represents other non-native speaking countries. We can attest to the fact that many students in Cameroon, Chad, Congo and so on, have enormous difficulties in writing the argumentative genre. Our experience has shown that students from these countries cited above cannot convince their readers using the argumentative genre. From the citations above, you can see the need to know the argumentative skills if you might one day compete with other international students in international examinations. The next discussion is on types of argumentations.

3.5 Types of Argumentative Writings

Much has been highlighted on the notion of argumentation and its various approaches. Among these authors is The College Board (2014). The College Board (2014:32) tells us that there are three mayor different approaches of argumentative writings:

-Classical argument.

-Rogerian argument

-Toulmin argument

The three approaches of argumentation mentioned above were invented by different scholars in different periods and in different geographical areas. But they seem to have many things in common. Considering the fact that many students do not have a clear idea of what an argument is all about and its major approaches, the discussion below focuses on these three major approaches of argument. The discussion is drawn from The College Board (2014:32) and notes by an unknown author entitled "3 Types of Argument: Classical, Rogerian, Toulmin.

3.5. 1 Classical Argument

The oldest of all the three approaches to argument cited above is the classical argument. In the discussion above, Mercier and Sperber (2013:100) tell us that WEIRD people that are people from western educated industrialized rich democratic countries inherited critical and logical thinking from the Greek civilization. The classical argumentative discourse was one of those critical and logical ways of expressing feelings and thoughts. Talking about the classical argument, The College Board (2014:32) explain:

Although Aristotle and Cicero devised a system of argumentation over 2,000 years ago, the elements of classical oration still influence contemporary attitudes and styles of argumentation. Anyone writing prior to the twentieth century had no other model than classical oration; therefore, many of the world's greatest speeches and documents are written using that structure. Even the more contemporary Rogerian and Toulmin models are based upon the components of classical argument. Some examples of arguments that use the classical model include the following:

- "Debtors' prisons" by Samuel Johnson

- "On war" by James Boswell
- What to the slave is the fourth of July" by Fredrick Douglass
- Shakespeare's Sister" by Virginia Woolf
- "Letter from a Birmingham Jail3" by Martin Luther king Jr.
- "Affirmative Action: The price of preference "by Shelby Steele

Based on the discussion above, The College Board (2014) highlights and reminds us that the ancient Greek philosophers are the ones who introduced the classical argument. We are also told that the contemporary Rogerian and Toulmin models are based on this line of thoughts that was invented by the Greek philosophers. The College Board (2014) also states some studies that are based on the classical argument as you can read above. Unfortunately, The College Board (2014) does not tell us the structure of the classical argument. However, in this study, the structure of the-Classical Argument and when to use it with an example is drawn from the notes by an unknown author entitled "3 Types of Argument: Classical, Rogerian, Toulmin". According to these notes, the structure of the classical argument goes thus:

1. **Introduction (Exordium):** Capture the audience's attention. Introduce the issue and create exigence for your claim. Why is this issue? Why do we need to pay attention?

2. **Statement of Background (Narratio)** Supply the context needed to understand the case you present. What circumstances, occurrences, or conditions do we need to be made aware of?

3. **Proposition (Partitio)** State your position (claim/thesis), based on the information you have presented, and outline the major points that will follow. The partitio divides the background information from the reasoning.

4. **Proof (Confirmatio)** Present your reasons, subclaims, and evidence. Establish inferences between claim and support. Provide additional evidence for subclaims and evidence, where necessary. Explain and justify assumptions.

5. **Refutation (Refutatio)** Anticipate and refute opposing arguments.

In this section you demonstrate that you have already considered the issue thoroughly and have reached the only reasonable conclusion.

6. Conclusion (Peroratio) Summarize the most important points. Make a final appeal to values, motivations, and feelings that are likely to encourage the audience to identify with your argument

Looking at the structure of the classical argument above, we observe that the structure is made up of six elements: Introduction (Exordium), Statement of Background (Narratio), Proposition (Partitio), Proof (Confirmatio), Refutation (Refutatio), and Conclusion (Peroratio)). Talking about the instances in which the classical argument can be used the notes entitled "3 Types of Argument: Classical, Rogerian, Toulmin" states:

– More direct

– More aggressive

– To establish power

– When the audience already respects you or

– When the audience needs to get something from you.

From the citation above the notes entitled "3 Types of Argument: Classical, Rogerian, Toulmin" highlights some five moments that we can use the classical argument-more direct, more aggressive, to establish power, when the audience already respects you, and when the audience needs to get something from you. An example of a talk that used the classical argument according to entitled "3 Types of Argument: Classical, Rogerian, Toulmin" is. "I have a dream speech". More about the classical argument can be read from the books cited above.

Summary of Classical Argument

At the outset of this study, we observed that intellectuals operate in the academic world in which they "learn at second hand, from what other people have written, rather than from their own experiences". As we can see, the Greek philosophers introduced the concept of an argument many years ago. Modern scholars call that form classical argument, and it has influenced the other forms. Based on the classical argument, we learn that it is used in situations which are more direct, more aggressive, when the audience already respects you or when the audience needs to get something from you and to establish power. A keen and curious student can determine the minds of mankind during that period with the help of these purposes for which this form of argument was used because we are also hinted that Martin Luther king used it in his famous speech "I have a dream speech". Apart from Martin Luther King who used this type of argument, we are also told that it is used in works such as "Debtors' prisons" by Samuel Johnson, "On war" by James Boswell ,What to the slave is the fourth of July" by Fredrick Douglass ,Shakespeare's Sister" by Virginia Woolf, "Letter from a Birmingham Jail3" by Martin Luther king Jr.,"Affirmative Action: The price of preference "by Shelby Steele. At the end, the elements of classical arguments are (Introduction (Exordium), Statement of Background (Narratio), Proposition (Partitio), Proof (Confirmatio), Refutation (Refutatio), and Conclusion (Peroratio)). Everything said and done, much about the classical types cannot be handled in a study of this scale. So students should consult more books on this type of argument for a deeper understanding. The next chapter handles the Rogerian Argument.

3.5.2 Rogerian Argument

Like the classical argument, the Rogerian argument in this study has been explained by The College Board (2014:32) and the notes by an unknown author entitled "3 Types of Argument. For example, according to The College Board (2014:32), the Rogerian argument is explained thus:

Carl Rogers, an American psychologist, developed a more contemporary and nonconfrontational method of argumentation. Rhetoric scholars Richard E. Young, Alton L. Becker and Kenneth L. Pike identified four stages of Rogerian argument.

1) Introduction

- Describes an issue, a problem, or conflict with sufficient evidence.

- Demonstrates respect for alternative positions

2 Contexts

- Describes the contexts in which alternative positions may be valid

3 Writer's position

- States a position on the issue
- Present circumstances in which that position would be valid

4 Benefits to opponent

-Explains to opponents how they would benefit from adopting the writer's position

As we can observe above, unlike the classical argument that was invented by the Greek philosophers, Rogerian argument was introduced by Carl Rogers, an American psychologist. The discussion above states that some scholars have identified four stages of the Rogerian argument: introduction, contexts, writer's position, and benefits to opponent. However, just like the classical argument above, The College Board (2014:32 does not give us more details. In this study, a deeper knowledge on the elements that make up the Rogerian argument has been identified in the notes by an unknown author entitled "3 Types of Argument: Classical, Rogerian, Toulmin" thus:

1. **Introduction of Problem**: State the problem you hope to resolve. By presenting your issue as a problem you raise the possibility of positive change. Often opponents will want to solve the same problem.

2. **Summary of Opposing Views**: As accurately and neutrally as possible, state the views of the people with whom you disagree. By doing this you show that you are capable of listening without judging and have given a fair hearing to people who think differently from you.

3. **Statement of Understanding**: Also called the statement of validity. Show that you understand that there are situations in which these views are valid. Which parts of the opposing argument s do you concede? Under which conditions might you share these views?

4. **Statement of Your Position**: Now that readers have seen that you've given full consideration to views other than your own, they should be prepared to listen fairly to your views. State your position.

5. **Statement of Contexts:** Describe situations in which you hope your views will be honored. By showing that your position has merit in specific contexts, you recognize that people won't agree with you all of the time. However, opponents are allowed to agree in part and share common ground.

6. **Statement of Benefits**: Appeal to the self-interest of your opponents by showing how they would benefit from accepting your position; this concludes your essay on a hopeful, positive note.

Looking at the structure of the Rogerian argument above, we observe that like the elements of the classical argument as discussed above, the structure of the Rogerian argument is also made up of six elements: Introduction of Problem, Summary of Opposing Views, Statement of Understanding, Statement of Your Position, Statement of Contexts, and Statement of Benefits. Like the classical argument, the Rogerian argument also has specific situations in which it can be used. Talking about the conditions that favour the use of the Rogerian argument, "3 Types of Argument: Classical, Rogerian, Toulmin" states:

– With an audience who you don't relate to

– With an audience who doesn't share your views

– With an audience who has authority over you

– With an audience who is overly sensitive

Based on the citation above we realize that the situations in which the Rogerian argument are supposed to be used are different from those of the classical argument. However, "3 Types of Argument: Classical, Rogerian, Toulmin" tells us that a good situation in which Rogerian argument was applied was in "Queen Elizabeth's speech at Tilbury". In fact, these messages can push us to carry out more research if we are up to the task.

Summary of Rogerian Argument

In the course of reading through the situations in which the classical argument could be used, we observe that it is used in aggressive situations. The American psychologist, Carl Rogers, seemed to have studied the classical argument and introduce a type of an argument that is nonconfrontational. Like the classical argument, Rogerian argument also has six elements- . Introduction of Problem, Summary of Opposing Views, Statement of Understanding, Statement of Your Position, Statement of Contexts and Statement of Benefits. Based on its nonconfrontational approach, the situations in which the Rogerian argument can be used in include— With an audience who you don't relate to, with an audience who doesn't share your views, with an audience who has authority over you, with an audience who is overly sensitive, etc. From our reading above, we also learn that a good case in which the Rogerian argument was used was in "Queen Elizabeth's speech at Tilbury". So our students might go further to investigate more about the "Queen Elizabeth's speech at Tilbury" and other cases to understand how the Rogerian argument was well applied on an audience who you don't relate to and in a non-aggressive way.

3.5.3 Toulmin Argument

Besides the classical and the Rogerian arguments, the last type of argument to be highlighted in this study is Toulmin argument. Talking about Toulmin argument, The College Board (2014:32) narrates:

Stephen Toulmin, a British philosopher is credited for developing a "practical tool for understanding and shaping arguments in the real world". Lunsford and Ruszkiewicz ,p. 132). Rather than designate a certain organization plan for an argument, Toulmin model presents critical components that should be included in any type of argument:

Claim: Presents a controversial or debatable claim the writer plans to defend

Evidence: Provides reasons and examples to support the claim from a variety of sources (personal experience, anecdotes and observations, facts and statistics, authorities or experts in the field of study)

Warrant:

- Makes a logical and persuasive connection between a claim and the evidence supporting it

- Proposes a general principle that enables the writer to justify the move from a reason to a specific claim

- Presents a shared value or principle with the audience

Qualifiers: Includes words and phrases that place limits on claims

Conditions of rebuttal: Addresses potential objections/alternatives viewpoints.

Right up to this moment, we have examined two types of arguments: the classical and the Rogerian arguments. It has been highlighted that the classical argument can be used in aggressive situations, whereas the Rogerian argument is nonconfrontational. At this moment that we are focused on the Toulmin model, it should be noted that it is used by scientists to construct and promote knowledge. However, according to The College Board (2014:32), some excellent examples of works that have exploited the Toulmin model include:

1 "In praise of the F word" by Mary Sherry

2 "The separation of church and state" by Stephen L. Carter

3 "If Black English Isn't a Language, Then Tell Me, what Is?" By James Baldwin

4 "On Natural Death" by Lewis Thomas

In the discussion above, like the classical argument, The College Board (2014:32) also enlightens us on some key works in which more about the Toulmin model can be found. This suggests that more information about the Toulmin model can be examined in these works. So our students should consult these works to learn more about the Toulmin model. However, like the other two approaches above, the version of the Toulmin model according to the document entitled the "3 Types of Argument: Classical, Rogerian, Toulmin" narrates:

The twentieth-century British philosopher Stephen Toulmin noticed that good, realistic arguments typically will consist of six parts. He used these terms to describe the items.

1. **Data**: The facts or evidence used to prove the argument

2. **Claim**: The statement being argued (a thesis)

3. **Warrants**: The general, hypothetical (and often implicit) logical statements that serve as bridges between the claim and the data.

4. **Qualifiers**: Statements that limit the strength of the argument or statements that propose the conditions under which the argument is true.

5. **Rebuttals:** Counter-arguments or statements indicating circumstances when the general argument does not hold true.

6. **Backing**: Statements that serve to support the warrants (i.e., arguments that don't necessarily prove the main point being argued, but which do prove the warrants are true.)

From the discussion above, we learn that like the other two types of arguments, the Toulmin model is also made up of six elements: data, claim, warrants, qualifiers, rebuttals and backing. Talking about when to use the Toulmin model, the document entitled the "3 Types of Argument: Classical, Rogerian, Toulmin" narrates:

– When speaking to the scientific community

– When you are trying to put the facts at the forefront of your argument

– When your audience is very logical and rational

Based on the citation above, we now know that the Toulmin model of an argument is designed for intellectual discussions. It is logical, but does not identify the element of acknowledgement. The same document tells us that a good example of a study that used the Toulmin model is John Gage's "The Shape of Reason".

Summary of the Toulmin Model

In the course of reading through the three types of arguments, we have observed that these different argumentative approaches are designed for different purposes. We have seen how the classical type was used in "I have a dream speech", and the Rogerian arguments was used in "Queen Elizabeth's speech at Tilbury". The Toulmin model on its part is most used in the academics due to its logical orientation. Its main elements are data, claim, warrants, qualifiers, rebuttals, backing. It can be used in the following situations: – When speaking to the scientific community, when you are trying to put the facts at the forefront of your argument, when your audience is very logical and rational etc. From the discussion above, we read that a good example of the Toulmin model can be found in John Gage's "The Shape of Reason".

3.6 Elements of an Argumentative Writing

At this level, especially in this study, we are already informed of the three main types of argumentative approaches: -Classical argument, Rogerian argument and Toulmin argument. From the classical argument to the modern Toulmin argument, we have also observed that within each argument, there are elements which must be maintained when using any of the arguments. For now, our focus is on the main elements and not the order in which they should appear in an argument. Talking about some of these main elements, Stab (2015: 620) comments:

The internal structure of an argument consists of several argument components. It includes a claim and one or more premises (Govier 2010). The claim is a controversial statement and the central component of an argument, and premises are reasons for justifying (or refuting) the claim. Moreover, arguments have directed argumentative relations, describing the relationships one component has with another. Each such relation indicates that the source component is either a justification for or a refutation of the target component.

From the citation above, a keen reader can already identify some of the main components of an argument. However, besides the citation above, Booth, W. C.; Colomb, G. G. & Williams, J. M., (2003:113) state:

When you know enough to start planning your research report, you should have a tentative but clear understanding of your question and why it might matter to your readers, and a tentative but reasonably specific answer. You should have a list of reasons that support your claim and evidence to support those reasons, and some idea about the kinds of questions and objections your readers would be likely to raise, were they there in front of you. You won't be able to imagine all of their questions, nor will they expect you to. But you must anticipate at least the questions that generate the five elements of an argument and answer them before they're asked.

Although Booth et al. (2003) in the citation above focus on the academic domain or they use the Toulmin argument, we can see the importance of knowing the five importance elements of an argument. In another move to illustrate these five elements, Booth et al. (2003:114) further explain:

In a research report, you make a claim, back it with reasons based on evidence, acknowledge and respond to other views, and sometimes explain your principles of reasoning.

Talking about the five elements of an argument, Booth et al. (2003: 115) list:

1. What do you **claim**?

2. What **reasons** support that claim?

3. What **evidence** supports those reasons?

4. Do you **acknowledge** this alternative/complication/objection, and how do you **respond**?

5. What **principle (warrant)** justifies connecting your reasons to your claim?

As already mentioned above, the five elements of arguments listed above are based on Booth et al. (2003). Some students may want to see the element of data which is identified in Toulmin argument. It should be noted that data is synonymous to evidence or facts. At this moment in this study, a keen reader might have realized that there are four authors whose elements of an argument have been identified: classical, Rogerian, Toulmin and then the scholars, Booth et al (1995,2003) who elaborated on any of the three main types. The table below is a summary of the components of the main types of arguments including the one of Booth et al (1995, 2003) for a deeper understanding.

Classical	Rogerian	Toulmin	Booth et al (1995, 2003)		
Introduction (Exordium):	**Introduction of Problem**	Data	Claim		
Statement of Background (Narratio)	**Summary of Opposing Views**	Claim	Reason		

Proposition (Partitio)	Statement of Understanding	Warrants	Evidence		
. Proof (Confirmatio)	Statement of Your Position	Qualifiers	Acknowledgement		
Refutation (Refutatio)	Statement of Contexts	. Rebuttals	Respond		
. Conclusion (Peroratio)	Statement of Benefits	Backing	Principle (warrant		

Looking at the table above, we observe that there are certain elements that are common in all the arguments. The problems we might face is the equivalence of certain phrases or Latin words to single concepts in the modern English language and the ordering of these elements in individual argument. For example, we might not know whether "statement of background" in the classical argument has the same meaning as "claim" in the Toulmin model. However, our aim here is to identify the elements of each argument and then to analyze the problems highlighted above in subsequent sections especially in chapter five of this study.

3.7 Conclusion

Everything said and done, this chapter has examined the following concepts: the difference between a debate and an academic argument, the definition of an argumentative writing, the differences between argumentative and persuasive, the importance of argumentative essay, types of argumentative writings, and elements of an argumentative writing. An introduction study of this nature cannot sol-handedly examine the complex features of an argumentative discourse. However, it has been of prime importance for this chapter to reveal some importance qualities of an argument writing. For example, the ability to know the differences between an argumentative discourse and a debate, the differences between an argumentative writing and persuasive writing, and to highlight the various types of arguments known in discourse were deemed the core of this chapter. With these core concepts already identified, the chapter then highlights some minor qualities of an argument such as the definitions of an argumentative writing and some elements of an argument. With these basics features of an argumentative writing discussed in this chapter, we think that a sense of direction has been established in the argumentative discourse in our students' academic lives. Students can now use this knowledge as a stepping stone to carry out more findings on these features and other related feature in order to extend their skills in the argumentative writing and other forms of writing. This is possible if they exploit the tools of curiosity and critical thinking which have been discussed in chapter one of this study.

Chapter Four - The Introduction Part Of An Essay

4.0 Introduction

In the chapters above, we have observed some various descriptions of the Five- Paragraph Essay and some qualities of the argumentative essay. Unlike the Five –Paragraph Essay which has only five paragraphs: one introduction paragraph, three paragraphs for the body and one conclusion paragraph, the advanced argumentative essay can have more or less than five paragraphs, depending on the topic under discussion. For example, there are some advanced argumentative essays which have two paragraphs in the introduction section. Other advanced argumentative essays may have more than four paragraphs in their bodies and so on. Despite the many numbers of paragraphs in argumentative essays, the paragraphs of the body have the same purpose because they are all aimed at convincing readers instead of merely informing people as is the case with most logical thoughts of the Five –Paragraph Essay. Students of the higher level of learning need to acquaint themselves with these realities in order to succeed in their academic lives. This chapter therefore analyses how Moves can be identified and how they are related in the introduction paragraph of an essay. It is structured into two parts, the first sections examine the main ideas of an introduction and the second part examines how these main concepts appear as a Move or how they combine to form a Move, which is the basic unit of analysis in an introduction. This is necessary because some advanced essays have one paragraph introductions, whereas others have two paragraphs as their introduction paragraphs.

4.1 The Introduction Section of an Essay

Many scholars have examined the introduction part of essays (Franklin et al, 1986; love,1998; Afful, 2005; Ho, 2008; Kum, 2016;). However, from the works of these scholars cited above, we learn that in order to identify the introduction part of an essay, two criteria are needed: the structure and the function. The discussion below focuses on the functions and then the structure of the introduction section of an essay.

4.1.1 The Functions of the Introduction Section of an Essay

With regards to functions, the introduction paragraph of an essay has many roles. The first function of the introduction of an essay is to capture the interest of a reader. Experience has shown that once the introduction of an essay fails to capture its readers' interest in order to arouse their curiosity, many readers do not read the remaining parts of the writing. In fact, they immediately stop to read the essay at the level of the introduction as soon as it is poorly crafted. In order to capture the interest of readers in the introduction paragraph, experts use some tactics such as quotations, proverbs, anecdotes, questions, and so on. The second function of the introduction of an essay is that it contains the thesis statement of an essay. The thesis statement is the main point or the main idea that runs through the essay. Some writers often liken the thesis statement of an essay to the spinal cord of the human body because it joins all parts of an essay into a single whole. As soon as the thesis statement of an essay is not well highlighted, many readers find it very difficult to understand the essay at the level of its logic, its structure, its coherence, and even its linear nature. The third function of the introduction section of an essay is to state the various divisions that are found in an essay. Some writers state the structure of their essay in the introduction section of the essay. This may be before or after the thesis sentence. The fourth function of the introduction part of an essay is to orientate the reader towards the body of the essay and finally, the introduction of an essay serves as an eye- opener for the reader because it reveals important issues in the whole essay which the reader might have never known.

4.1.2 The Structure of the Introduction Section of an Essay

Talking about the structure, the introduction section of an essay is the first paragraph out of many paragraphs of an essay. However, unlike the five-paragraph essays, advanced essays may have two paragraphs within the introduction section and more paragraphs in the body section. The introduction section is easily recognized because it has the shape of an inverted pyramid. This is so because ideas found in the introduction section flow from a general to a specific perspective. These ideas are found in sub sections known as Moves. As already seen above, the introduction section of an essay occupies 10% of the total essay. The figure below is the physical representation of an introduction of an essay.

The parts of an essay

Introduction

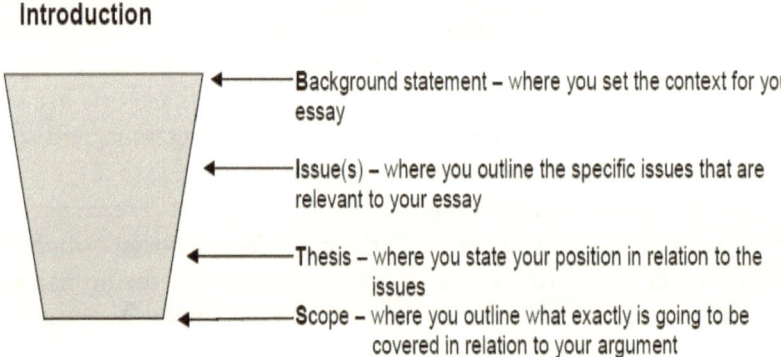

SOURCE: Essay writing from the English for Uni website

A keen look at the figure above shows that the introduction section has the shape of an inverted pyramid. If you look keenly at this introduction above, you may observe that there are four arrows indicating each section. The first arrow indicates (**Background**), the second arrow indicates (**Issue**), the third arrow indicates (**Thesis**), and the last arrow indicates (**Scope**).

4.2 Analysis of Moves of the Introduction Section of an Essay

The introduction paragraph of an academic genre whether it is the five paragraph essay, a longer essay, a research article or a conference paper and so on is made up of three Moves. However, depending on the level, the message, the purpose, and so on, some introductions can have two paragraphs, and others can indicate four Moves. Talking of the conditions that demand four Moves and how they can be distributed in the introduction section of a long essay, Rao et al. (2007:55) state:

of course, if there is the need for instance, if the essay is long or complex, so if your introduction is roughly 300 words, you might choose to split it into two paragraphs, with moves 1 and 2 in the first paragraph, and moves 3 and 4 in the second paragraph (you can see this is the introduction to the sociology essay above pp 53-54). If your introduction is short, you might need only one paragraph and cover all the 4 Moves.

The concept of whether or not an introduction should have three Moves or four Moves, or whether or not an introduction should have one paragraph or two paragraphs depends on your understanding of the discussion below. Although students use the word analyses on daily bases, many of them are not familiar with its real meaning. It might sound trivial, but the truth is that many common words are often minimized by learners. However, Rao et al. (2007:24) suggest that: "Analysis means breaking something down into its component parts and understanding how they relate to one another" From the definition above, it should be recalled that the breaking down of introductions into their various parts in order to understand how each part relates to one another (analysis) was first carried out by Swales in the 1980s, (Kum, 2016). Swales (1981) collected 48 articles introductions in scientific research papers covering three majors: 16 hard science articles, 16 biology medicine articles and 16 social science articles (education management and language). (kum, 2016). After a closed examination, Swales observed that these introductions contained repeated patterns, which were similar to one another. These repeated patterns were named by swales as a system of rhetorical or discourse analysis known as "Move Analysis". Swales identified four Moves:

Move 1 establishing the field

Move 2 summarizing previous research

Move 3 preparing for present research

Move 4 introducing the present research

. Besides the explanation above, a brief account on the origin of the 4 Moves has been highlighted by Rao, Chanock and Krishnan, (2007:53) thus:

The classic '4 Moves of the introduction' were first identified by J. Swales in 1981(Aspects of article introductions', Aston ESP Research Report No. 1, Language Studies Unit, University of Aston Birmingham). The original article analyzed introductions to scientific journal articles. The '4 Moves' have been adapted since then by many academics and students to suit their needs, as indeed we too have done.

The quotation above describes the origin of the four move system. However, many scholars found the four Moves pattern confusing and difficult to apply. Swales then reworked on his analysis and came up with three Moves backed by steps or strategies (Kum, 2016). Swales in 1990 revised the model and called it "create a research space (CARS)" the create a research space (CARS) model has tree moves. Under each move, they are steps or strategies that enables us to identify each Move. The discussion below illustrates the three Moves and their various Steps.

Move1: Establishing a Territory

Step1 claim centrality and/ or

Step2; making topic general action (s) and or

Step3 reviewing terms of previous research

Move 2 Establishing a Niche

Step 1 A counter claiming or

Step 1 B indicating a gap or

Step 1 C question raising or

Step 1 D containing a tradition

Move 3 Occupying the Niche

Step 1 A outlining purposes or

Step 1 B announcing present research

Step 2 announcing principal finding

Step 3 indicating research article structure

With the CARS model already established above, we should remind ourselves that those three repeated patterns which Swales identified are known as "Moves". Everything said and done it is important to know that condor (2000) defines a Move as "a sub-communicative functional unit, used for an identifiable purpose which contributes to the overall communicative purpose of the text". Talking about a Step, Yang (2009) defines a Step as "a rhetorical strategy or technique employed by a writer to realize the purpose of a Move."

Looking at the structure of the introduction above, we observe that it is labeled with four arrows. This suggests that the authors illustrate the various parts of an introduction. For example, the authors highlight: **Background, Issue, Thesis, and Scope**. Now, look at the same introduction below.

Introduction

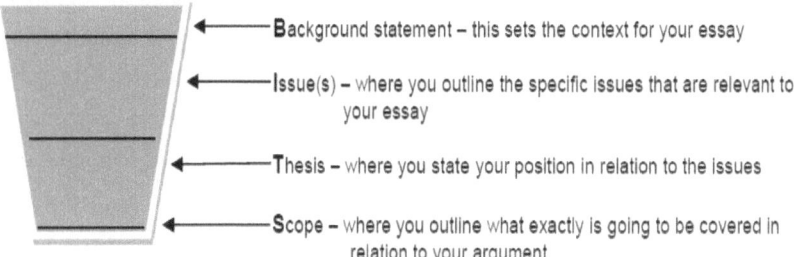

Source: **Essay writing from the English for Uni website**

In this second introduction above, we observe that the authors go further to divide the introduction into three main parts. The first part has one arrow that indicates **B**ackground statement – this sets the context for your essay, the second part also has one arrow which indicates **I**ssue(s) – where you outline the specific issues that are relevant to your essay, and the third section or last section has two arrows: **T**hesis – where you state your position in relation to the issues, and then the **S**cope – where you outline what exactly is going to be covered in relation to your argument. These three parts of the introduction are known as "Moves". In other words, Move 1 has the part **B**ackground statement – this sets the context for your essay, Move 2 has the part **I**ssue(s) – where you outline the specific issues that are relevant to your essay and Move 3 has the parts **Thesis** – where you state your position in relation to the issues, and then the **Scope** – where you outline what exactly is going to be covered in relation to your argument. We can summarize the information above thus:

Move 1(Background statement – this sets the context for your essay)

Move 2 (Issue(s) – where you outline the specific issues that are relevant to your essay)

Move3 (Thesis – where you state your position in relation to the issues and Scope – where you outline what exactly is going to be covered in relation to your argument)

From the discussion above, we can conclude that the order of ideas of the introduction above is **BITS (Background, Issue, Thesis, Scope)**.

Besides the arrangement above another introduction can have the order **BIST (Background, Issue, Scope, Thesis)**. That means only "S" **(Scope)** changes it position with "T" **(Thesis)**. Thesis takes the last position instead of Scope. The summary of this organization looks thus:

Move 1 (Background statement – this sets the context for your essay)

Move 2 (Issue(s) – where you outline the specific issues that are relevant to your essay)

Move 3 (Scope – where you outline what exactly is going to be covered in relation to your argument and Thesis – where you state your position in relation to the issues)

A keen look at the discussion above shows that there are two introductions: the one having the organization **BITS (Background, Issue, Thesis, and Scope)**, and the other one having the arrangement **BIST (Background, Issue, Scope, and Thesis)**. These two introductions are similar because they both have three Moves but differ in that the first one ends with the Scope whereas the second one ends in the Thesis. Based on the explanation above, we can now see that the last Move of an introduction is made up of two important items: Thesis and Scope. These two items of Move 3 (Thesis and

Scope) can be interchanged; one can come before the other and vice versa.

Talking about long essays with 4 Moves in the introduction section, it is because some writers consider Scope as a Move and the Thesis as another. However, as we have seen above, all these items are under Move 3. Using this model, we can then analyze the introduction of an essay by identifying each Move and then by showing how these Moves relate to one another. It should be noted that Moves are of various sizes and names but must contain a proposition or a main idea. The table below shows the different names of Moves in the introduction section, given by some scholars.

MOVE	SWALES (1990)	AFFUL (2005)	ANDERSON (1993)
1	Establishing a territory	Contextualizing issue(s)	Orientation
2	Establishing a niche	Engaging closely whit issue(s)	Justification
3	Occupying a niche	Previewing structure of entire essay\ stating purpose	Focus on your paper

The table above indicates three different scholars: Swales (1990), Afful (2005) and Anderson (1993). As we have mentioned above, Swales (1990) worked on the introductions of articles. The two other scholars: Afful (2005) and Anderson (1993) worked on essays. Whether the move analysis was carried out on the introduction section of research articles or the introduction section of essay, these findings all applied the theoretical framework of the introduction section that Swales (1990) established. The discussion below focuses on the analyses of the three Moves that Swales (1990) identified. No matter the level, a good mastering of each Move and its various steps will enable you to handle the introduction section of any academic genre whether the

Five-paragraph essay, Six- paragraph essay or any advanced pierce of writing with relative ease. The phrases are drawn from many writers such as Kum (2016), Swales (1990), Afful (2005) and Anderson (1993), and so on.

4.2.1 Move 1: Establishing a Territory

This move often describes the general layout, field, context or topic. In fact, it introduces a broader perspective of your topic or field of research. This can be attained by using any of these steps or strategies:

step1, claiming centrality;

step2, making topic generalization;

step3, reviewing item of previous research

In the lines below we describe each of these three steps and the phrases that are common in each of them.

Step1: Claiming Centrality

If the writer chooses to use this step or strategy in move 1, he or she will state how the topic of the essay or research is useful, important, relevant or worth investigating or writing on. These are some of the phrases that are common in this strategy, technique or step.

- The effect of -----has been stated extensively in recent years

- Of the many ----- have been the most widely studied

- The effect of ---- have received considerable attention

- Many investigations have recently turned to…

- A large body of data concerning ----- has been reported

- In recent years, there have been many papers describing…

- Recently there have been wide interest in ------

- In recent years, researchers have become increasingly interested in------

- The possibility of----- has generated interest in-----

- Knowledge of------- has great important for------

- The study of------ has become in important aspect of-----

- The central issue in------ is the validity of-----

- --- are believed to play an important role in-----

- The well-know----- phenomena------ have been favorable topic for analysis both in---

- A long standing problem has been to obtain more information on...

- The explication of the relationship between ...and...is a classic problem in farming

Step 2: Making Topics Generalization

Another writer or even you can decide to choose step 2 or strategy 2 instead of step1 above in writing or stating move1. If the writer chooses step 2 he or she will not be talking of the importance or usefulness of the topic. Instead the writer will be talking of the current state of knowledge, thought, practice or description of phenomena of the topic. The phrases below are those that are common in this strategy.

- The general features of------ are well known

- It is generally accepted that-------

- There is now much evidence to support the thinking that

- People believe that-----

- It is commonly suggested that------

- A standard procedure for assessing------ has been------

- Trout are believed to be relatively immobile

- An increase of mallards in eastern North America has been well documented

- Such methods are often criticized for------

- Plumage coloration is known to influence mate selection in mallards

- Comparisons of spatially separated population fend to consist of-----
-

- The history of this illness has been well studied------

- This plant, animal is generally looked upon-----

Step 3: Reviewing Items of Previous Works

Many writers might prefer to use step 3 or strategy 3 in their move 1. In this step instead of stating the importance of the topic as in step 1 or describing general or popular knowledge about the topic as in step 2, the writer is expected to cite or quote any authority who has talked about the topic or to introduce a popular proverb and so on that will highlight the relationship or the popularity or the importance of the topic to the present study. The phrases common in those strategies are:

- Smith (1984) found------

- Kum (2016) defines ------

- Nkemleke (2000) suggested that-------

- Finding by Neba (2017) suggests that-------

- There is a proverb that-------

- It has been suggested that ------

Using any one of the three steps discussed above implies you have written move 1. We now focus on move 2 of the introduction section of an essay or a research paper.

4.2.2 Move 2: Establishing a Niche

As already highlighted above, many authors use different names for each Move. For example, talking of Move 2, Swales (1990) calls it **Establishing a Niche**, Anderson (1993) terms Move 2, **Justification**, Afful (2005) names it "**Engaging Closely with Issue(s)** ", Rao et als (2007) says **Focus** and lynch ( ) looks upon it as **Focus on Your Papers**. From these various names of move 2, we can suggest the main idea that runs through in Move 2. In fact, after you must have given a general view of the topic in Move 1, Move 2 demands you to establish a base, a focus, or a center of your topic. You can establish a base of your topic by showing that the previous finding was not complete, or that you agree with the research or topic and you want to Shed more light on it. In order to attain these wishes, you will use any of the steps or the strategies that are common of move 2:

Step 1 A, counter claiming;

Step 1 B, indicating a gap (in previous research);

Step 1 C raising a question (about previous research),

Step 1 D continuing a tradition

Like move1, the discussion below explains all the steps of Move 2.

Steps I A: Counter-Claiming

The most common feature of this step or strategy is that it often follows Step 3 **reviewing items of previous research** of Move 1. It comes in to introduce an opposing view point or it comes in to pin point some of the weaknesses in the previous finding which was described in Move1, step 3. Some of the phrases common in step 1A of Move 2 are:

However, this view is challenged by recent data showing...

However, these studies have failed to recognize the...

However, recent work in our findings suggest that...

...but the experiments were performed, on...and are therefore...

...these approaches become increasingly unreliable when...

Step I B: Indicating a Gap (in previous research)

Unlike step I A above that closely follows step 3 of Move 1, step I B "indicating a gap" follows steps 2 of Move 1 (making topic generalization). In other words, step I B in Move 2 follows step 2 of Move 1, and its intention is to show the gap that exists in that topic generalization of step 2 in Move 1. Some phrase common in this strategy (step IB) include:

-A considerable amount of research has been ...but little research...

...has been extensively studied. However, less attention has been paid to...

-As a result, no comprehension theory appears to exist.

-Despite the importance of...few researchers have studied...

-Research has tended to focus on...rather than...

-The only reported study to date of...covered a limited range of...

...studies have appeared previously in the literature but measurements were restricted to...

-The properties of...are still not completely understood

-Evidence on this question is presently inconclusive

Step I C: Raising a Question (about previous research)

Step I C can follow any of the steps in Move 1. Phrases common in step 1C are:

-However, it is not clear whether the use of ...can be modified to...

-In spite of these early observations, the mechanism...has remained unclear

-The question remains ...

-How much has seal population actually decreased?

Step I D: Continuing a Tradition

Step I D can follow any of the steps in Move 1 and is signaled by logical connectors, such as therefore hence, as a result, consequently, and so on. Common phrases in step Id includes:

-These differences need to be analyzed

-Hence, additional studies of...are needed

-It is desirable to carry out surveys of...

-it is interesting to compare

From the explanation above, we observe that:

Steps I A: **Counter-Claiming** of Move 2 follows step 3 **Reviewing Items of Previous Research** of Move 1.

Step I B: **Indicating a Gap (in previous research)** of Move 2 follows steps 2 **Making Topic Generalization** of Move 1

Step I C **Raising a Question (about previous research)** can follow any of the steps in Move 1.

Step I D **Continuing a Tradition** can follow any of the steps in Move 1

4.2.3 Move 3: Occupying the Niche

Like the other two Moves discussed above, Move 3 also has many names by different scholars. Swales (1990) calls it **Occupying a**

Niche, Anderson (1993) names it as **Focus on your paper,** Afful (2005) says Previewing **Structure of Entire Essay/Stating Purpose** and Rao et als (2007) term it **Signpost structure of argument.** At this moment it should be noted that many essays or research papers end in move 3. Move 3 is very important because it contains the thesis statement of your essay. These statement is the aim or the purpose of your essay. In other words, the main idea that you want to tell your readers. Rao et al (2007) liken the thesis statement to our spinal cord, which supports our skeleton. Apart from the thesis statement, Move 3 also contains the scope of your essay or it shows the structure of your essay, it fills the gap raised in Move 2 or it continues with the tradition also raised in Move 2. In order to attain your goal in Move 3, you will still use steps or strategies. The steps of Move 3 include:

Step I A: out lining purpose (why);

Step 1 B: Announcing present research (what? where, who, why)

Step 2: Announcing main finding;

Step 3: indicating structure of the paper;

Step 4, Evaluation of finding).

like the other Moves above, the rest of the discussion below explain each step of Move 3.

Step IA: Outlining Purposes (why?)

In this strategy, the writer introduces the solutions to the problems he or she has highlighted in move 2. In fact, the writer states his aim of the study and why it is necessary. Common phrases are:

-The aim of this essay is to…

-The purpose here is o document…

-The aim of the present study was to…

-The objective of this essay

-Our purpose was to describe, narrate etc.

Step I B: Announcing Present Research (what, where, how, why, who)

This step is a bit different from step IA in that it might not be necessary linked to solution from move 2. Step I B actually sets out to describe what the paper aims to do without only limiting it Self to move 2. Common phrases are:

_In this study we suggest a 3 step process...

In this essay, we propose a.... algorithm...

In this paper, we attempt to develop a...

In this letter, we provide a new approach to...

In this essay, we describe novel algorithm for...

In this paper, we present a system of...

This paper evaluates the effect on...

This research presents data on...

This essay focuses on a strategy for

The present study tests...

-This thesis proposes a formal procedure for...

-This paper introduces a novel architecture for...

Step 2: Announcing Main Findings

Step 2 of Move 3 is a delicate step because not all discipline might accept it. Step 2 focuses solely on results that were established from previous findings. In this situation, we might suggest that this step is inclined toward advanced learners. However, common phrases of step 2 include:

-In this paper we agree that ...

-This approach provides effective...

-Our results indicate that this method is effective in...

Step 3: Indicating Structure of the Paper

Some scholars such as Rao et al. (2007) suggest that this step 3 can be another Move, not a step. They call it **Signpost structure of argument**. Well as earlier said, it depends on the length of your essay. Some advanced essays are longer than our Five-paragraph essay and so deserves more discussion. However, step 3 is all about stating how your essay is structured. But in a five paragraphs essay, the structure is already known so your theses statement (step IA, IB) should be well stated. Common phrases include:

-We have organized the rest of this paper in the following way

-This essay is structured as follows

-The remainder of this paper is divided into five sections

Step 4: Evaluation of Findings

Step 2 and Step 4 of Move 3 are almost the same but that in step four, more discussion is needed on how you evaluate the finds and not only stating them. Common phrases include:

-The advantages are more …

-The high level of …

-More disadvantages were incur …

-The joy from those…

4.3 Thesis Sentence

Many students have scored very low marks in their essays, not because their language was poor, not because their ideas were irrelevant, not because their organization of ideas was incoherent, and so on, but because they failed to respect the contract they signed with their readers or that they did not sign a contract with their readers at all. The contract you sign with your readers when writing an essay is known as the thesis statement. The thesis statement is so important in an essay to the point that it has been given different names. Some scholars call it a "contract", others name it the "spinal cord", of an essay, and in the argumentative genre, the thesis statement is known as the "main claim" or just a "claim". Based on the discussion above, it has been highlighted that a thesis statement alternates with the scope in some advanced writings in the introduction. There are many essays that the thesis statement appears before the scope and there are equally some essays that it appears after the scope. Following the analysis above, the thesis statement is the core of Move 3. This suggests that the thesis statement occupies the last position in an introduction. The discussion below highlights some important characteristics of a Thesis statement such as qualities, some types of thesis statement, choosing a thesis statement, structure of a thesis statement, some differences between facts and theses statement.

4.3.1 Differences between the Topic of an Essay and its thesis Statements

Some students may find it very difficult to make a distinction between a topic and a thesis statement of an essay. A topic often contains an issue or a question that needs to be answered or solved. The thesis statement can be likened to the answer to that question or a solution to that issue based on an opinion. So your opinion or position to an issue or a problem raised in a topic is your thesis statement or your claim. More on this can be read from Writing Center English 800 Center thus:

While the topic is what the paper is about, the thesis defines your opinion or position on that particular topic. For this reason, it is important to develop a tentative or working thesis statement early in composing your essay because it will help guide your thoughts and possible research. When you have decided on your essay's topic, you can begin to develop your thesis by examining your topic, perhaps doing some exploratory reading and writing, or reflecting and pulling from class discussions or conversations with classmates and friends. A writer develops a thesis by asking questions about the topic and by focusing on a basic point or question which the topic raises. The answer to such a question will be your thesis: what you think about a specific topic. The topic is your question, and the thesis your answer to that question.

The citation above reminds us that a topic is the general idea of any writing and a thesis statement is your position or opinion about the topic. A good example of a topic and a position or an opinion that forms a thesis statement can be seen in this unknown author below thus:

Topic: Should teens be able to buy violent video games?

Thesis: Teens should not be able to purchase violent video games because they are not mature enough to handle the content, it can increase aggressive behavior later in life, and violent video games desensitize players to real-life violence.

The citation above indicates how a question has been raised in the topic and how a position, an opinion or a claim has been developed from that question. In answering the questions above, many positions can be realized: those that are for, those that are against like the example above, and those that are neutral or even confused. The discussion below focuses on the structure of a thesis statement.

4.3.2 Structure of a thesis statement

A sound knowledge of the structure of a main claim in the argumentative writing can help to foster our understanding of the thesis statement or the main claim. Many scholars have identified the structure of the thesis statement. Although some use different appellations of the various parts, they have the same semantic sense. Look at the illustrations below from Writing Center English 800 Center:

TOPIC	OPINION	REASONS OR SUPPORTING EVIDENCE
Attending a community college like CSM	makes sense	since the cost is low and the quality of instruction is high.

TOPIC	OPINION	REASONS OR SUPPORTING EVIDENCE
Cell phone use while driving	should be banned,	for it creates an unsafe environment not only for drivers using them but also for other people in nearby vehicles.

In the illustration above, the authors demonstrates the structure of a thesis statement. Looking at the illustrations very keenly, you may observe that a thesis statement is made up of three parts: the topic, the opinion, or claim, and the reasons for making the main claim. So the formula is topic + opinion + reason. This is the core structure of a thesis statement. However, some scholars may use other appellations for each part rather than topic + opinion + reason. In this sense, look at the illustration below from unknown author.

CONSTRUCTING A STRONG THESIS

o How do you write a good thesis statement?

o Topic + belief/claim(using an active verb) + prongs / main points = Strong thesis

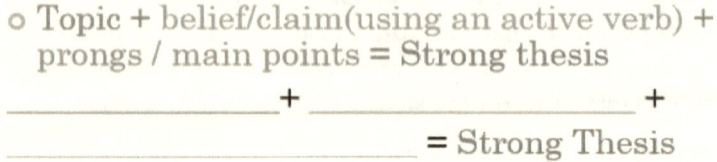

Teens should not be able to purchase violent video games because they are not mature enough to handle the content, it can increase aggressive behavior later in life, and violent video games desensitize players to real-life violence.

Unlike the first scholar who used topic + opinion + reason for the structure of a thesis statement, the second author above talks of topic + belief/claim + prong/main points for the structure of a thesis statement. These two illustrations above suggest that many names can be given to any part of the thesis statement. For example opinion can be called belief or a claim and the reason section can be called prongs or main points. More on the different appellations of these parts of a thesis statement can be seen in the example below drawn from RedRocks Community College Writing Center (2019) thus:

Parts of a thesis (claim + road map):
- **Claim or main idea:** This part states the main idea of the essay.
  ✓ **Example:** *Being a vegetarian is better than eating meat...*
- **Road map:** This part lists the major supporting reason(s) discussed in the body of the essay. Note that not all instructors require this part; always consult your professor's instructions.
  ✓ **Example:** *... because it is healthier, less expensive, and doesn't harm animals.*
- **Claim + Road Map = Entire Thesis Statement**
  ✓ **Example:** *Being a vegetarian is better than eating meat because it is healthier, less expensive, and doesn't harm animals.*

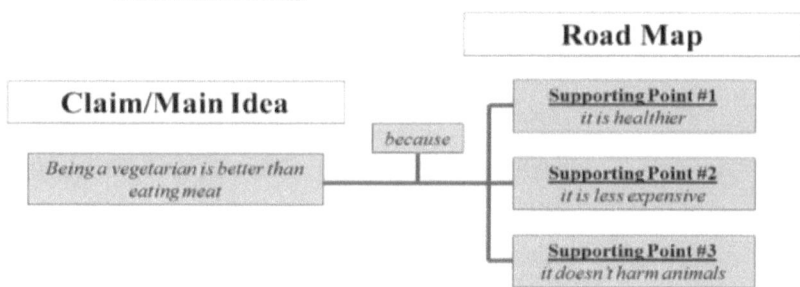

The illustration above of the structure of a thesis statement has no topic as was the case in the first and second examples above. The structure of the third example is just main claim + road map. We neither have topic + opinion + reason nor topic + belief/claim + prong/main points. This only suggests that you must be vigilant whenever your thesis statement has to be used. However, a normal thesis statement is made up of a topic + a claim + reasons. An argument is made up of topic+ claim+ reasons+ evidence. The last example of the structure of an argumentative main claim in this study is adapted from Surdzial,(2019) thus:

Thesis Structure:

1. *Your claim/assertion*

2. The reasons/evidence to support this claim (or categories of analysis)

3. **The order in which you'll present your reasons and evidence**

Examples:

➢ *Tutors should not write essays for their students* because the students will not benefit or grow as writers from this form of assistance since **the students do not learn how to identify and fix their mistakes by themselves.**

> *The public would benefit from additional legislation limiting gun ownership* because such <u>legislation will reduce the number of casualties from</u> **suicides, domestic abuse, and mass shootings**.

In the thesis statement above, Surdzial,(2019) gives us this formula- *claim/ assertion*+ <u>reasons/evidence</u> + **order or scope**. This suggests that the author combines thesis statement and the scope as we have seen in the structure of the introduction above. In order to illustrate the different parts of the structure of the thesis statement above, the author italicizes the claim; he underlines the reasons and darkens the scope. A sharp student can further analyze the two examples above by identifying the two topics: "Tutors" and "the public" respectively.

Now that you can identify the parts of an argumentative thesis statement, we think that more examples of the division of thesis statement is very necessary for your acquaintance. We think that a sound knowledge of the structure above can enable students to identify the parts of other essay genres such as the persuasive, compare and contrast, and so on. It is for this reason that Blinn College- Bryan Writing Center Spring 2023 was consulted. In this document, more than ten thesis statements have been cited and their various parts identified. The rest of the discussion below highlights the study in Blinn College- Bryan Writing Center Spring 2023. As already mentioned above, Blinn College- Bryan Writing Center Spring 2023 has identified, analyzed and discussed many thesis statements for your deeper understanding thus:

1. **Causal Argument**

   What it does: Examines a cause and its effects, states an effect and traces the effect back to its causes, or debunks an existing cause-and-effect argument.

   Include in your thesis: Topic (cause OR effect) and statement of the effects OR the causes; or an existing argument and the reasons why it is invalid.

   Example thesis: Climate change [Topic (cause)] endangers life on earth because [Claim] it is leading to an increase in catastrophic weather events [Effect 1], warmer average temperatures [Effect 2], and a rise in sea levels that threaten coastal communities [Effect 3].

2. **Compare and Contrast Argument**

   What it does: Evaluates the similarities and the differences of a particular topic. You can think of "compare" as discussing similarities and "contrast" as discussing differences.

   Include in your thesis: Topic (the item, process, situation, or solution; or the literary element or theme), claim about similarities, claim about differences, evidence to support both claims. The thesis statement will often include words such as "although," "even though," and "while."

   Example thesis: Although Gilman's "The Yellow Wallpaper" [Topic, part 1] and Ibsen's *A Doll House* [Topic, part 2] both explore the subjugation of married women in the late nineteenth century [Similarity], the authors use characterization [Difference 1] and point of view in distinct ways to portray different outcomes: a descent into madness in the case [Difference 2 / Evidence 1] of Gilman's protagonist and a greater sense of individuation in the case of Ibsen's Nora. [Evidence 2]

3. **Definitional Argument**

    What it does: Examines the nature of a word or a concept, a person, an event or a situation, or an object.

    Include in your thesis: Topic (the term, situation, or phenomenon you are defining), category, criteria for meeting this category, your claim.

    Example thesis: American Sign Language [Topic] should be considered [Claim] a foreign language [Category] for the purpose of a college graduation requirement because it is not a language used within most American families, [Criterion 1] and it is usually learned outside of the family setting. [Criterion 2]

4. **Ethical Argument**

    What it does: Assesses whether a person, thing, or action is right or wrong through an examination of either principles or consequences, or both.

Include in your thesis: Topic, claim of whether the topic you are analyzing is right or wrong, the consequence(s) or the principle(s) that determine the rightness or wrongness of the topic.

Example thesis (consequences): Recycling [Topic] consumer products, packaging, and other waste is a positive behavior [Claim] to encourage in local residents because it keeps waste out of the landfill [Consequence 1], reuses manufacturing resources instead of requiring new ones [Consequence 2], and is healthier for the environment [Consequence 3].

Example thesis (principle): Recycling [Topic] consumer products, packaging, and other waste is the right action to take [Claim] because it is the duty of citizens to serve as good stewards of the earth [Principle].

5. **Evaluation Argument**

    What it does: Assesses whether a person, thing, or action is a good or a bad member of its category through an examination of the criteria determining goodness or badness.

    Include in your thesis: Topic, category, claim as to whether the topic you are analyzing is good or bad, criteria for a good or bad member of this category.

    Example thesis: From the point of view of customers, Facebook [Topic] is a poor medium [Claim] for conducting business transactions because it does not keep personal and financial information secure [Criterion 1], it is constantly changing [Criterion 2], and it is more time-consuming than a regular website [Criterion 3].

6. **Literary Analysis Argument**

    What it does: Analyzes the text of a short story, play, or poem and makes a claim about how various literary elements illustrate the theme of the piece, revealing how these literary elements and the theme work together to create meaning for the audience.

Thesis Statement Types & Models
Blinn College – Bryan Writing Center
Spring 2023

Include in your thesis: Title of the literary piece, genre, author, theme, statement of how the author uses literary elements (character, tone, setting, imagery, point of view, etc.) to illustrate the theme.

Example thesis—Short story: Nathaniel Hawthorne's [Author] short story [Genre] "The Birth-Mark" [Title] illustrates the destructive powers of perfectionism [Theme] through the author's adept use of symbolism [Lit. Element 1] and foreshadowing [Lit. Element 2].

Example thesis—Poem: Adrienne Rich's [Author] 1955 poem [Genre] "Living in Sin" [Title] builds an extended metaphor [Lit. Element 1] rich in imagery [Lit. Element 2] and symbolism [Lit. Element 3] to convey the disillusionment that often occurs in the early years of marriage [Theme].

7. **Persuasive Argument**

    What it does: Persuades the audience that your position on this issue has merit or to believe as you would like them to believe.

    Include in your thesis: Topic, claim, evidence.

    Example thesis: Climate change [Topic] threatens the health and safety of all Americans [Claim] because of the increase in air pollution [Evidence 1], the rise in the number of days with record-breaking heat [Evidence 2], and the greater frequency of catastrophic weather events [Evidence 3].

8. **Pro/Con Argument**

   What it does: Examines an issue from different perspectives and offers a recommendation based on a careful analysis of both the positive and the negative aspects of the issue.

   Include in your thesis: Topic, summary of pros, summary of cons, claim.

   Example thesis: Proponents of higher education maintain that college graduates earn more and experience better physical and mental health, while opponents state that college is not appropriate for everyone and that student loan debt is crippling. However, a careful analysis of both sides of the "should you get a college education?" argument reveals that the advantages of a college degree outweigh the disadvantages.

   (Annotations: Topic, Pro 1, Pro 2, Con 1, Con 2, Topic (restated), Claim)

9. **Proposal Argument**

   What it does: Identifies a problem or a need, proposes an action-based solution(s), and demonstrates feasibility.

   Include in your thesis: Topic (problem/need), claim, possible solutions to the problem.

   Example thesis: The governments of all fifty states in the United States should promote measures to limit global warming by educating consumers, by giving tax incentives to green businesses, and by developing public transit systems.

   (Annotations: Topic, Claim, Solution 1, Solution 2, Solution 3)

Thesis Statement Types & Models
Blinn College – Bryan Writing Center
Spring 2023

10. Rhetorical Analysis Argument

What it does: Examines the organization and effectiveness of a written or visual argument.

Include in your thesis: Author's or artist's name, title of the work, topic of the analyzed work, analyzed work's claim, your claim (whether the rhetoric is effective, partially effective, or not effective), evidence supporting your claim using rhetorical strategies (ethos, pathos, logos, kairos).

Example thesis: In his humorous article, "Eat and Croak," [Title] Maynard G. Finnegan [Author] effectively uses [Claim] pathos, ethos, and logos [Rhetorical Strategies 1, 2, 3] to convince his audience that genetically modified foods [Topic of the article] may not be a consumer's best choice [Claim of the article].

Example thesis: Kathryn Tyler's [Author] article, "The Tethered Generation," [Title] on the adverse effects of technology on millennials [Topic of the article] creates a somewhat successful argument [Claim of the article / Claim, part 1] through her use of logical organization [Rhet. Strategy 1], appropriate sources [Rhet. Strategy 2], and on-level language [Rhet. Strategy 3] suitable for her audience but falls short with her omission of technology's benefits [Claim, part 2].

11. Rogerian Argument

What it does: Identifies an issue and acknowledges opposing positions while also presenting evidence for your own position in a fair and respectful way with the intent of opening up dialogue between you and the audience. The thesis is often delayed until the end of the essay.

Include in your thesis: Topic, acknowledgment of the opposing viewpoint, a balanced presentation of your own viewpoint with a summary of the already-presented evidence.

Example thesis: While civilian gun ownership is acceptable for personal protection [Writer's Viewpoint], the idea to eliminate gun control laws is not the best solution [Opposition Viewpoint]. Agreeing that pursuing responsible gun ownership [Topic] is a step in the right direction to reduce the number of accidents [Evidence 1], keep guns away from children [Evidence 2], and reduce access to guns capable of unleashing mass murder [Evidence 3].

The discussion above has identified many thesis statements. The authors identify, explain and illustrate the various parts of the thesis statements. Students must take this advantage and learn how to write or recognize the structures of thesis statements in general and those in their domain in general. The discussion below focuses on some main kinds of thesis statements which are very important at the higher levels.

4.3.3 Some kinds of thesis statements

The discussion above focused more on the division of thesis statements into their various parts. This section examines the main differences amongst some key thesis statement that you may meet not long from now. Talking about the different types of thesis sentences, ResearchLeap ( ) narrates:

Your thesis statement will depend on what kind of paper you are writing.

What is the paper's purpose? —to convince?, to explain?, to analyze?

Argumentative Thesis Statement. An argumentative paper takes a position
or makes an assertion or a claim and supports or justifies the position, assertion, or claim with reasons and evidence. An argumentative paper seeks to convince the reader that your position, assertion or claim is true. An
argumentative thesis tells your reader what your argument is and what supporting evidence or reasons you will present.

For example, "Smoking should be banned in all public places."

Explanatory (Expository) Thesis Statement. An explanatory paper explains or acquaints your reader with something (your topic). An explanatory thesis statement tells your reader what you will explain and what
aspects or parts of the topic will be considered.

For example, "Chinese labor played an important role in western railroad
expansion."

Analytical Thesis Statement. An analytical paper evaluates an issue or
idea, usually by considering its various aspects or parts, and presents this
evaluation to the reader. An analytical thesis statement tells your reader what issue or idea you are analyzing, what aspects of the issue or idea you are evaluating and how you will be presenting your analyses.

For example, "An analysis of the ferruginous hawk reveals two kinds of
flight patterns: patterns related to hunting prey and patterns related to

Many writers have suggested that the most important essay genres that higher student needs are the argumentative, the expository and the analytic. Although all essay genres are very important, we feel that a sound base in the argumentative genre is very imperative because it builds knowledge and does not only analyze or explain knowledge. The discussion below handles some qualities of thesis statements.

4.3.4 Qualities of a thesis statement

Talking about the qualities of a thesis statement, Messenger et al. (2013-2014 :19) state:

A thesis statement is a sentence that:

-Identifies the limited topic and the main idea of your essay.

-Usually appears as the last sentence in the introductory paragraph.

-Lets the reader know what you are trying to prove or demonstrate.

Besides the citation on a thesis sentence above, there are some good qualities of a thesis sentence. Courtesy the Odegaard Writing & Research Center () explains:

Despite the differences from discipline to discipline, a good thesis will generally have the following characteristics:

1. **A good thesis sentence will make a claim.** This doesn't mean that you have to reduce an idea to an "either/or" proposition and then take a stand. Rather, you need to develop an interesting perspective that you can support and defend. This perspective must be more than an observation. "America is violent" is an observation. "Americans are violent because they are fearful" (the position that Michael Moore takes in Bowling for Columbine) is an argument. Why? Because it posits a perspective. It makes a claim. Put another way, a good thesis sentence will inspire (rather than quiet) other points of view. One might argue that America is violent because of its violent entertainment industry. Or because of the proliferation of guns. Or because of the disintegration of the family. In short, if your thesis is positing something that no one can (or would wish to) argue with, then it's not a very good thesis.

2. **A good thesis sentences will control the entire argument.** Your thesis sentence determines what you are required to say in a paper. It also determines what you cannot say. Every paragraph in your paper exists in order to support your thesis. Accordingly, if one of your

paragraphs seems irrelevant to your thesis you have two choices: get rid of the paragraph, or rewrite your thesis. Understand that you don't have a third option: you can't simply stick the idea in without preparing the reader for it in your thesis. The thesis is like a contract between you and your reader. If you introduce ideas that the reader isn't prepared for, you've violated that contract.

3. **A good thesis will provide a structure for your argument.** A good thesis not only signals to the reader what your argument is, but how your argument will be presented. In other words, your thesis sentence should either directly or indirectly suggest the structure of your argument to your reader. Say, for example, that you are going to argue that "American fearfulness expresses itself in three curious ways: A, B, and C." In this case, the reader understands that you are going to have three important points to cover, and that these points will appear in a certain order. If you suggest a particular ordering principle and then abandon it, the reader will feel betrayed, irritated, and confused.

Another scholar that highlights the qualities of a thesis statement is Whitaker (2009). The author gives a detailed summary of the importance of the thesis sentence. From her findings, we observe that the thesis sentence is an opinion; it shows the purpose and so on. Below is a quotation from Whitaker (2009)

The thesis statement is the most important sentence in your paper. If someone asked you, "What does your paper say?" your answer would be your thesis statement. Everything you write will support this statement.

A good thesis statement usually includes

Main idea of the paper. ONE idea. The entire paper is based on this statement.

Your opinion or point of view. The thesis statement is not a fact nor a question, but your view of the topic and what you want to say about it.

Purpose of the paper. From the thesis, it should be clear what the paper will do.

Answer to the research question. Ask yourself the question and then answer it with your thesis. Is it truly an answer? (if not, change the question or the answer!)

An element of surprise. This means that the thesis is interesting, engaging, and perhaps not so expected.

Clarity. It should be understandable after one reading and have no mistakes.

From the citations above, we can imagine the importance of a thesis sentence in the life of any essay. Considering the importance of the thesis sentence in an essay, we must remind ourselves that the thesis sentence appears in the last sentence in Move 3, the thesis sentence guides the reader, the thesis statement is a contract between you and your reader, the thesis sentence should be a complete sentence, it should be specific and must have a single idea. In a way to emphasis the importance of the thesis statement in an essay, **Courtesy the Odegaard Writing & Research Center ( ) explains:**

No sentence in your paper will vex you as much as the thesis sentence. And with good reason: the thesis sentence is typically that ONE sentence in the paper that asserts, controls, and structures the entire argument. Without a strong persuasive, thoughtful thesis, a paper might seem unfocused, weak, and not worth the reader's time.

Besides the quotation above, one most important thing we must know about a thesis sentence is that there are many types of thesis sentences. As already seen above, the thesis sentence of an expository writing is not the same as the one for argumentative essays. There are these varieties at the level of the thesis sentences based on the topic that give the bodies of essays different logical patterns.

4.3.5 Changing statements of facts into arguable thesis statements

In the discussion above we have examined some qualities of thesis statements. Most thesis statements are developed from topics or facts in different domains. However, the quotation below shows some examples of statements of fact and how they can be transformed into arguable thesis statements from an unknown scholar.

<u>Statement of fact</u>: Smoking can cause health problems.

<u>Arguable thesis statement</u>: The government should ban smoking altogether.

<u>Statement of fact</u>: Small cars get better fuel mileage than 4x4 pickup trucks.

<u>Arguable thesis statement</u>: The government should ban 4x4 pickup trucks except for work-related use.

<u>Statement of fact</u>: On average, people with college degrees earn more money in the workplace.

<u>Arguable thesis statement</u>: A college degree should not be required for the _____ profession.

<u>Statement of fact</u>: Foul language is common in movies.

<u>Arguable thesis statement</u>: The amount of foul language in movies is disproportionate to the amount of foul language in real life.

As you might have seen so far, facts are not good for most arguments. For example it is a fact that the sun rises from the East and sets in the West every day. This is a fact that we all know. There is no controversy in such a phenomenon, and so there can be little or no argument from many scholars to this happening. However, many insightful scholars can generate a controversial topic from facts and create new knowledge from there. More on this will be seen in other sections.

4.3.6 Steps in Constructing a Good Thesis Statement

The section above has suggested how thesis statements can be developed from facts. In other words, thesis statements can be built from a broad concept to a sound manageable one. To choose and construct an arguable thesis statement demands some basic steps. Some of these steps have been highlighted by Ozagac (2004) thus:

In this kind of essay, we not only give information but also present an argument with the PROS (supporting ideas) and CONS (opposing ideas) of an argumentative issue. We should clearly take our stand and write as if we are trying to persuade an opposing audience to adopt new beliefs or behavior. The primary objective is to persuade people to change beliefs that many of them do not want to change.

Choosing an argumentative topic is not an easy task. The topic should be such that

• it should be narrowed down

X Marijuana should be considered illegal. (Not a good topic because it is too general. In some medical cases, marijuana is prescribed by the doctors and the patients are encouraged to use it in case of suffering from too much pain)

√ Selling and using marijuana in public places should be considered illegal.

• it should contain an argument

X We should decide whether we want a bicycle or a car. (our stand is not clear: do we support having bicycles or cars?)

√ If we are under the age of 30 and want a healthy life, we should definitely get a bicycle instead of a car.

X Are you one of those who thinks cheating is not good for students? (a question cannot be an argument)

√ Cheating helps students learn.

X Considering its geological position, Turkey has an important geopolitical role in the EU. (facts cannot be arguments)

√ Considering its geopolitical role, we can clearly say that the EU cannot be without Turkey.

• it should be a topic that can be adequately supported (with statistics, outside source citations, etc.)

X I feel that writing an argumentative essay is definitely a challenging task. (feelings cannot be supported; we cannot persuade other people)

Although much has been examined on thesis statements and their qualities, the writer above reminds us that an argumentative thesis stamen does not only inform, it examines the pros and the cons in argumentative writing. The discussion below highlights some differences between an arguable thesis statement and an informative thesis statement.

4.3.7 Differences between Argumentative or Informative thesis Statements

Some thesis statements are informative in nature. These can be mistaken for argumentative thesis statements. The examples below come from unknown source.

1. ARG Censorship is the best way of controlling the minds of the citizens.

2. ARG Newspapers should not identify victims of sexual assault without their consent.

3. INF Parents control their children's TV viewing habits in three ways.

4. ARG In war journalism, it is never appropriate to show on the news how a country's soldiers suffer in combat.

5. ARG The only way to receive high ratings for a TV series is to cast attractive actors or actresses.

6. INF There are common practices that advertisers use to sell products.

7. INF Politicians use various strategies to influence the media during their election campaigns.

8. INF There are two main ways of manipulation in print media; false balancing, which means focusing on only one side of an argument; and slighting of the content, which aims at giving so much emphasis to style and so little to the actual substance.

We conclude the analyses of the introduction section of an essay or a paper with good examples introduction. The first example is a three-move introduction and the second example is a four-move introduction.

Example1: Three-Move Introduction

The example below is an introduction of an essay which is made up of three moves. It was adopted from Kum (2016: 110). In this introduction, Move 1 is normal size, Move 2 is underlined, and Move 3 is italicized.

Most researchers are of the assumption that the size of class will prove a significant determinant of the degree of success of students. **Move 1**

This raises the question of, what is the ideal class size? And what is considered as a large or small group? In terms of numerical strength, the national policy on education (1977 revised in 1981) specified 20 in pre-primary schools, 30 in secondary schools. **Move 2** *This essay will agree that these smaller groups or classes are likely to perform better than those of the larger groups or classes as, the teacher easily interact with the students and coax better performance from each of them given their limited size.* **Move 3**

If you were to analyze the introduction above, you might say that the writer respects the structure of an introduction section. For instance, the idea starts from a general perspective (Most teachers...), to a specific perspective (question), and (solution). In Move 1, the writer uses step 2 **Making Topics Generalization or** (current state of knowledge). In Move 2 which is underlined, the writer uses strategy or Step I C **Raising a Question (about previous research),** and in Move 3 which is italicized, the writer uses strategy or step 2 **Announcing Main Findings** (agrees).

Example 2: Four- Moves Introduction

From the discussion above, we observe that there are many essay topics that might require four Moves. These advanced forms of writing demand you to have a solid base in our five paragraph essay. Once you can identify the three moves in our five paragraph essay, you can handle any introduction of an essay topic with confidence. The discussion below focuses on an introduction that contains four Moves. It is adapted from Rao et al. (2007:53,57). In the Four-Moves introductions below, Move 1 is underlined, Move 2 is italicized, Move 3 is normal and Move 4 is darkened,. The question goes thus:

"Discuss Putnam's view about the loss of 'social capital" in developed societies. What in your judgement should be done (if anything) to reverse this loss?"

As countries modernize and societies expand globally, away from closed-knit communities that were more common in the past, social cohesion is becoming less prevalent, evidenced by phenomena such as the isolation of individuals and families (Smith, 1998,p.7) (**Move 1**) *Critics such as Putnam developed the term social capital, formed on analogy with the more familiar idea of economic capital, to label the process of community development, indicated by the networks, values and norms of action that link* *individuals within a community* **(reference)**. *There is general consensus that social capital has decreased in western societies over the last three decades (reference). As social capital has decreased, communities have become more aware of its value for maintaining a heathy society, and sociologists are debating different strategies to rebuild community reserves (references).*

This essay examines theories behind the concept of social capital, and the main manifestations of the loss of social capital as exemplified in twenty-first century Australia. (**Move 2**). It considers evidence of the loss of social capital in the areas of inter- personal, inter- community and interstate relationships, along with the serious consequences and possible remedies (**Move 3**). **Having considered the evidence, this essay concludes that, in an increasingly diverse society, social communities need to be rebuilt, not by replication of prototypes which worked in previous centuries but by new models involving government, media, family, and individual participation which take into consideration the paradoxical modern need for being a part of society while at the same time being free to be highly individualistic in our social behavior.** (**Move 4**).

As you must have noticed, the Four-Move introduction above ties with the essay topic it is trying to solve. In order to discuss Putnam's view, the writing in Move 1 uses **Step 3: Reviewing Items of Previous Works** by citing (Smith, 1998, p.7). In Move 2, the writer uses **Step I D: Continuing a Tradition** and focuses on Putnam's view. In Move 3, the writer uses **Step I B: Announcing Present Research (what, where, how, why, who)** by signposting and stating solutions to be attained in the essay, and in Move 4, the writer uses **Step 2: Announcing Main Findings** by mentioning the thesis or the answer to the problem raised in Move 2. This is an example of a **BIST (Background, Issue, Scope, Thesis)** introduction.

The next introduction below has not got Move 4. You can now analyze the various steps or strategies the writer has used in order to achieve his aims, based on the question or problem posed to him.

Example 3: Introduction for Your study

From the samples of introductions above, you can observe that there are introductions with three Moves and others with four Moves. The number of Moves might depend on the type of problems you intend to solve, the discipline, the genre, and so on. Have a look at the introduction below.

"Chocolate is a healthy food". Discuss.

Background statement which draws the reader into the issue	Since Spanish explorers brought back chocolate from the new world, chocolate consumption has become a worldwide phenomenon. At first, chocolate, a derivative of the cacao bean, was consumed as a drink, only later achieving mass popularity in tablet or bar form. However, chocolate's inherent popularity does not equate to it possessing healthy properties, as suggested by the title. The realities of chocolate are more down to earth: a number of these realities will be addressed in this essay. Chocolate has chemical properties that can influence mood and there is possible evidence for some positive impacts of chocolate on cardiovascular health. Yet, such positive attributes are counterbalanced somewhat by the argument that, in some instances, chocolate can be viewed as a drug rather than a food. Moreover, there is the possibility of some correlation between over-consumption of chocolate and obesity. Thus, it will be argued that despite chocolate's positive effect in some cases on mood and the cardiovascular system it has also been linked to addiction and obesity.	Additional information to the background statement
Issue suggested by the title		Scope of the essay

Thesis statement

Source: **Essay writing from the English for Uni website**

4.4 Conclusion

This chapter has highlighted some important features of the introduction section of an essay. For example, we learn that the introduction part of an essay has the shape of an inverted pyramid. This shape reminds us that ideas in the introduction paragraph should flow from the general to the specific perspective. Moves are the units that enable us to realize this shape. The three moves that make up the introduction part of an essay are each further divided into steps or strategies. These steps are identified through some key sentences that are common in each step. We have equally been told that the introduction section plays the role of bait. As a bait, the introduction part of an essay should attract a reader to read our essay even if he or she hadn't the intention to do so. In view of the vital importance of the introduction to an essay, our students are demanded to spend a lot of time and energy to master the various Moves and steps that are needed at the introduction section of an essay. Unlike the body section of essays that might demand many logical patterns depending on the nature of the essay, the introduction sections of many writings are the same. In fact, ideas often run from the general to specific point of view. A sound knowledge of the introduction section of your essay suggests an interesting essay ,so much effort is needed from you at this section.

Chapter Five - The Body Part Of An Argumentative Essay

5.0 Introduction

The introduction section of an essay has been established above. It is now your duty to read through the various Moves and the strategies that are used in order to realize, or to determine a Move. As already mentioned, after the introduction section of an essay, there is the body of the essay. It is in the body of an essay that you justify your thesis statement. We are of the opinion that knowledge is a continuous process. This chapter therefore begins by reminding you of the bodies of the Five Paragraph Essay that you might have known before or you might have read in Kum (2023). After the revision section of these bodies especially from Kum (2023), the rest of the sections in this chapter examine the body components of the argumentative essay.

5.1 Revision of the Body of the Five-Paragraph Essay

From the structure of an essay above, the body part of an essay is the one found in the middle of an essay. It is situated between the introduction and the conclusion. The diagram below shows the structure of the body part of the Five –Paragraph Essay.

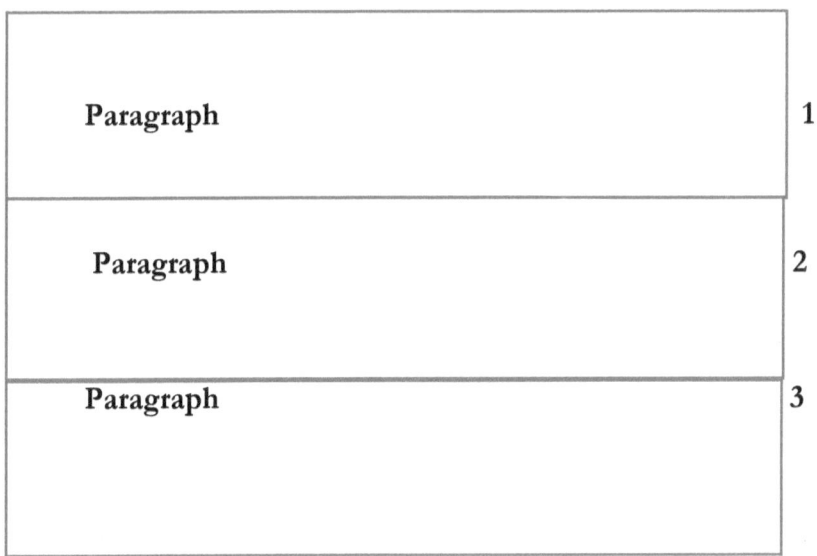

BODY OF A FIVE –PARAGRAPH ESSAY

Under normal conditions, the body of the Five Paragraph Essay starts from the second paragraph of an essay. But there are certain cases that the introductions of very long essays may take two paragraphs. In responding to this question, "Can I have more than one paragraph in my introduction?» Rao et als (2007:55) responded:

Of course, if there is the need –for instance, if the essay is long or complex so if your introduction is roughly 300 words, you might choose to split it into two paragraphs, with moves 1 and 2 in the first paragraph, and moves 3 and 4 in the second paragraph (you can see this in the introduction to the sociology essay above pp.53-54). If your introduction is short, you might need only one paragraph and cover all the 4 moves.

The citation above highlights the fact that there can be exceptions. But traditionally, the introduction part of the Five Paragraph Essay occupies the first paragraph. That said, it should be noted that unlike the introduction part that comprises one paragraph, which is further divided into Moves and then Steps or Strategies, the body of our Five –Paragraph Essay is made up of at least three paragraphs. Talking about a paragraph Ncheafor (2010:9) says:

"A paragraph is a unit of written information which treats one central idea that forms part of the central theme of the whole piece of writing or complete text".

From the quotation above, we learn that a paragraph is a unit that comprises of a single idea that forms a part of the main message. it is worth mentioning that the function of a paragraph is to assist readers to process and understand an idea. As already mentioned above, the body of an essay is made up of paragraphs. The rest of the discussion below focuses on the analysis of some bodies of the five-paragraph essay.

5.1.1 Analysis of the Body of the Five-Paragraph Essay

In the course of analyzing the introduction part of an essay, we observed that the paragraph of an introduction is divided into moves which are further divided into steps. But the paragraphs of the body of an essay are divided into sentences. Linguists define a sentence as *a group of words that has a subject and a predicate or verb and expresses a complete thought.* In this light, we can now suggest that a Move is different from a sentence because a Move can be a sentence or many sentences. However, the body of an essay is analyzed based on the logical arrangement of ideas.

In sections above on logical pattern of the introduction section of an essay, we observed that an introduction of a Five-Paragraph essay has only one pattern in which to arrange ideas. This one and only pattern is from a general perspective to a specific one. At the level of the body section of an essay, the story is completely different. The body part of an essay depends entirely on the thesis statement of the essay. If the thesis statement of an essay demands a chronological arrangement of ideas, the body of the essay should respect that arrangement. If on the contrary the thesis statement suggests a cause and effect arrangement, the body of the essay should also respect that ordering. Based on the fact that the order of ideas in the body paragraphs respects the thesis sentence, the discussion below focuses on various orders of the Five – Paragraph Essay.

5.1.1.1 Chronological Order

Unlike the main idea and the supporting details order that focuses on main ideas and then the supporting details, the chronological order is about telling a complete story from the beginning till the end. In this logical pattern, Ideas are arranged in the order in which they occurred. The chronological order on most parts comprises of transitional and supporting sentences. National Geographic Learning ( ) tells us that:

*In an essay with chronological organization, each paragraph ends with a **transitional sentence**.*

Transitional sentences have two purposes: (1) to signal the end of the action in one paragraph, and (2) to provide a link to the action of the next paragraph. These sentences are vital because they give your story unity and allow the reader to follow the action easily. The following example is from Essay 8 on page 43, Paragraphs 2 and 3. Notice how the ideas in the last sentence of Paragraph 2 (the transitional sentence, underlined) and the first sentence of Paragraph 3 (underlined) are connected.

2   *This was my first visit to the international terminal of the airport, and nothing was familiar. I could not make sense of any of the signs. Where was the check-in counter? Where should I take my luggage? I had no idea where the immigration line was. I began to panic. What time was it? Where was my plane? <u>I had to find help because I could not be late!</u>*

3   *<u>I tried to ask a passing businessman for help, but my words all came out wrong.</u> He just scowled and walked away. What had happened? I had been in this country for a whole semester, and I could not even remember how to ask for directions. This was awful! Another bus arrived at the terminal, and the passengers stepped off carrying all sorts of luggage. Here was my chance! I could follow them to the right place, and I would not have to say a word.*

From the citation above, we learn the functions of transitional sentences and also two examples of transitional sentences that are underlined at the end of paragraph 2 and the beginning of paragraph 3. These ways of talking in a chronological order gives your essay a sense of unity and enhances understanding. However, some people call chronological order, time order, others say narration order and still some think it is the sequence of events. From the explanation above, it is right to think that the narrative essay falls under this arrangement of ideas. Experts of essay represent the chronological order in a diagram known as the "Freytag's Pyramid." The Freytag's Pyramid is different from the pyramid of the conclusion in that it has strings attached to its base. The diagram below shows the Freytag's Pyramid that must be used whenever our essay has a chronological or a narrative.

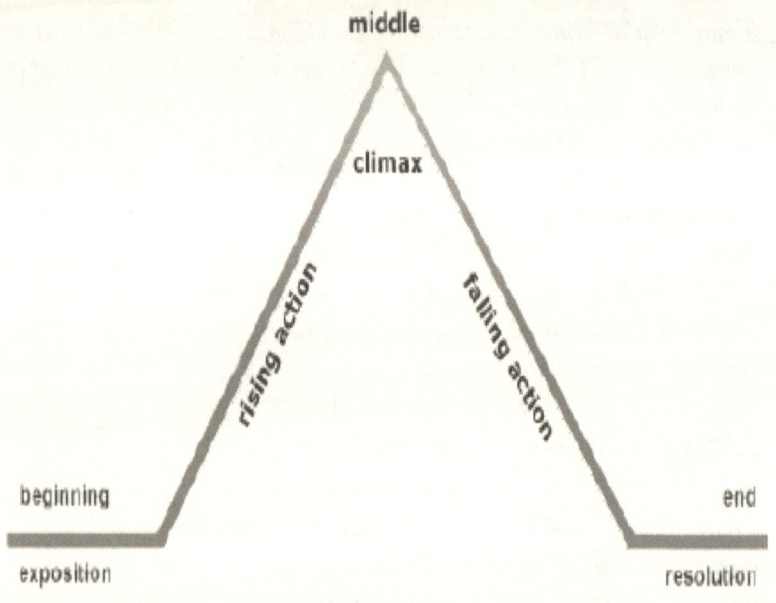

DIAGRAM FREYTAG PYRAMIND
Adopted from International Reading Association NCIE Marcopolo

Plot Structure Components

Climax: The turning point. The most intense moment (either mentally or in action.

Rising Action: the series of conflicts and crisis in the story that lead to the climax.

Falling Action: all of the action which follows the Climax.

Exposition: The start of the story. The way things are before the action starts.

Resolution: The conclusion, the tying together of all of the threads.

FREYTAG PYRAMIND

Adopted from International Reading Association NCIE Marcopolo

The diagram above has 5 main points the beginning, the rising, the climax (middle), the falling and the end.

Every story starts somewhere (beginning), the story then start development which includes conflicts, meetings, crisis and so on (rising), the rising reaches the highest point which can be intense excitement, intense anger, intense frustration, killing, beating, and so on, (climax) From the climax, which is the highest moment in the story, the same story start reducing in action, in the number of people, in the number of discussion (falling) and at the end, decisions, results, solutions, conclusions are reached, that finally brings the story to an end (end).

Like the introduction section, knowing how ideas are arranged in a chronological order is not enough. The next thing to know is how to construct these ideas into this one whole. There are words that can help you produce ideas in a chronological order. This is important because English discourse is writer responsible, that is it is the rule of the writer to guide his/her reader. So in order to ease understanding in this order, words known as signals include: first, secondly, next, then, now, after, as soon as, later, formerly, furthermore, in addition, besides, finally and so on.

5.1.1.2 Spatial Order

Many descriptive essays limit themselves to the spatial order. In fact, spatial order is an approach in description that shows the relationship between things based on space. Another name of spatial order is order of location. It makes use of words such as above, beside, to the left, south, east etc.). In view of the popularity of spatial order in the descriptive essays, we wish to take this opportunity under spatial order to highlight some interesting approaches in description which might entice or broaden our students' knowledge in the descriptive genre. It should also be noted that, in the descriptive subgenre, the aim is to paint a picture of something that you have seen, experienced or even heard on the mind of your audience. A good descriptive essay enables us to see, to hear, to touch, to taste, or to smell whatever is being described. In order to attain these objectives, writers resort to many approaches or order. Some of these orders are natural order, angle of vision, camera angles and perceptual salience [see Brown and Yule,1983]. In the discussion below, we are going to explain these approaches and cite an example for each.

A) Natural order

The first order that can be linked to spatial order is natural order. In this sub order, description is done base on the natural manner in which things happen or are positioned. Natural order also ties very well with narrative or chronological order, but it is also common in the descriptive approach. For example, in the course of describing your house to a stranger, you might start with the name of the quarter in which your house is located, the road that links to your house, then some prominent features such as a petrol station, a church, a school, a tall building that might be nearer or around your house before describing how your house looks like and so on. But, if you just start by describing your house without first mentioning the quarter in which it is found, then you might confuse your reader or audience. In other words, in a natural order, we describe features or things that are known before the features that are unknown.

B) Angle of vision

Besides the natural order, there is there is the angle of vision order. Fillmore [1981] in Brown and Yule [1983] suggests that the order in which an action or a happening is observed is different from the natural order. This means that some incidents can be described based on the location from which the writer or speaker observes the happening. For instance, if there is a fire outbreak from a house, the speakers who watched the fire outbreak from the southern part of the huge building might give a different description from those who were standing to the northern, eastern or western side of the house. In fact, the description of the fire incident above will be based on the position of the writer when he was observing the huge flame. From the explanation above, we observe that angle of vision is an order of description based on the location of the writer and what he or she saw from that location.

C) Camera angle

Another approach in description is known as "camera angle". It was Kuno and Kaburaki [1977;627] in Brown and Yule [1983] who suggested that certain descriptions are based on feelings. The authors state:

The speaker's empathy, his sympathy with one point of view rather than another, may also lead to a particular choice of lexis [Brown and Yule,1983;147]. As we have read from this quotation above, the Camera angle suggests that the manner in which a speaker or a writer feels towards an occasion, towards an action, towards a person and so on. can influence the way he or she describes that occasion, that action, that person and so on. For instance, if a fight breaks out between KUM and Kang and you, the writer feels pity for KUM, you might describe the fight in a way that your audience will feel pity for KUM. But if on the contrary, you, the speaker thinks or feels, that KUM should be punished, you can also describe the fight in a way that your audience will want KUM to be punished. From the explanation above, we understand that Camera angle hinges much on emotions.

D) Perceptual salience

Finally, Van Dijk [1977;106] in Brown and Yule [1983;145] suggests that another approach to description is perceptual salience. In this order of description, the more salient entity will be mentioned first. This means that in the course of describing an event, a thing, a person, and so on, things that can be seen first, or big things will always be mentioned first before those that cannot be seen or are smaller. Van Dijk [1977] gives this pattern in Brown and Yule [1983;145]

General	-	particular
Whole	-	part /component
set - subject	-	element
Including	-	included
Large	-	small
outside	-	inside
possessor	-	possessed

A keen observation of perceptual salience order suggests that it is a sub order to the natural order of description. However, a sound knowledge of their existence might deepen our critical thinking.

The diagram below summarises the nature of the descriptive genre, irrespective of the various approaches.

Description:

DIAGRAM OF DESCRIPTION

Source for Olympic Selections: http://www.stanford.edu/~arnetha/expowrite/info.html

Assume that I have been asked to describe any important annual festival in my culture. Using the diagram above, I will put my annual festival, "ukuum" in the middle and the other branches are the three days that the ukuum festival takes. In my essay, the first paragraph of the body will be day one activities, paragraph two will be day two activities and paragraph 3 will be day three activities.

Like the narrative essay, the descriptive essay also has its common phrases, or words that must be used in order to paint a vivid picture of what you are describing on your audience mind. Some of these words include: opposite, above, inside, under, within, nearby , next to, beside, between, below, behind, in front of, away ,over ,across, toward ,along, close by , on ,in ,west ,south ,to the south ,elsewhere , next to, and many adjectives,

5.1.1.3 Order of Importance

In his lectures on principles of organization of ideas or information Friedlander (2009) states order of importance as one of the four main principles. Order of importance is so important that we meet it in economic, under scale of preference, we also meet it in welcome speeches when hierarchy is maintained from the President of the Republic to the sub divisional officer, we also meet it in our essay at the level of plan, where we are compelled to organise our ideas from the most attractive one to any others

The problems we often observe in students writing is that they do not understand the meaning of importance. Students often consider the meaning of importance from the semantic view point (great) and not the pragmatic view point (context).

Learners must be careful to understand what the marker or the reader wants to see or read or know first not only what is important. For instance, your reader might be interested in the least privilege person in your village. In this situation, you better start from the poorest person in your village to the richest person. Do not think that as the poorest person in your village is not important, you should begin your first paragraph of the body of your essay with the richest person because he or she is far important than the poorest person. As you can see, you have not respected the order of this particular essay, because you started talking of the most important person instead of the least important people as your marker or audience wants to know. In fact, order of importance depends on what the audience wants. It can begin from the smallest to the small, or from the oldest to the old and vice versa. So the question here should be which order is needed. The diagram below might help you to list the order that is needed for a particular purpose.

1. _____
2. _____
3. _____
4. _____

It should be mentioned that unlike the chronological order that items are narrated the way they occurred, order of importance is based on the purpose of the ordering. You will also observe that in "the main idea and the supporting details ordering" above, the main ideas in each paragraph are of equal weight or importance, whereas in "the order of importance ordering", the main ideas in each paragraph is inferior to the other as you move from the first paragraph to the second then the third. The diagram above shows how you can list your item in the order that is needed. The most needed, then the need. Signal words in this order include: First, second, third, finally, ending, important, principal, primary, next, last, more, least, less, major, chief, central, key, most, then, later, now, and so on.

5.1.1.4 Compare and Contrast Order

Many students have difficulties to handle this order. They sometimes do not know how or what to compare and how or what to contrast. After their comparison, some do not know how to present their arguments. In view of all these problems, it is necessary to highlight, at the outset that the best tool to use in this order is the Venn diagram.

<u>Comparison/Contrast:</u>

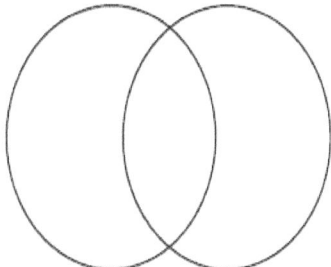

Source for Olympic Selections:

http://www.stanford.edu/~arnetha/expowrite/info.html

The Venn diagram will enable you to arrange your ideas into three sections. In circle A, you write only the characteristics that are unique or pertinent to that particular item. In circle B, you also list the elements that are unique only to that particular item. The space of intersection will be used to list all the characteristics that are common to both the two items. If this is done, then you will have a clear organizational plan to begin with your writing. The discussion above can be seen in Strunk, and white [1993;220]. In this book, apples and oranges are being compared and contrasted. The two fruits are presented thus:

    EDIBLE

    WARM COLOR

    ROUND SHAPE

    SIMILAR SIZE

    CONTAIN SEEDS

    GROW ON TREES

    GOOD FOR JUICE

    NAMES BEGIN WITH VOWELS

    SIMILAR PESTICIDE THREATMENT

    UNSUITABLE FOR MOST SPORTS

Using these common characteristics above that apples and oranges share, we can now fit them on our Venn diagram in the space of intersection. The rest of the work now is to look for those characteristics that are only common to apples and fill them on the space only for apples and the same thing for those characteristics that are common only to oranges. When our Venn diagram is filled, we can now begin with our write up.

In the course of writing, we make sure that our thesis statement is reduced enough in order for us to cover the similarities and differences. it should actually state the reason why you are comparing and contrasting any of the two items, and so on.

Your first paragraph may discuss those characteristics that are common to both apples and oranges. Paragraph two might explain the characteristics that are unique to the apples, while paragraph three may examine the characteristics that are common only to the orange. Your conclusion can now summarise the similarities and differences that have been discussed in the body of your essay and then the conclusion ends in your own point of view.

Like the previous orders, the language that should be used when comparing must be different from the one you use when you contrast.

At the level of comparison, you should use words such as: also, as well as, both, correspondingly, compared to, in comparison, in the same way, just as, like, likewise, resembles, share, similarly, the same as, too.

At the level of contrast, you should use words such as: although, as opposed to, but, despite, differs from, even though, however, instead, nevertheless, on the contrary, on the other hand, in contrast, in spite of, unlike, whereas, while, yet.

5.1.1.5 Cause and Effect Order

From the name, many students think that this order only deals with one cause and one effect. This might not be true because there might be one cause and many consequences, many causes and many consequences or many causes and one consequence. This suggests that students should know what to write and how to write it.

This order demands you to demonstrate why or how something occurred, and the consequence that emanated from that cause what these effects will be in the nearest future. You are expected to reduce your theses statement to a logical way that can be managed. To be more convincing, you might be asked to illustrate the causes or effects that are more important and those that are not. In order to attain this goal, diagrams like the one bellow might help you in one way or another.

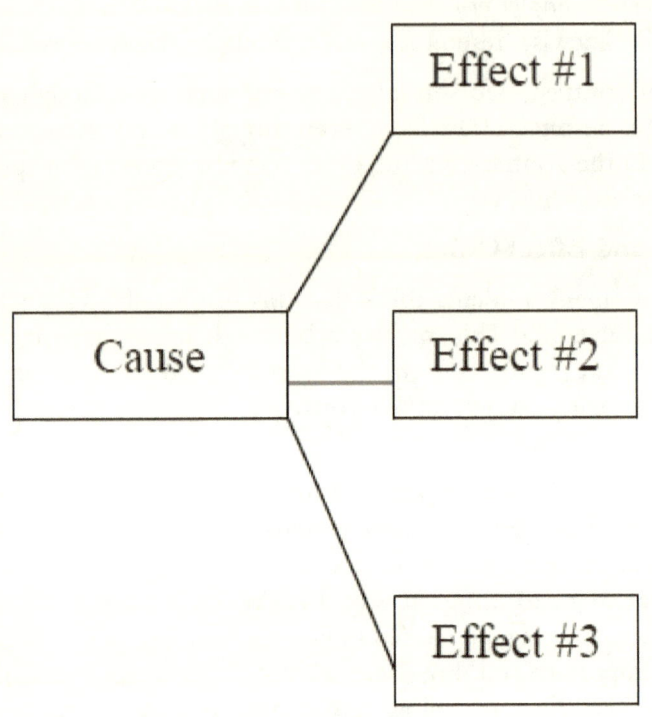

ONE CAUSE MANY EFFECTS

Source for Olympic Selections: http://www.stanford.edu/~arnetha/expowrite/info.html

THREE CAUSES ONE EFFECT

ONE CAUSE ONE EFFECT

Like the other orders, signal words in this order include:

Cause

Because, causes, creates, due to, for this reason, if this…then, leads to, on account of, produces, this

Effects

As a result, consequently, hence, in effect, resulting, since, therefore, this.

5.1.1.6 Problem and Solution Order

As the name suggests, problem and solution order Seeks to present a problem and gives a solution or solutions or even no solution. Many writers can observe a problem and end up not suggesting a solution. But an ideal problem and solution is an order in which a writer presents a problem and ten propose a solution or solutions. The diagram below Suggest a visual picture of a problem and solution order

Problem/Solution:

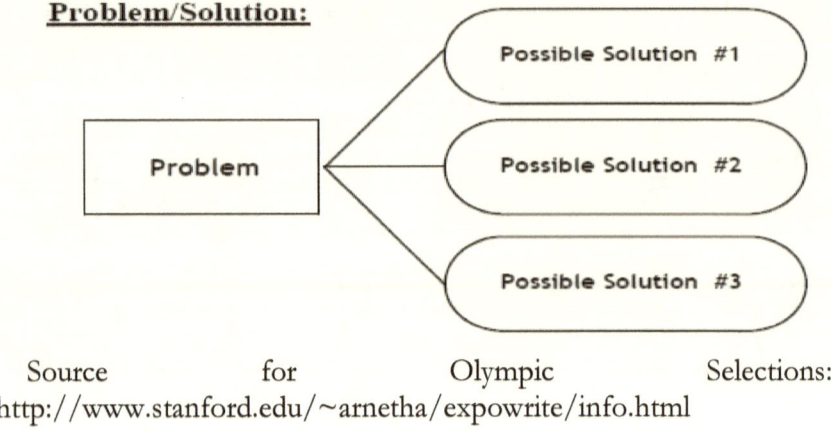

Source for Olympic Selections: http://www.stanford.edu/~arnetha/expowrite/info.html

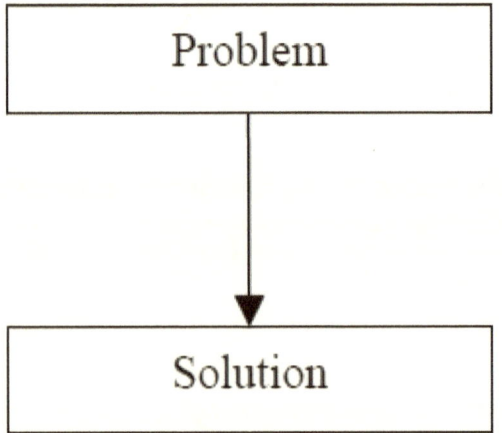

Source for Olympic Selections: http://www.stanford.edu/~arnetha/expowrite/info.html

Signal words include: answer, challenge, need, difficulty, improve, indicate, issue, plan, dilemma, plan a need, problem, propose, remedied, resolve, respond to, solve, suggest.

5.1.1.7 Process Order

Some students complain that they cannot make out the difference between the chronological order

And the process order. Chronological order talks more of events, while process order focuses more on the various steps needed to attain a goal. In another light, we might look upon the process order as a sub form of the chronological order. However, in the process order, you describe the various steps that are needed to do something. For instance, the various steps to cook kwakoko, the various steps to write an essay, the various steps to raise a child, the various step to plant tomatoes and so on. The diagram below suggests a picture of process writing.

Step 1

Step 2

Step 3

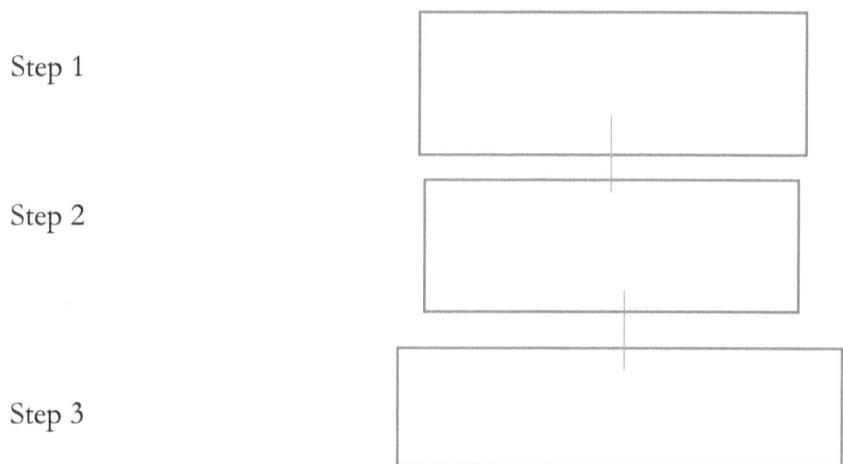

The diagram above resembles that of "order of importance". The difference is that process order deals with steps in a whole life cycle while order of importance handles individual concepts in a define context.

Signal words here include:

accordingly, after that, begins, following steps, how to, in the process of, series, sequence, stages, then, first, second, third next, last, finally.

5.1.1.8 Classification Order

Classification order is all about dividing a whole concept into its various sub members. It has some similarities with analysis but analysis Looks at every minute relationship of a whole in order to understand the complete whole. so classification is not too detailed like analyses.

For example, we can classify workers according to their skills, according to their grades, according to their functions, according to their ages and so on. We can also classify trees according to their species, their geographical locations, their functions and so on. We can even classify subjects in classrooms under larger group, for example science subjects, arts subjects and so on. teachers, clouds, countries, dresses, dances, songs, music, drinks, shoes and so on can also be classified under certain criteria. An essay of classification can be made interesting by stating the purpose of your classification. you can also mention the criteria you are using for the classification. The diagram below shows the classification of kingdoms on earth

Kingdoms

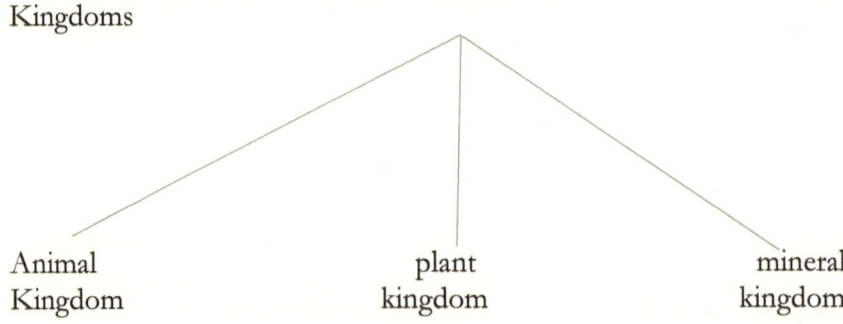

Animal Kingdom   plant kingdom   mineral kingdom

From the diagram above, you can now describe each kingdom in a paragraph by giving detailed and pertinent characteristics of each. Signal words in this order include: categories, classified as, classes, classification, comprises, composed of, different stages of division, elements, features, groups, kinds, types, varieties, ways, and so on.

5.1.1.9 Listing Order

Listing order can be a series of ideas, reasons, examples, people, food, houses, facts, opinions that support the main idea. In this order, you might not maintain the order of importance because each member has the same importance. Listing order might also be different from classification in that it can be too broad but classification often has a unique source that needs pertinent elements.

The diagram below might shed more light on listing order.

Item 1--------

Item 2 --------

Item 3 --------

Words under this order include the following first, second, as well as, least several, the following, in fact, in addition, furthermore, besides, a number of, most important,

5.2 The Body Structure of the Advanced Argumentative Essay

Many scholars of essay have talked about the structure of an essay. For example, Nelson (2014) tells us that an essay is made up of three parts: the introduction, the body and the conclusion. The introduction part is the first part of an essay and occupies 10 percent of the entire essay. After the introduction part, there is the body of the essay. Unlike the introduction part, the body part of an essay makes up 80 percent of the whole essay. Talking about the conclusion part of an essay, the authority mentioned above reminds us that the conclusion part of an essay occupies 10 percent of the whole essay. Like any essay, the argumentative essay is also made up of three parts-the introduction, the body and the conclusion. Depending on the topic, purpose, or the context under discussion or the field of study, the argumentative essay can be made up of four paragraphs, five-paragraphs or more. For a deeper understanding of the argumentative essay in this study, the body section of an argumentative essay will be examined under two main levels: the paragraph level and the general body level.

5.2.1 Approaches to Paragraphs Organization of an Argumentative Essay

The argumentative approach to writing is very important for the success of students. However, many students do not know how to handle this particular genre. At the level of the paragraph of an argumentative writing, an argumentative paragraph can only be pro side, contra side or mixed (pro view and contra view). In view of this unpredictable nature of the argumentative paragraph, the discussion below comprises of three approaches to the analysis of an argumentative paragraph- the common approach, which examines only elements of the pro side, and the deep approach, which also examines elements of the pro side but in more detailed. The last approach under the paragraph level is the deeper approach which examines all the elements of the pro sides and those of the contra sides.

5.2.1.1 The Common Approach Paragraph Organization of an Argumentative Essay

At your elementary level to essay writing, you were taught that the paragraph of the body of an essay is made up of some elements. More on these elements can be read from Blau et al (1998). For example, Blau et al (1998:342) tell us "one useful way of organizing your writing is by supporting a main idea with details". Under this logical way of arranging ideas in an essay, you were expected to know the following:

- Topic sentence
- Explanatory or controlling sentence
- Supporting sentences
- Summarizing transition sentences

In an attempt to shed light on each sentence and its functions, Azariadis (2018:3-4) contends.

*A **topic sentence** appears at the beginning of the paragraph. The topic sentence conveys the main idea you wish to explore in the paragraph. It usually takes the form of a broad, general statement or assertion.*

*The topic sentence is followed by an **explanatory or 'controlling' sentence**. The function of the controlling sentence is to explain, elaborate on or focus the main idea you have introduced in the topic sentence. Its function is to direct the discussion or the reader's attention to a specific area of concern. The important thing to note is that the controlling sentence provides the reader with an aspect or element of the topic. The controlling sentence signals to the reader what it is the writer will develop.*

*Following the controlling idea are a group of sentences called **supporting sentences**. They are called supporting sentences because they provide evidence to support (or in some cases refute) the controlling idea/sentence. This is needed because often the controlling idea takes the form of an opinion or viewpoint which needs substantiating. Supporting details may include examples, statistics, citations from published research and quotations. The supporting details serve to strengthen your argument; they persuade the reader of the validity of your reasoning!*

*Finally, academic paragraphs include a concluding sentence (sometimes called a **summarizing transition**) that summarizes or rounds off the points made in the paragraph and leads into the topic sentence of the next paragraph. This final sentence is also known as a 'summarizing transition'.*

From the quotation above, we learn that in the main idea and its supporting details approach to ordering ideas, there are some key concepts to know. These important concepts are: Topic sentence, Explanatory or controlling sentence, Supporting sentences and Summarizing transition sentences. The scholar above explains each of these types of sentences and it is up to you to read more on these concepts. Talking about the functions of a topic sentence, Jean-Wyrick says:

Most body paragraphs present one main point in your discussion, expressed in a topic sentence. The topic sentence of a body paragraph has three important functions:

1. It supports the thesis by clearly stating a main point in the discussion.

2. It announces what the paragraph will be about

3. It controls the subject matter of the paragraph. The entire discussion—the examples, details, and explanations—in a particular paragraph must directly relate to and support the topic sentence.

In the common approach discussed above, students are told that the body of an argumentative essay is made up of a topic sentence, backed by an explanatory or controlling sentence, then by
Supporting sentences and lastly by summarizing transition sentences. Many students often find it very difficult to determine the meaning of a topic sentence, the meaning of an explanatory or controlling sentence, the meaning of supporting sentences and lastly the meaning of summarizing transition sentences. Because of this lack of knowledge, students often abandon the argumentative genre for the narrative, the descriptive, the expository, the analytic, and so on. It is for this reason that we have decided to name this elementary approach a common approach to the elements of an argumentative essay. As you can observe, this approach examines only the pro side of an argumentative paragraph without the contra side. Although the next approach below also examines the pro side of an argumentative paragraph, it is more detailed and identifies key words that can help you produce a good pro side paragraph of an argumentative essay easily.

5.2.1.2 A Deep Approach to Paragraphs Organisation of an Argumentative Essay

As already mentioned above, this section takes a deep step into the understanding of the body paragraph of an argumentative essay. The deep step in this section is not to change the various stages or sentences mentioned above, but to reduce them to common concepts or words that our students can feel or know easily. In order to solve this problem, we will use the same elements of the body of an argumentative essay discussed above, and equate them to the commonly cited simple and short elements of the body paragraph of an argumentative essay. The juxtaposition goes thus:

- Topic sentence (claim)
- Explanatory or controlling sentence (reason)
- Supporting sentences (evidence)
- Summarizing transition sentences (warrant, qualifiers etc.)

The presentation above shows that *a topic sentence* is the same as a "claim" or an "assertion", *an explanatory or controlling sentence* is the same as a "reason", *the supporting sentences* are the same as the "evidence" and the *summarizing transition sentences can be* "warrant", "qualifiers" etc. We now know the new names for topic sentence, explanatory or controlling sentence, and the supporting sentences in an argument. In the rest of the discussion below, we are going to use the words claim or assertion, reason and evidence instead of topic sentence, explanatory or controlling sentence, and the supporting sentences that you have been used to. Claim, reason and evidence are very important in an argument because they are the core elements of the body paragraph of an argumentative essay. Besides using the new concepts of assertion or claim, reason and evidence in the discussion below, we will also illustrate how they are combined to form a core argument. That said, although many scholars have examined how the elements above are combined to form a convincing paragraph, this study adapts the combination illustrated by Shuster. This is so because it is short, detailed and very simple to understand. According to the author, a complete argument is made up of three parts:

-Assertion,

- Reasoning

-Evidence,

These three components according to the author are abbreviated ARE. Note that unlike The College Board (2014) which calls them "critical components", Shuster reminds us that they are abbreviated "ARE". This might suggest their importance in the existence of an argument. In describing these three components, Shuster gives the definition of each and the examples in which they can be used in order to deepen our understanding. The citation below is a summary of Shuster explanation:

An assertion is usually a simple statement, such as "Homework is a waste of time", "Television news is boring," or "Tomato soup is better than grilled sandwiches". An assertion is the thesis statement or the main point of an argument.

Reasoning is the "because" part of an argument as in the following examples:

- Homework is a waste of time because it takes time away from other activities that are more important".

- Television news is boring because it doesn't talk about issues that are relevant to me"

- "Tomato soup is better than a grilled cheese sandwich because it is more nutritious ". At the level of evidence, Shuster continues:

"Just as reasoning supports an assertion, evidence supports reasoning. There are many different kinds of evidence, ranging from expert testimony or statistics to historical or contemporary examples. As students learn the ARE framework for argumentation, it is helpful to encourage them to begin with the most basic and common form of evidence: the example. This also allows students to practice the verbal cue "for example".

- Homework is a waste of time because it takes time away from other activities that are more important. For example, we end up doing worksheets of math problems instead of getting outside and getting fresh air and exercise".

- Television news is boring because it doesn't talk about issues that are relevant to me. For example, I never see stories about the issues that kids deal with every day".

- Tomato soup is better than a grilled cheese sandwich because it is more nutritious. For example, tomato soup contains important vitamins such as Lycopene, while grilled cheese sandwiches really don't have that much nutritional value at all.

Many students are very familiar with the combination above. From the discussion above, the author explains assertion or claim, reason and evidence. He further demonstrates how these components can be combined to form the core of an argument. For example, we learn that the part of reason is joined to the claim by the word "because "and the part that contains evidence is joined to reason by the phrase "for example". Talking about the core of an argument, Booth, Colomb and Williams (1995, 2003:138) state:

Readers look first for the core of an argument, for its claim and

two kinds of support: reasons and evidence. In the sequence of

reasons, they see the outline of the logical structure of its support.

If they do not see that structure, they are likely to judge your

argument shapeless, even incoherent. Evidence, on the other

hand, is the bedrock of your argument, the established body of

facts that readers need to see before they accept your reasons. If

they don't accept your evidence, they are likely to reject your reasons,

and with them your claim. So once you know your claim,

your next task is to assemble the reasons that support it, and the

evidence on which those reasons rest.

The discussion above highlights the main elements of the argumentative writing and how they can be combined to form the core of an argument. At this level of the deep approach of this study, we have learnt the new appellations for the topic sentence, the explanatory or controlling sentence, and the supporting sentences. They are claims, reason and evidence respectively. We have also known how they are combined to form the core part of an argument. The deeper approach section below highlights all the elements of an argument and some examples of how they are combined.

5.2.1.3 A Deeper Approach to Paragraphs Organisation of an Argumentative Essay

At your level of education, one might think that you already know the various structures of a sentence. However, for the revision of non-language students, we know that a sentence has four structures: the simple, the complex, the compound, and the complex-compound. Amongst the sentence structures cited above, we are interested in the complex sentence. A complex sentence is a sentence that has two clauses: an independent clause and a dependent clause. This particular grammatical structure is further divided into two rhetorical sentences: the periodic sentence and the loose or cumulative sentence. A periodic sentence is a complex sentence that begins with a dependence clause and ends in an independence clause. For example, **Because he was hungry, thirsty and sick, Kum came to our house"**. In this sentence, the part, *Because he was hungry, thirsty and sick,* is known as a dependent clause and the remaining part *Kum came to our house* is called the independent clause. So a periodic sentence begins with a dependent clause and ends in an independent clause. On the other hand, a loose or cumulative sentence is a complex sentence that instead begins with an independent clause and ends in a dependent clause. For example **Kum came to our house because he was hungry, thirsty and sick.** As a good student, you might have observed that it is the same sentence with the same meaning but just that the independent clause has been placed before the dependent clause. The main difference between a periodic sentence and a loose sentence is that in a periodic sentence, more words cannot be added to it at the end but with a loose sentence, many new items can be added to the sentence at the end to make it long, longer and even the longest. For example, we can say **Kum came to our house because he was hungry, thirsty and sick and so had to meet my father for an immediate help which he did.**

Based on the discussion above, we can now liken an argumentative writing to a loose sentence that can accept many new items which can help to shed more light on a particular concept. In other words we are saying that apart from the core elements of an argument which we have highlighted above such as claim, reason and evidence, there are other elements that can join them to build a solid and a convincing argument. In view of the great importance of the argumentative essay for our academic success, the discussion below analyses each element of the paragraph of an argumentative essay and how they are linked to each other for a convincing whole. This is necessary because according to Booth, Colomb and Williams (2003), an academic argument attracts and motivates intellectuals to think together in order to have "the best answer to a hard question". But before we embark on the analysis of each part of an argument, let look at the difference between an argument and an opinion.

5.3 The Difference between an Opinion and an Argument

The discussion below sheds more light on the meaning of an argument and an opinion. Talking about the difference between an opinion and an argument, Shuster (writes:)

There is a difference between an opinion and an argument. An opinion is an expression of preference; it does not require any support (although it is stronger with support). An opinion is only the first part of an argument.

The structure and the functions of a thesis statement has been examined in chapter three of this study. Since the structure of an essay depends on the nature of the thesis statement, it may be of great importance for you to have a look once more on the structure of a thesis statement above for a better understanding of the structure of the topic sentence. However, the citation above reminds us that *An opinion is only the first part of an argument.* This suggests that certain ideas must be added to an opinion in order for this opinion to become an argument. In this sense, we can then summarize that an argument is therefore an opinion plus another idea. In the body of an essay, an opinion plus another idea forms an arguable sentence known as the Topic sentence. Due to the importance of a topic sentence in a paragraph in particular and the body of an essay in general, the discussion below focuses first on the nature of a topic sentence.

5.4 Elements of Argumentative Paragraphs

This section examines elements that make up the paragraphs of argumentative writings. Paragraphs are divided into two: the pro paragraphs and the con paragraphs. The section begins with the identification of elements of the pro paragraphs.

5.4.1 Pro Paragraph

Scholars of the argumentative genre know that an argumentative essay should have two types of paragraphs or two ways of looking at the same problem. The pro paragraph usually stands for your own points of view on any controversy. It is the paragraph that you write in order to back up your claims. Elements of these pro points of view include:

5.4.1.1 A Topic Sentence

In the section on the thesis statement, we mentioned that another name for the thesis statement is a main claim. Main claim because there are sub claims or just claim under the main claim. These main claims are made up of topic sentences, which must be developed in each paragraph. We know that a topic sentence is to a paragraph just like a thesis statement or a main claim is to an essay. The citation below gives a detailed summary of a topic sentence. It is adapted from Writing Center English 800 Center:

WHAT IS A TOPIC SENTENCE?

As you know, college students are required in their classes to express their ideas effectively in coherent, unified, and well-developed essays. Each essay is composed of several paragraphs, and each paragraph should express a different point or aspect of the thesis. Usually the first sentence of a paragraph but sometimes the last sentence or in another position in the paragraph, the topic sentence identifies for the reader the main point of a paragraph. If this sounds similar to the preceding section on the thesis statement, that's because the thesis is essential to an essay just as the topic sentence is the unifying force in a paragraph. An effective topic sentence must therefore be clearly related to the essay's thesis statement.

The topic sentence in a paragraph functions much like the thesis does in an essay; it sets up a reader's expectations about what the controlling idea is. In fact, topic sentences often act like mini thesis statements. Like a thesis statement, a topic sentence makes a claim of some sort, but unlike the thesis which is more general, it attempts to explain only one specific aspect of the thesis. Also, as in the case of the thesis statement, when the topic sentence makes a claim, the sentences in the paragraph which follow must explain, describe, or prove it in some way.

WHAT IS A TOPIC SENTENCE GOOD FOR?

A good topic sentence

• is a complete sentence

• can be located anywhere in the paragraph (although it is often the first sentence)

• accurately summarizes the main point of a paragraph in one sentence and reflects the paragraph's main purpose

• serves as a contract between the reader and the writer

• promises that the writer will stick to the idea it expresses throughout the paragraph

• is not too narrow and broad enough to require further explanation or evidence

In a thesis, the writer first states the topic (what the paragraph is about) and then the arguable assertion or opinion about that topic. Similarly, a good topic sentence usually has two parts, the topic and the key words that state the writer's assertion or opinion about the topic. Consider the following sentence.

Racquetball is a superior sport for several reasons.

TOPIC KEY WORDS

In this sentence, racquetball is the topic because it is what the paragraph is about. "Superior sport" are the key words because they state an opinion about the topic, racquetball. The topic sentence identifies and limits what will be discussed in the paragraph. In such a paragraph, the writer would have to identify through personal experience, examples, facts, or reasons why racquetball is superior to other sports.

In the citation above, the explanation, the functions and the structure of a topic sentence has been discussed. Although well analysed, we still hope that the citation above on a topic sentence may arouse your curiosity to read other works in order to acquire more knowledge that relates to a topic sentence. For further understanding of a topic sentence, look at the example below once more drawn from RedRocks Community College Writing Center (2019):

Parts of a thesis (claim + road map):
- **Claim or main idea:** This part states the main idea of the essay.
  - ✓ Example: *Being a vegetarian is better than eating meat...*
- **Road map:** This part lists the major supporting reason(s) discussed in the body of the essay. Note that not all instructors require this part; always consult your professor's instructions.
  - ✓ Example: *...because it is healthier, less expensive, and doesn't harm animals.*
- **Claim + Road Map = Entire Thesis Statement**
  - ✓ Example: *Being a vegetarian is better than eating meat because it is healthier, less expensive, and doesn't harm animals.*

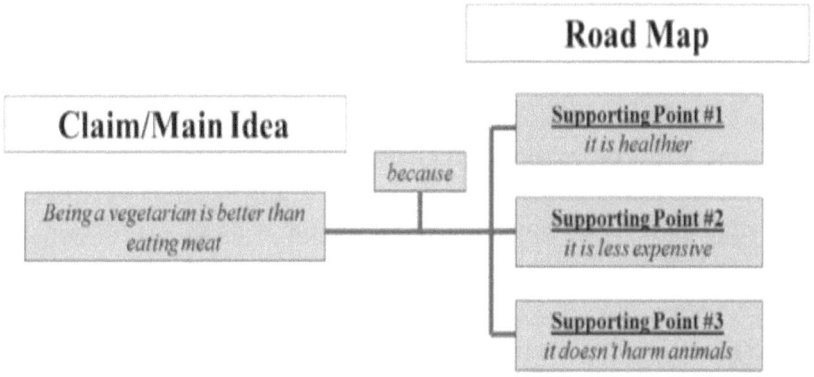

From the diagram above, the main claim is **Being a vegetarian is better than eating meat because it is healthier, it is less expensive, and it doesn't harm animals.** Based on this thesis statement, you may have three topic sentences:

1) Being a vegetarian is better than eating meat because it is healthier.
2) Being a vegetarian is better than eating meat because it is less expensive
3) Being a vegetarian is better than eating meat because it doesn't harm animals

Each topic sentence represents a paragraph that must be backed by facts or evidence and even warrant or general knowledge. Like the main claim, a topic statement is made up of parts. The discussion below focuses on the parts of a topic sentence.

The Structure of the Topic Statement

In order to understand the structure of a topic sentence better, we may be compel to look at the section above once more which highlights the difference between an opinion and an argument. Under that section, there is a summary that says "In the body of an essay, an opinion plus another idea forms an arguable sentence known as the Topic sentence". The other idea which should be added to an opinion in order to form a topic sentence is known as "reason". With this revelation done, we can now suggest that the structure of the topic sentence is made up of an opinion + a reason. Just like the thesis statement, the topic sentence is made up of two parts: the opinion or claim and a reason. The main difference between a thesis statement and a topic statement is that a thesis statement or the main claim can have one or more reasons, whereas topic sentences often have only one reason on which you have to justify in the body paragraph of an argumentative essay. Since a topic sentence is made up of two main parts: an opinion and a reason, in the sections below we are going to examine each of these parts.

A) Claim of a topic sentence

The claim section of a topic sentence is the opinion part. Booth et al (2003 :116) define a claim thus: *a claim is any sentence that asserts something that may be true or false and so needs support:* As you can see, a claim is the opinion part about your topic. Being an opinion, a claim can be true or false. Look at the examples of opinion, or claim or assertion below from some writers cited above such as Booth et al (2003) and Shuster.

EXAMPLE

The world's temperature is rising.

Homework is a waste of time

Television news is boring

Tomato soup is better than a grilled cheese sandwich

Tutors should write essays for their students

One of the most important characteristics of a claim is that it can be true or false. So we can render the positive examples or opinions above into negative ones thus: In the example above, we can maintain the topic but change our claim or our opinion from a positive to a negative one. For example,

The world's temperature is not rising

Homework is not a waste of time

Television news is not boring

Tomato soup is not better than a grilled cheese sandwich

Tutors should not write essays for their students

As we have observed so far, a topic sentence is made up of two parts: a claim and a reason. In other words, the sentences above are only opinions, or claims or assertion. We can further divide the claims above into two parts: its topic and its opinion. For example the topics of the claim above include: *the world's temperature, homework, television news, tomato soup, and tutors* and their opinions are, is not rising, is a waste of time, is boring, is better than a grilled cheese sandwich, should not write essays for their students respectively. They may become arguments when we add reasons to them. The other name for reason is the explanatory or controlling sentence. In most cases, controlling sentences are added to a claim with the help of a subordinating conjunction such as "because" in order to form an argument and no longer an opinion. The next talk below is based on an explanatory or controlling sentence.

B) Explanatory or Controlling Sentence (Reason)

An explanatory sentence is the subordinate sentence that is added to the main sentence that contains a claim. In a single word, an explanatory or controlling sentence is known as a reason. A reason is the idea that justifies your claim. Talking about a reason in an argumentative essay, Booth et al. (2003: 116) note: "A reason is a sentence supporting a claim, main or not". Besides this definition, Booth et al. (2003: 116) further explains the relation between a claim and a reason thus:

At the core of every research report is your claim, the answer to your research question, along with two kinds of support for it.

The first support is at least one **reason, a sentence or two explaining**

why your readers should accept your claim. We can usually join a claim and a reason with ***because:***

The examples below show the position of a reason and how it is linked to the claims above by "because". They are still drawn from Booth et al. (2003:116):

The emancipation of Russian peasants was an empty gesture *claim*

because it did not improve the material quality of their daily lives. *reason*

TV violence can have harmful psychological effects on children *claim*

because those exposed to lots of it tend to adopt the values of what they see. *Reason*

At this level, we now know that a topic sentence is divided into two parts: a claim and a reason. The structural formula of a topic sentence may look thus: **a claim + a reason.** A good language student may agree with us that a topic sentence is a complex sentence, which is made up of an independent sentence and a dependent sentence. The independent sentence comprises of an opinion or a claim. The dependent sentence is known as the reason and must be linked to the main sentence by a subordinating conjunction such as "because". Other subordination conjunctions that can link a reasoning sentence to the main sentence include: after, that, in order to, since, so that, though, unless, until, when, whenever, where. Wherever, whether, while, although, as, as if, as long as, as soon as, before, even, even if, even though, if, in order, and so on.

We now know the structure of a topic sentence: **a claim + a reason.** It should be noted that the most important part of a topic sentence is the reason. It is the most important part of an argument because the weakness or the strength of a claim is backed by a reason and everything about evidence is determined by a reason. Talking about the nature of a reason, Booth et al. ((2003:138) narrate:

Readers use reasons to decide whether to believe your claim, but

they also use them to understand the structure of your report.

Reasons outline the logic of your argument, and if each major reason is the point of a section, they outline the report as well.

For a complex argument, each reason will be supported with sub reasons that serve as the points of subsections of the report.

The citation above has stated some functions of a reason- it helps readers to believe a claim, it defines the structure of an essay because if the thesis statement has one reason, the body of the essay might have one paragraph. If there are two reasons in the thesis statement, the essay may also have two paragraphs and so on. The reason also gives more meaning to the logical nature of an argument and more reasons can be used to support other reasons that might intend become claims. The section below illustrates how a claim can be supported by two reasons.

Claim with more Reasons

At this level, we now know that after a claim is a reason. It should be noted that there are many instances in which a claim can be followed by many reasons or other reasons giving birth to other reasons in more complex writings. More on this has been highlighted by Booth et al. (2003:117) thus:

These terms can get confusing, because a reason is often supported by more reasons, which makes that first reason a claim in its own right. In fact, a sentence can be *both* a reason *and* a claim at the same time, if what it states (1) supports a claim and (2) is in turn supported by another reason:

Booth et al. (2003:117) gives us the two examples below:

Example 1

TV violence can have harmful psychological effects on children *claim 1* because **those exposed to large amounts of it tend to adopt the values of what they see** *reason 1 supporting claim 1 / claim 2 supported by reason 2* **Their constant exposure to violent images makes them unable to distinguish fantasy from reality.** *reason 2 supporting reason1 / claim 2*

Example 2

Although many believe that school uniforms help lower the incidence of violence in public schools, the evidence is at best weak, **because no researchers have controlled for other measures that have been instituted at the same time as uniforms** *reason 1* **and because the data reported are statistically suspect.** *reason 2*

The aim of these two examples above is to highlight the idea that not all reasons in advanced writings are linked to the main sentence by a subordinating conjunction as we have seen so far. For instance, example 1 above has not got any subordinating conjunction such as because, but there are two reason in it. So far, we have seen how a reason can support a claim and how two reasons can support a claim or another reason. We have also observed some of the functions of a reason and how a reason is often introduced by "because". According to Booth et al. (1995, 2003) "Reasons can be based on reasons, but ultimately a reason has to be grounded on *evidence*". At this level, it should be noted that your topic + your opinion + your reason have given you a concrete argument. In other words, your complex sentence of a topic sentence and a controlling sentence have given you a good argumentative stand. You now need many supporting sentences to convince your readers to belief in your opinion or claim. These supporting sentences are known as evidence or data. The discussion below focuses on supporting sentences or evidence or data.

5.4.1.2 Supporting Sentences (Evidence or Data)

In many cases, students put up very interesting topic sentences and controlling ones but fail to convince their reader with their data or supporting sentences. As you have seen so far, the single word for supporting sentences is evidence or data. The nature of evidence in an argument can be captured in the citation below from Booth et al. (2003: 117-118) thus:

In casual conversation, we usually support a claim with just a reason:

We should leave *claim* **because it looks like rain.** *Reason*

We don't ask, what evidence do you have that it looks like rain? (unless someone thinks he's a meteorologist: Those aren't rain clouds; they're just . . .). When you address serious issues in writing, though, you can't

expect readers to accept all your reasons at face value. Careful

readers behave more like that would-be weatherman, asking for

the evidence, the data, the facts on which you base those reasons:

Based on the citation above we are presented with this argument which goes thus:, "We should leave *claim* because it looks like rain. *Reason*". Because there is no evidence to prove the reason that "it looks like rain" this argument might not convinced some people. The audience might ask the question; why do you think "it looks like rain"?, others might remind you that this is the dry season and there is no rain, still others might tell you that those types of cloud do not bring rain. In such a situation, you need more evidence to convince your audience to believe in your reason that "**it** looks like rain". As we can see evidence is very importance in an argument because it supports a reason. Talking about evidence, Booth et al. (2003: 117-118) say:

At least in principle, *evidence* is something you and your readers

can see, touch, taste, smell, or hear (or is accepted by everyone

as just plain *fact—the sun came up yesterday morning*). It makes

no sense to ask, *where could I go to see your reasons?* It does make

sense to ask, *where could I go to see your evidence?*

When people talk about evidence, they typically use foundational metaphors

(as have we): evidence is *hard reality, solid proof,* something

we can *see for ourselves*. It's the *bedrock,* the *solid foundation* on which

we build arguments

The citation above reminds us that evidence is something that we can see, touch, taste, smell or hear. In other words, evidence has much to do with our five senses. In a way to foster understanding, the differences between reason and evidence has been highlighted in

Booth et al. (2003: 140) thus:

• Reasons state why readers should accept a claim. Researchers can think up reasons; they don't think up evidence (or at least they do so at their own risk).

• Evidence is what readers accept as fact, at least for the moment. They think of evidence as "hard" reality, evident to anyone able to observe it.

In the citation above, we observe that some critical people can easily think of a reason to some claims that are made but not evidence. For example in the argument "We should leave *claim* because it looks like rain. *Reason*", some critical people can immediately suggest a reason to your claim that "We should leave" by saying: "is it because of the rain that is threatening to fall"? So a reason can be known by an audience but evidence is always provided. Most people will always ask this question "how do you know all these things"? You have to convince them by providing enough evidence from good and reliable sources that we are going to see below.

Sources of Evidence

The importance of sources of evidence cannot be underestimated because without a good source, many people cannot believe an argument. Below are some common sources:

Anecdotes

Case studies

Data and Facts

Statistics Quotes from authority/expert testimony

Examples

Personal experience

or

☐ *Facts*

☐ *Examples*

☐ *Definitions*

☐ *Comparison*

☐ *Statistics*
☐ *Experience*
☐ *Analysis*
☐ *Prediction*
☐ *Demonstration*
☐ *Expert opinions*
☐ *Anecdotes/Reflections/Observations*
☐ *Quotations*

The list above suggests sources from which evidence can be gotten. But in view of the importance of evidence in every domain, Booth et al. (2003: 125) highlight some particular qualities in some fields. The citation below highlights the warning from the authors and then some qualities of evidence found in some fields thus:

This does not mean that what you learn in one class is useless in another. All fields share the elements of argument we describe here. But you do have to watch for what's distinctive in how a field handles those elements and be flexible enough to adapt— trusting, at the same time, the skills you already command. You can anticipate this problem as you read by noting the kinds of evidence used by the sources you consult. Here are just a few of the different kinds of evidence to watch for in different fields:

☐ personal beliefs and anecdotes from writers' own lives, as in a first-year writing course;
☐ direct quotations, as in most of the humanities;
☐ citations and borrowings from previous writers, as in the law;
☐ fine-grained descriptions of behavior, as in anthropology;
☐ statistical summaries of behavior, as in sociology;
☐ quantitative data gathered in laboratory experiments, as in

natural sciences;

- photographs, sound recordings, videotapes, and films, as in art, music, history, and anthropology;
- detailed documentary data assembled into a coherent story, as in some kinds of history or anthropology;
- networks of principles, implications, inferences, and conclusions independent of factual data, as in philosophy.

Just as important, note the kinds of evidence that are never used in your field. Anecdotes enliven literary history but rarely count as good evidence in sociological explanations; fine-grained narratives are crucial in many anthropological reports but are irrelevant in an argument about subatomic physics.

Your field of study may not be known but we hope that the examples above can orientate you in one way or the other. In argument, many cases of evidence are often introduced by a clause that often starts with "for example"... Look at these examples below drawn from Shuster above. The portion of evidence starts with for example and has been highlighted.

- *Homework is a waste of time because it takes time away from other activities that are more important.* **For example, we end up doing worksheets of math problems instead of getting outside and getting fresh air and exercise".**

- *Television news is boring because it doesn't talk about issues that are relevant to me.* **For example, I never see stories about the issues that kids deal with every day".**

- *Tomato soup is better than a grilled cheese sandwich because it is more nutritious.* **For example, tomato soup contains important vitamins such as Lycopene, while grilled cheese sandwiches really don't have that much nutritional value at all".**

As we saw above, evidence is often introduced by the phrase "For example" However, in many advanced writings; the phrase "for example" does not always begin evidence. The two examples below are drawn from Booth et al. (2003:143). They combine claim, reason and evidence. Like the examples, the portion of evidence has been highlighted thus:

Example 1

TV violence can have harmful psychological effects on children *claim 1* because those exposed to large amounts of it tend to adopt the values of what they see.*reason 1 supporting claim 1/claim 2 supported by reason 2* Their constant exposure to violent images makes them unable to distinguish fantasy from reality.*reason 2 supporting reason 1/claim 2* **Smith (1997) found that children ages 5–9 who watched more than three hours of violent television a day were 25 percent more likely to say that most of what they saw on television was "really happening."***evidence supporting reason 2*

Example 2

Emotions play a larger role in rational decision-making than most of us think,*claim* because without the help of the emotional centers of the brain, we cannot make rational decisions.*reason* **Persons whose brains have suffered physical damage to their emotional centers cannot make even simple, everyday decisions.***Evidence*

The citations above have highlighted different ways of presenting evidence in an argument-with a "for example" clause and without a "for example" clause. At this level, many scholars of the argumentative genre know that the core structure of an argumentative writing has been examined. Some intelligent students might question the complete nature of the discussion above because the phrase "core elements" or "core structure" suggests that there are still other elements of an argument that have not yet been identified. Besides this, some students who know the complete structure of an argumentative essay may know that a complete argumentative essay must have a pro side and a contra side, but the discussion above has only focused on the pro side.

This means that the contra side of an argument has not yet been handled. It is for these reasons that the discussion below focuses on the counter elements of an argumentative writing that may add more to understanding and to the complete structure of an argument.

5.4.2 Counter Paragraph

After having established your argument: claim. Reason and evidence, you must state a thesis statement with an opposing view. It is made up of acknowledgement and a respond or rebut or a counter claim. At this level, it should be noted that unlike the thesis statement that starts with an independent sentence, the counter thesis often begin with a dependent clause. The dependent sentence often stands for an acknowledgement whereas the main clause suggests your respond, rebut or counter claim. Because the counter thesis is made up of an acknowledgement and a respond, the discussion examines these two qualities. They are drawn from Oshima and Hogue (2006).

(1) [DC Despite the claims that curfew laws are necessary to control juvenile gangs], [IDC curfew laws are clearly unconstitutional].

(2) [DC Although there are certainly reasons to be cautious with stem cell research], [IDC I believe that its potential benefits far outweighs its dangers].

In the two examples above, DC stands for Dependent Clause and IDC stands for Independent Clause. As you can observe, these two examples begin with subordinate conjunctions (despite and although).This means that an acknowledgement comes first, then the rebut. That is the nature of most counter argumentative thesis statements. However, the next talk below focuses on acknowledgement and later the response, which are the two main parts of a counter argument.

5.4.2.1 Acknowledgement

At the outset of chapter three of this study, it is mentioned that an argumentative discourse is 'a thoughtful conversation with amiable colleagues, a conversation in which you cooperatively explore a contestable issue that you all think is important to resolve, a conversation that aims not at coercing each other into agreement, but at cooperatively finding and agreeing on the best answer to a hard question" (Booth, W. C.; Colomb, G. G. & Williams, J. M., 2003). In fact, it is a friendly conversation between or amongst friends on a controversial issue or over a hard question that needs the best answer. In order to embark on such a conversation, friends must accept or acknowledge other friends' view points before they can put forward their own argument. By acknowledging another person's point of view or opinion, before you put forward your argument, you create a friendly atmosphere for positive thinking and active participation. Talking about acknowledgement, Booth et al. (2003:151) state:

As you know by now, the core of your argument is a claim backed

by a reason based on evidence. You thicken that core by assembling

more reasons, perhaps supporting each with yet more reasons,

then laying down a base of evidence on which all those

reasons rest. But if you plan your argument only around claims,

reasons, and evidence, your readers may think that your argument

is flatfooted, even naive. You will seem less like an inquirer

amiably engaging intelligent but feisty colleagues in conversation

than like a lecturer droning at an empty room.

Since your readers won't be there as you draft your report, you

have to *imagine* them asking questions, not just the predictable

ones that readers ask about any argument, but ones about yours

in particular. It's when you can acknowledge and respond to that

imagined questioning, to suggested alternatives and to outright

objections, that your report not only speaks in your voice but

brings in the voice of others. That's how you most effectively establish

a working relationship with readers.

The citation above suggests that by acknowledging other peoples' points of view, your writing "brings in the voice of others" and makes your argument more of a complete search for knowledge which involves many people than an individual work. This is very importance because many scholars know that knowledge cannot be constructed by a single individual. The citation above amongst many other things highlights that "since your readers won't be there as you draft your report, you have to *imagine* them asking questions…" You have to imagine the questions that others can ask in order to acknowledge them before responding. Due to the importance of the questions that you may acknowledge in your argument, the discussion below focuses on the sources of these questions that your readers might ask you in your argument.

Possible Sources of Your Readers' Questions

There are many ways that people can use in order to reduce or to discredit the power of your argument and render it very useless. Although these ways might differ based on levels, ages, occupations, tastes, popularity and so on, this study highlights those that are very common at the advanced level writings. Some of these sources of counter arguments include: irrelevance, insufficiency, incorrect, and so on.

Irrelevance

At the advanced level, many of your opponents including your teachers, your markers, your examiners, your colleagues are very educated and deeply insightful in your domain in particular and others in general. These people can easily identify irrelevant points, approaches, organizations, words, sentences in your argument and use this particular tool to discredit your argument. So you must see into it that your argument is relevant to the topic, to the idea, to the context (time, place, people etc.), to the age, and so on.

Insufficiency

Many students fail because their points are not sufficient to the theme they are supposed to handle. In fact, their data, evidence, and so on are not sufficient to support a reason. Using the tool of insufficiency, your opponents can reduce the power of your argument. So in order to convince your audience, your argument must be impregnated with sufficient points, sufficient reasons, sufficient proofs, sufficient data, and so on.

Incorrect

Many people use misleading information, wrong opinions, general beliefs, emotions, incorrect language, incoherence organization, wrong approaches, and so on to push certain arguments to others. Careful opponents are often good to identify these incorrect thoughts, deeds, speeches, organizations, etc. and they then use them to reduce the strongest argument to zero. It is therefore up to you to see into it that your argument is freed from inappropriate organizations, inappropriate language; inappropriate ideas and so on because your opponents will use these incorrect issues against your argument.

Possible Questions from your Readers

In general, you now know that your reader can identify areas of irrelevant, areas of insufficiency, or areas of incorrectness in your argument and he or she can exploit any or all of these lapses to reduce the power of your argument. As we can see, acknowledgement reveals many things in an argument because besides all the importance of Acknowledgement discussed so far, acknowledgement also reveals peoples strength and weaknesses. For example, when you acknowledge too much, your essay reveals a weakness in your argumentative skills because it suggests that much research was not carried out by you or you are very ignorant or stubborn in your field. And when you acknowledge too less you might be looked upon as being proud and authoritative. However, in order to put up a good acknowledgement, it might be very necessary to know areas that can provide your reader with many questions against your argument as has been highlighted above. However, some possible questions that can come from your readers and which may need your acknowledgement before you counter act have been identified by Booth et al. (2003) .In a more specific manner, these authors identify two major ways that can generate questions in an argumentative discourse. These two ways according Booth et al. (2003:151) include:

- They may question its intrinsic soundness: the clarity of your claim, the relevance of your reasons, and the quality of your evidence.
- They may ask you to consider alternatives—a different way of framing the problem, evidence you haven't considered, warrants that you might not have thought of.

Based on the citation above, we observe that your readers can generate questions within your argument (claim, reason and evidence) or out of your argument (alternatives). In a way to solve the first section of internal argument, Booth et al. (2003:152) focus their possible question from the claim and the evidence, The citation below is divide into two parts-first questions and second questions.

First, your readers may ask these questions on your problem:

1. Why have you defined the problem in that way? If there is a problem, it involves not what you raise but this other issue.
2. Why do you think there is any problem here at all? I don't see any serious costs if it is not solved. Maybe there is no problem.
3. What kind of problem is this? Is it conceptual or pragmatic? Maybe it should be framed differently. Now question your solution:
4. Exactly what kind of solution are you proposing? Does your claim ask me to understand something or to do something? Your solution is conceptual but your problem is practical (or vice versa)
5. Have you stated your claim too strongly? I can think of exceptions and limitations.

6a. Why is your conceptual answer better than others? It doesn't fit in with all this other well-established knowledge.

6b. Why is your practical solution betters than others? I think it will cost too much and create new problems.

Second, your readers may question your support, focusing first on your evidence. Some objections probe your evidence:

1. I'd like to see a different kind of evidence. We need hard numbers, not anecdotes. (Or, we want to hear about real people, not cold numbers.)
2. It isn't accurate. The numbers don't add up.
3. It isn't precise enough. What do you mean by "many"?
4. It isn't current. There is more recent research on this.
5. It isn't representative. You didn't get data from . . .
6. It isn't authoritative. Smith is no expert on this matter.

The toughest objection, however, is usually this one:

7. You need more evidence. One quotation does not establish a pattern.

Talking about questions that can come out of your argument, Booth et al. (2003:152) raised three main topics:

Alternatives in Your Sources

"But there are causes in addition to the one you claim

"But what about these counterexamples?"

"I don't define X as you do. To me, X means.

The discussion above reminds us that there are very critical thinkers who can question any part of your argument. We aim at building your minds in this domain so that more hard work can come from you. The next talk highlights some main areas that need your acknowledgement in many arguments.

Main Elements to be acknowledged

At this level, you may now see where your opponents can raise ideas to discredit your argument. You must acknowledge all these before responding. However certain areas are too common that they demand your acknowledgement. Some of them are:

Acknowledging Questions You Can't Answer

Selecting Alternatives to Respond To

Many students have had problems because they failed to acknowledge some questions and alternative points of view from their opponents. Always acknowledge question that you cannot answer instantly and also alternative solutions or evidence, reason from your opponents.

Phrases for acknowledgement

The talk below focuses on some common phrases that are often used to indicate the beginning of an acknowledgement. But before you read these phrases, you should bear in mind that acknowledgement always start with subordinated clauses. Some key subordinate conjunctions that indicate acknowledgement include: although, though, even, even though, and so on. However, San Antonio College Writing Center states the following acknowledgement phrases:

1) Although the space program yields important scientific discoveries

2) Some argue that the space program costs too much, saying that the prices for scientific discoveries made by the program are too high.

3) Some believe that the current warning messages are enough,

(4) Some people feel that the United States should have a national health care plan like Canada's.

(5) Many (may/might) think that genetically engineered crops are a grave danger to the environment.

(6) Smokers say that they have a right to smoke.

(7) It may be true that the U.S. constitution gives citizens the right to own weapons.

(8) Some people feel that the United States should have a national health care plan like Canada's; however, others feel that government should stay out of the health care business.

(9) Although/Even though many think that genetically engineered crops are a grave danger to the environment, such crops can have alleviate world hunger and malnutrition.

(10) Smokers say that they have a right to smoke in spite of the fact that/despite the fact that smoking will kill them.

(11) While/whereas it may be true that the U.S. constitution gives citizens the right to own weapons, the men who wrote the Constitution lived in a different time.

Besides the acknowledgement phrases above Ozagac, (2004) states:

-Opponents of this idea claim / maintain that ...

-Those who disagree /

-Those who are against these ideas may say / assert that ...

-Some people may disagree with this idea.

Besides the phrase that indicate acknowledgement above, we can also read more about acknowledgement and its dismissal phrase, or acceptance phrases from Booth et al. (2003) . Talking about acknowledgement and some particular cases and particular words, Booth et al. (1995, 2003:161-163) report:

When you respond to an alternative or objection, you can mention and dismiss it or address it at length. We offer these expressions roughly in that order, from most dismissive to most respectful. (Brackets and slashes indicate alternative choices.)

1. You can dismiss an objection or alternative by introducing it with **despite, regardless of, or notwithstanding:**

[**Despite/Regardless of/Notwithstanding**] Congress's claims that it wants to cut taxes, *acknowledgment* the public believes that . . . *response*

Use **although, while, and even though** in the same way:

[**Although/While/Even though**] there are economic problems in Hong Kong, *acknowledgment* Southeast Asia remains a strong . . . *response*

2. You can signal an acknowledgment indirectly with **seem, appear, may, and could**, or with an adverb like **plausibly, justifiably, reasonably, surprisingly, or even certainly:**

In his letters, Lincoln expresses what [**seems/appears**] to be depression. *Acknowledgment* But those who observed him . . . *response* This proposal [may have/plausibly has] some merit, *acknowledgment* but we . . . *response*

3. You can acknowledge alternatives by attributing them to an unnamed source or to no source at all, which gives a little weight to the objection:

It is easy to [**think/imagine/say/claim/argue**] that taxes should . .

There is [**another/alternative/possible**][**explanation/line of argument/account/possibility**].

Some evidence [**might/may/can/could/does**][**suggest/indicate/ point to/lead some to think**] that we should . . .

4. You can attribute an alternative to a more specific source, giving it more weight:

There are [**some/many/a few**] who [**might/may/could/would**] [**say/think/argue/claim/charge/object**] that Cuba is not . . .

Note that researchers sometimes weaken their case by prematurely downgrading those they will disagree with:

Some naive researchers have claimed that . . .

The occasionally careless historian H has even claimed that . . .

It's usually best to save your criticism for the response, and to direct it at the work rather than the person.

5. You can acknowledge an alternative in your own voice, with a passive verb or with an adverb such as **admittedly, granted, to be sure,** and so on, conceding it some validity:

I[**understand/know/realize**] that liberals believe in . . . , but . . .

It is [**true/possible/likely/certain**] that no good evidence proves that coffee causes cancer. . . . However, . . .

It [**must/should/can**] be [**admitted/acknowledged/noted/conceded**] that no good evidence proves that . . . Nevertheless, . . .

[**Granted/Admittedly/True/To be sure/Certainly/Of course**], Adams has claimed . . . However, . . .

We [**could/can/might/may/would**] [**say/argue/claim/think**] that spending on the arts supports pornographic . . .

Much about acknowledgement has been highlighted. After acknowledgement. You must respond to those contra views. The discussion below focuses on the element of respond.

5.4.2.2 Respond or Rebut

What actually differentiates an argumentative essay from a persuasive essay is the ability to put forward a counter argument that is very sound and convincing. In fact, your ability to convince your audience in an argumentative essay or argumentative speech hinges a lot on your ability to handle your counter argument or to refute other claims with vigor. The importance of the counter argument is so deep that it shapes or orientates the patterns of any argumentative essays or speeches toward a logical discourse. More about a counter argument can be read from many scholars. However this unknown writer states:

The most important technique in persuading readers that your viewpoint is valid is to support it in every paragraph, but another strong technique is to write a good **counterargument** that goes against your thesis statement. Introducing this counterargument adds credibility to your essay. It shows that you understand more than one point of view about your topic.

After you provide a counterargument, you must give a **refutation**, or a response to the counterargument, that either disproves it or shows it to be weaker or less important than your point.

In simple terms, imagine that you are having an argument with a friend about your topic. She disagrees with your opinion. What do you think will be her strongest argument against your point of view? That is your counterargument. How will you respond to her counterargument? Your answer is your refutation.

Look at the following excerpt from "The Best Classroom" on pages 167–169. The counterargument is in italics and the refutation is underlined.

> Though studying abroad offers many advantages, *some may argue that a semester or a year abroad is nothing but a vacation. Yes, it is true that some students choose to treat studying abroad as a vacation rather than the rich academic experience that it can be.* The bad actions of a few students should not invalidate study-abroad programs as a whole. In fact, in a long-term study of 3,400 students, Dwyer and Peters (2004) found that a large number said studying abroad had an impact on their world view (96 percent), increased their self-confidence (96 percent), and gave them the skill sets they needed for the career they chose (76 percent). Clearly, studying abroad is not just a party.

The writer above suggests that a counter argument should either disprove or reveal the weaker or the less important aspects of your opponent's argument or point. The answer you give in order to illustrate that your opponent's points are irrelevant, weaker, of less important is known as your refutation or response. In this same vein of the importance of a counter argument, Booth et al. (2003:118) narrate:

A responsible researcher supports a claim with reasons based on evidence. But thoughtful readers don't accept a claim just because you back it up with *your* reasons and *your* evidence. Unless they think exactly as you do (unlikely, given the fact that you are making an argument), they will probably think of evidence you haven't, interpret your evidence differently, or, from the same evidence, draw a different conclusion. They may reject the truth of your reasons, or accept them as true but deny that they are relevant to your claim and so cannot support it. They may think of alternative claims you did not consider.

In other words, your readers are likely to question *any* part of your argument. So you have to anticipate as many of their questions as you can, and then acknowledge and respond to the most important ones. For example, as readers consider the claim that children exposed to violent TV adopt its values, some might wonder whether children are drawn to TV violence because they *already* are inclined to violence of all kinds. If you think readers might ask that question, you would be wise to acknowledge and respond to it:

The citation above still reminds us of curious and critical readers who can question any part of an argument. This reinforces the concept of you thinking more about what your readers can eventually question in your argument which demands you to acknowledge and then respond.

A respond is much closed to an acknowledgement to the point that when an acknowledgement is positive, a positive respond is needed. Likewise, when an acknowledgement is negative or neutral the respond too is negative or neutral. In a counter argument, an acknowledgement sometimes forms the claim and respond is always the reason. But in most cases, your respond is your claim and needs a lot of supports (reason, evidence) to make it very convincing. As we have already indicated above, you will respond to instances of irrelevance, incorrect or insufficiency identified in your argument by your opponents or by your readers. Look at the possible questions above and see how you can respond to them if asked by your opponents or readers. The example below is a passage that reveals the real nature of a refutation. It is drawn from an unknown scholar.

1. Topic: Mandatory retirement for pilots

   Thesis statement: Pilots should be required to retire at age 60 to ensure the safety of passengers.

   Counterargument: Some people may believe that older pilots' experience can contribute to flight safety.

   Refutation: _While this may be true for a handful of pilots, the vast majority of people report weaker eyesight, hearing, and motor skills as they age._

Look at the passage above and learn the main thesis statements, then you see how the counterargument is framed and then the convincing refutation the writer puts up. You can then also develop your own argument and put up a refutation.

Phrases that Indicate a Respond

Respond in an argument is often characterized by some signaling words of the contrary sense such as but, however, nevertheless etc. Look at the citation below from Booth et al. (2003:163)

Begin your response with contradicting language like **but, however, or on the other hand**. After you state your response, offer some support for it, because that response is a claim. You can respond in ways that range from tactful to blunt.

1. You can regret that you don't entirely understand:

But [I do not quite understand how . . ./I find it difficult to see how . . ./It is not clear to me how] X can claim that, when . . .

2. Or you can note that there are unsettled issues:

But there are other issues here . . ./There remains the problem of ...

3. You can respond more bluntly, claiming the acknowledged position is irrelevant or unreliable:

But as insightful as that may be, it [ignores/is irrelevant to/does not bear on] the issue at hand.

But the [evidence/reasoning] is [unreliable/shaky/thin].

But the argument is [untenable/weak/confused/simplistic].

But the argument [overlooks/ignores/misses] key factors. . . .

Besides the examples above, the ones below are common words that may help you in your effort to put up a counter argument.

Transitional phrases and connectors in argument essays help the reader to follow the logical development of the argument. These transitions can be used to connect sentences, ideas, and paragraphs. Here are some common transitions and connectors for developing support in your argument and for addressing a counterargument.

Transitions and Connectors That Develop a Point Further			
additionally	correspondingly	furthermore	moreover
also	for example	in a similar manner	similarly
besides	for instance	likewise	what is more

Transitions and Connectors That Address a Counterargument			
although	even though	nevertheless	still
but	however	nonetheless	though
conversely	in contrast	on the other hand	while
despite	in spite of	some people might say	yet

With the explanation done, the example below is an argument that contains claim, reasons, evidence and acknowledgement and response. It is necessary because it combines all the elements of an argument discussed so far in the body of an argumentative writing in this study. The passage is drawn from Booth et al. (2003:118-119)

TV violence can have harmful psychological effects on children*claim 1* because those exposed to large amounts of it tend to

adopt the values of what they see.*reason 1 supporting claim 1/ claim 2 supported*

by reason 2 Their constant exposure to violent images makes

them unable to distinguish fantasy from reality.*reason 2 supporting reason 1/ claim 2* Smith (1997) found that children ages 5–9 who watched more than three hours of violent television a day were25 percent more likely to say that most of what they saw on television was "really happening."*evidence supporting reason 2* **It is conceivable, of course, that children who tend to watch greater amounts of violent entertainment already have violent values,***acknowledgment* **but Jones (1989) found that children with no predisposition to violence were just as attracted to violent entertainment as those with a history of violence.***response*

After the passage above the next discussion focuses on the warrant which is one of the most important elements of an argumentative writing.

5.4.3 Warrant

In a move to know to what extent my students understand the meaning of a warrant in an argument, I observed that many students had never heard of a warrant in the genre of an argument, let alone knowing its definition. However, it should be noted that a warrant in an argument sheds abundant light on the relevance or the relations that exist amongst the elements of an argument such as claim, reason, evidence, etc., Look at the illustration below to identify how a warrant works in an argument:

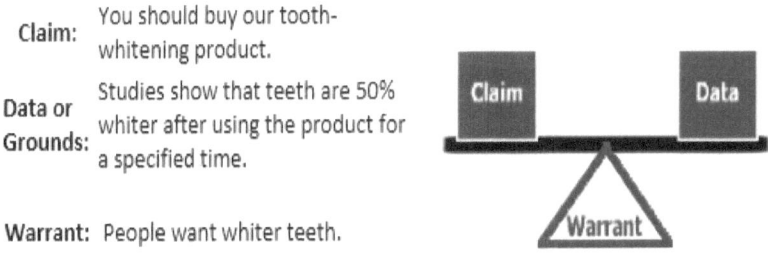

Claim: You should buy our tooth-whitening product.
Data or Grounds: Studies show that teeth are 50% whiter after using the product for a specified time.
Warrant: People want whiter teeth.

Source: Blinn College – Bryan Writing Center Spring 2023

The diagram above illustrates how a warrant can link a claim and its data or evidence. The authors begin by identifying a claim (You should buy our tooth-whitening product), followed by data or ground (studies show that teeth are 50 whiter after using the product for a specified time) and then a warrant (People want whiter teeth).This might help you to imagine the importance of a warrant. However, talking about the importance of a warrant in an argument, Booth et al. (2003:165) state:

Researchers owe their readers their best reasons, backed with more than enough of the best available evidence. But even if readers accept your reasons as true, they may still not accept your claim if they think your reasons are *irrelevant* to it. We explain and demonstrate the relevance of a reason to a claim with the fifth element of argument—a warrant.

The citation above has only highlighted the relationship between a claim and a reason. For example, it tells us that your readers might consider your claim very good but they might question your reason for the claim because it may sound irrelevant. This is true; however, students should also note that a keen opponent can question the relationship between your reason and your evidence too. So a warrant can be used to support your argument or show how any element relate to the other in a practical context. In fact, we learn that a warrant justifies the relevance amongst elements in an argumentative discourse. But what really is a warrant in an argumentative discourse? Booth et al. (2003:165) suggest: "A warrant is sometimes called a *commonplace,* a commonsense generalization about the world that everyone considers self-evident": A warrant can be a proverb, an idiomatic expression, a formulaic speech that is well known by a particular community that uses it. Warrants are very abstract in nature and might have different interpretations in the same community or in different groups. In view of these differences, warrants should be used appropriately in an argument. In order to illustrate the differences and the care that must be taken in order to use a warrant, Booth et al. (2003:120) state:

Think of a warrant as a principle claiming that a general set of circumstances predictably allows us to draw a general consequence. You can then use that warrant to justify concluding that a specific instance of that general consequence (your claim) follows from a specific instance of that general circumstance (your reason). But for that warrant to apply, readers must first agree that the specific circumstance (or reason) qualifies as a sound instance of the general circumstance in the warrant and that the specific consequence (or claim) qualifies as a sound instance of the general consequence. As you'll see, it is not easy to decide where to put warrants in the sequence of an argument, or even whether you need them at all. In fact, writers state warrants rarely, only when they think readers might question the relevance of a reason to their claim.

The citation above suggests that a warrant has a structure which must be acceptable by your reader. The structure of a warrant goes thus: a general circumstance leads to a general consequence. For example by saying "more men less work", more men (general circumstance) and less work (general consequence). In other words, the result (less work) comes from the general circumstance (more men). In order to understand the structure of a warrant better, look at the example below from Booth et al. (2003: 167)

• the specific circumstance (*Despite Congress's doubling the budget to reduce drug smuggling, the amount of drugs smuggled into this country has risen*) is a good instance of the general circumstance (*more resources are invested to prevent something but its incidence goes up*);

• the specific consequence (*We are wasting our money*) is a good instance of the general consequence (*resources have been wasted*).

The citation above reveals the two parts of a warrant: *circumstance* and *consequence*. These two parts can be expressed at a general level and at a specific level. At the general level, the citation illustrates these two parts thus: when *more resources are invested to prevent something but its incidence goes up* (general circumstance); therefore *resources have been wasted (general consequence)*.

At a specific level, the citation reduces the two parts to the American context by saying that

*Despite Congress's doubling the budget to reduce drug smuggling, the amount of drugs smuggled into this country has risen (*specific circumstance*) therefore We are wasting our money (*specific consequence*).* In order to have a good command of the structure of a warrant,

Booth et al. (2003: 167) suggest the following formulation: **When(ever) X, then Y.** Based on the structure of a warrant, there are many types of warrants. It should also be noted that in many advanced contexts, warrants are not mentioned because many people already know them. This type of warrant that is not mentioned in an argument is known as an implicit warrant and the warrant that is mentioned is known as an explicit warrant. The discussion below focuses on how the parts of a warrant can be united.

Ways to Unite Parts of a Warrant

As already highlighted above, warrants are often used in situations of limited understanding from a reader, especially when the critical reader does not see any relevance amongst elements in an argument. Warrants come in to shed abundant light on the relevance. Talking about the ways in which parts of a warrant can be united, Booth et al. (2003: 167) state:

But however it is stated, a warrant always has those two parts: a general circumstance and the general consequence that readers should infer. The parts can relate by cause-and-effect (Rain causes wet streets), one-thing-is-the-sign-of-another (Cold hands, warm heart),a rule of behavior (Look both ways before you cross the street), a definition (A three sided figure is a triangle),a principle of reasoning (Sufficient representative data are necessary for any reliable generalization), or by any other principle that links a condition and a consequence.

Based on the narration above, parts of a warrant can be related in the following situations:

Cause-and-effect

-The parts can relate by cause-and-effect (*Rain causes wet streets*),

Indexation

- one-thing-is-the-sign-of-another (*Cold hands, warm heart*),

-A rule of behavior

-a rule of behavior (*Look both ways before you cross the street*),

-A definition

a definition (*A three-sided figure is a triangle*),

-<u>A principle of reasoning</u>

-a principle of reasoning (*Sufficient representative data are necessary for any reliable generalization*),

- by <u>any other principle that links a condition and a consequence.</u>

Looking at the examples above, students should know that a warrant is an important speech unit that has at least two parts. The first part deals with a general situation or a general condition known in the society and the second part handles effects or consequences on that general condition. Students may look for good speech unit that can serve as a warrant in a particular situation. Some of them are proverbs, indices, definitions, cause and effect phenomena and so on. A well applied warrant shows how you have widely read in your domain. The discussion below focuses on good warrants in short arguments.

Warrants in Arguments

At this level, we have highlighted some important characteristics of a warrant. It should be noted that warrants are very important in an argument because it fosters understanding in an argument especially to non-members of a discourse community. The discussion below highlights how warrants are added to argument to enhance more understanding. In the first part, we present an argument without a warrant and in the second part we add a warrant to the same argument for you to see the role of a warrant. The warrant in each argument is darkened. The examples are drawn from Booth et al. (2003:121)

Argument with no warrant

So watch out going down the stairs, *claim* because the light is out. *reason*

The same argument with a warrant

When it's dark, you have to be careful not to misstep. *warrant* So watch out going down the stairs, *claim* because the light is out. *reason*

Argument with no warrant

Homosexuality must have a strong genetic component *claim* because so many of its characteristics appear in the feelings and behavior of children who have no contact with homosexuals but become homosexual adults. *Reason*

The same argument with a warrant

When children manifest behavior arising not from teaching or modeling, but spontaneously, that behavior is genetically based.warrant Homosexuality must therefore have a strong genetic component claim because . . .reason

Argument with no warrant

Data show that violence among children 12–16 is rising faster than among any other age group. *reason* Brown (1997) has shown that ...evidence We can no longer ignore the conclusion that TV violence, even in cartoons, is a destructive influence on our children today. *claim*

The same argument with a warrant

Few doubt that when we expose children to examples of courage and generosity, we influence them for the better. How can we then deny that when they are constantly exposed to images of sadistic violence, they are influenced for the worse?warrant Data show that violence among children 12–16 is rising faster than among any other age group.**reason** Brown (1997) has shown that ...evidence We can no longer ignore the conclusion that TV violence, even in cartoons, is a destructive influence on our children today.**claim**

The discussion above has highlighted some common warrants that are added to short arguments. Some very serious students may want to know why these warrants are only placed in front of the claims. This should remind you of the nature of an argumentative discourse that says that when writing, always think of the possible questions that your readers may ask and you answer those questions for them. Since I think that some students may ask the location of warrants in an argument, the discussion below focuses on the location of warrants in an argument.

Location of Warrants

Knowing a warrant is an achievement, and also knowing where to place the warrant in the structure of an argument is another further one. The position of a warrant in an argument is very important. Based on this assertion, there is one main important position for a warrant in an argument and other less important ones. Talking about the main position in which warrants appear in arguments, Booth et al. (2003:199) say:

Once you have determined whether to state warrants, you have to decide where to put the ones you will. Generally speaking, state a warrant before you offer your claim and its supporting reason.

From the citation above, we are told that warrants are often placed or mentioned before a claim. When you place your warrant before a claim, the warrant suggests to your reader many things about you and the argument. For example, the warrant summaries your argument, it also provide a sense of orientation to your reader and so on. The example below shows an argument without a warrant and just below the same argument; it is attached with a warrant before the claim. The example is from Booth et al. (2003: 200)

An argument without a warrant

Since most students at Oxford University in 1580 added nothing to their signatures, reason most of them must have been commoners.*claim*

The same argument with a warrant

In late-sixteenth-century England, only those few men called "gentlemen" could sign their names with an added "Mr.," and only the son of a gentleman could add an "Esq." *warrant* Since most students at Oxford University in 1580 added nothing to their signatures, reason most of them must have been commoners. *Claim*

Apart from placing or stating a warrant before a claim, there are certain moments when a warrant can be stated after a claim. In this case, Booth et al. (2003:200) say:

You can also state a warrant after a specific claim and supporting reason, as a kind of rhetorical flourish that seems to wrap up the argument on an emphatic note:

In fact, there are moments that certain claims are too specific for a particular culture, group or a particular discourse community. In such a situation, you might state your warrant after your main argument to emphasize your point of view. Although many experts use this way to state their warrants, students should learn all the ways of stating a warrant in an argument because it will help them to recognize a warrant in any position of an argument. Like the case above, the example below shows an argument without a warrant and the same argument with a warrant at the end of the argument. This example stills comes from Booth et al. (2003:200)

An argument without a warrant

We should have suspected all along that Thomas Jefferson had a relationship with his slave Sally Hemings, *claim* if only because there were so many contemporary reports of one. *reason*

The same argument with a warrant

We should have suspected all along that Thomas Jefferson had a relationship with his slave Sally Hemings, *claim* if only because there were so many contemporary reports of one. *reason* **After all, where there's smoke, there's likely to be fire.** *warrant*

The main aim of the illustration above is to remind you that although warrants are often placed before the claims, they can equally be placed on other portions of an argument. As already mentioned above, students should know how to recognize warrants in experts' writings before they start placing theirs in various contexts. There are some moments that warrants are being challenged. This is so because as we said above any part of an argument can be challenged especially by experts. So you should not think that as you have supported your argument with a strong warrant, it is above criticisms. So the section below identifies ways that warrants can be challenged.

Challenging the Warrants of Others

As we have seen above, warrants are common knowledge or sayings that are known by many people. Some warrants are known only to a particular group of people and so warrants can be challenged by experts, individuals, etc. In the examples below, we can see the same argument but different warrants (Booth et al, 2003:171)

The same argument

The population of Zackland must be controlled *claim* because it is outstripping its resources and heading for disaster. *reason*

The same argument but the warrant is made by an Economist

When countries A, B, and C exceeded their means, each collapsed. They tried to prevent collapse by every means other than population control, but it did no good. *reason* **When societies reach a point where their population exceeds their resources, the only way they can prevent collapse is to reduce their population.** *claim/warrant*

The same argument but the warrant is made by a Religious leader

It doesn't make any difference what the economic consequences might be; it is immoral to discourage married couples from having children. *claim* **When people are advised to defy God's will as revealed in our holy books, that advice is sinful.** *Warrant*

The same argument but the warrant is made by an American with their doctrine of "Yes we can"

It doesn't make any difference what the economic consequences might be; it is immoral to discourage married couples from having children. *claim.* **Whenever we put our minds to a problem of limited resources, we can solve it.** *Warrant*

Outdated warrant

Some warrants can be challenged because they are outdated. The case below is a good example of an outdated warrant

Nonhuman creatures are mere biological objects without any inner life and so should not be objects of pity or concern. *warrant* Since apes used in medical experiments experience nothing like human emotions or feelings, *reason* we should not waste money trying to make their conditions more comfortable. *claim*

Some insightful students may appreciate the section above because it reveals how intellectuals can indicate the limitation and the reduction of knowledge into certain domains. In fact, when the economist raised the argument above on the population of Zackland and placed his or her warrant, he or she thought that the warrant was the best for that argument. But we have seen two other experts from the field of religion and that of the American culture reducing the warrant only to the economists and not to the rest of the world. Beside the limitations of warrants above, we have also observed that some warrants can also be outdated and so we need a lot of precaution whenever we use a warrant in an argument. This is the real power of argument because it is aimed at creating new knowledge and reviewing the old ones. Argument teaches us not to be too authoritative in our speeches because there are many alternatives not known to us. That said, the next discussion focuses on some common types of warrants.

Kinds of Warrants

In the discussion above, we have observed that warrants are common thoughts, common beliefs, or proverbs used by people in particular situations to enhance further understanding in an argument. We have seen how the same argument can have a warrant from a religious perspective, from an economic perspective and from a cultural perspective and all of them are right and just. This suggests that there are many types of warrants. Booth et al. (2003:179-181)

Identified six types of warrants and their examples thus:

Warrants based on Experience

Where there's smoke, there's fire.

When certain insecticides leach into the ecosystem, eggshells of wild birds become so weak that fewer chicks hatch and the bird population falls.

Warrants based on Authority

When authority X says Y, Y must be so.

Warrants based on Systems of Knowledge and Belief

From mathematics: When we add two odd numbers, we get an even one.

From religion: When we commit adultery, we commit a sin.

From law: When we drive without a license, we commit a misdemeanor

General Cultural Warrants

Early to bed, early to rise, makes you healthy, wealthy, and wise.

Whenever a king wants to abuse his subjects, he may.

It is always wrong to mock someone from another culture.

Methodological Warrants

Generalization: When many cases of X have the quality Y, then X is characterized by Y.

Analogy: When X is like Y in certain respects, then X will be like Y in other respects.

Cause-effect: When Y occurs if and only if X occurs first, then X may cause Y.

Sign: When Y regularly occurs before, during, or after X, Y is a sign of X.

Warrants based on Articles of Faith

When a claim is directly experienced as revealed truth, that claim is true.

When a claim is in accordance with divine teachings, it must be true.

The citation above has highlighted some common warrants from some common domains. This might broaden your scope in one way or the other. The discussion below focuses on qualifiers which are also very important elements for an argument.

5.4.4 Qualifiers

In academics, there are two important voices: the tentative voice and the authoritative voice. Intellectuals hate the authoritative voice because it carries a tone of absolute confidence, which is not needed in knowledge building. This is so because no knowledge is absolute. Knowledge in its nature is constantly modified. A tentative voice in academics is highly appreciated for several reasons: It reveals your humility; it shows that you recognize other alternatives in your domain; your tentative voice also attracts many intellectuals in your domain and so on. The citation below highlights the importance of a tentative voice in an intellectual discussion. It is drawn from Booth et al. (2003:172) thus:

A warrant can be basically true but stated too generally. For example, here is that warrant about gun ownership with no qualifications or hedges:

In the eighteenth and nineteenth centuries, household objects were listed in wills.

That's too strong. Scaled back, it might be more acceptable:

In the eighteenth and nineteenth centuries, household objects **considered valuable by their owners** *were* **usually** *listed in wills.*

Based on the citation above, we observe that Booth et al. (2003) reject the first warrant *In the eighteenth and nineteenth centuries, household objects were listed in wills.* The reason for its rejection is that the warrant is too authoritative, too strong, and very crude and so can easily irritate, or provoke many criticisms from some intellectuals who might want to contribute in the argument. The authors remind us that for that warrant to be tentative, friendly, and promote understanding, we need to add some words that are known as hedges or qualifiers. When the authors added some hedges to the warrant, the warrant now reads like this *In the eighteenth and nineteenth centuries, household objects* **considered valuable by their owners** *were* **usually** *listed in wills.* As you can see, the warrant now is friendlier, not too generalized, and more convincing with the additions of the darkened words. Qualifiers are highly needed in an argument in order to solve a difficult problem. The discussion below focuses on the definition of a qualifier.

Definition

If you look at the elements of the three types of argument highlighted above, you will notice that the element of qualifier is mentioned in Toulmins model. Talking about a qualifier,

Blinn College – Bryan Writing Center Spring 2023 says:

A qualifier is a statement about how strong the claim is. For example, if you are claiming that stains on teeth are caused by drinking coffee, you might need to acknowledge that there may be other causes as well. Your qualified claim would be that drinking coffee is the most significant cause **(although perhaps not the only cause)** of stained teeth.

From the citation above, we observe that qualifiers in an argument are aimed at reducing the bitterness, the aggressive spirit, or the authoritative spirit that might destroy a friendly conversation. By so doing, a qualifier attracts more reasoning, more alternatives, more joy and so on. Look at the examples of claims below that have been hedged. They are drawn from Booth et al. (2003: 135).

We can conclude that the epicenter of the earthquake was fifty miles south-southwest of Tokyo, **assuming the instrumentation was accurately calibrated.**

We believe that aviation manufacturing will not soon match its late-twentieth-century levels, **unless new global conflicts lead to a significant increase in military spending.**

As you can see, the bold lines help to weaken the claim so that it should not appear too authoritative. For more examples of qualifiers look at the citation below from Rogerian number four element and Toulmin number six element thus:

6. When you finish your homework, you can play Luigi's Mansion until bedtime, and you will have good grades in school. **(Statement of Benefits)**

4. Birds will build a nest in your hair if it isn't clean and brushed. You don't want to be the stinky girl at school. **(Qualifiers)**

As already mentioned, sentence 6 and 4 above come from the Rogerian and the Toulmin's models. We now know that Toulmin calls it qualifier statement, whereas in the Rogerian model it is known as a statement of benefits. Although different names are used, we can see that both statements almost have a common sense between them. It should be noted that there are qualifiers as words and qualifiers as statements. The section below highlights some qualifying words according to words classes.

A Modal Verb

May

Might

Could

Would

B VERBS

Suggest

Seem

Appear

Think

C NOUNS

Possibility

Assumption

Probability

Potential

D ADVERBS

Usually

Probably

Certainly

Apparently

E AJECTIVES

Possible

Clear

Likely

Sure

As we have highlighted above, the function of a qualifier is to reduce the authoritative nature of a claim. We have seen examples above in which the qualifiers are phrases or sentences attached to claims. We have equally reminded ourselves that qualifiers do not only end at the level of sentences but also at the level of words. More about hedges will be handled in other studies.

5.5 The Academic Position of the Toulmin Model

At this moment, we think that much has been highlighted on the various approaches to an argument known to many scholars. As already mentioned above each of the approaches of an argument highlighted above has a context. This suggests that no argumentative approach is useless. This claim may be true judging from the fact that it is the context in which you are found that determines the type of an argumentative approach you have to use. For examples, when you are angry and want your message to reach your audience in that mood, you may use the classical approach to an argument. When you don't know your audience and so you need to be noncofrontational toward them, you may use the Rogerian approach. But when you are in an intellectual setting in which logic and reasoning are highly needed, it may be appropriate to use the Toulmin approach to an argument. In our analyses above, we have examined each element of an argument especially those that were identified by Toulmin. Although much has been said about the elements of an argument that were identified by Toulmin, we once more demand you to read the citation below on the elements of an argument put up by Toulmin. The citation is drawn from Maharani (2019: 300) thus:

According to Toulmin (1958) as stated in Nimehchisalem (2011, p.59), a good piece of argument commonly consists of six elements: claim [C]: the statement of the thesis, data [D]: the evidence providing proof for C, warrant [W]: the principle that bridges D to C implicitly/explicitly, proving the legitimacy of D, qualifiers [Q]: the linguistic cues that show the strength of the C,D or W, backing[B]:further support for W, rebuttal [R]:response to the anticipated objections against the arguments.

The author in the citation above has listed the elements common in Toulmins model. Since the Toulmins model is highly needed by students in their academic world, the discussion below focuses on a detailed talk on the Toulmin model from Rene (2007: 272-275) thus:

7. The Toulmin Model

A widely accepted argument analysis is the Toulmin's Model (1958, 1984, 1979, 2001). It is named after a current Harvard Professor, Stephen Toulmin, who, in his first work on the subject, 'The Uses of Argument' (1958), proposed that every good argument has six components. The first three are essential to all arguments, explicitly, 1) the claim, 2) the ground / support, and 3) the warrant. Furthermore, arguments may also contain one or more of three additional elements: 4) the backing, 5) the rebuttal and 6) the qualifier.

These components of argument structure proposed by Toulmin (1958) are described as follows:

7.1. Claims

• The claim is the main point of the argument.

• Plan a claim of your own by asking, "What do I want to prove?" Your response is your claim.

- Synonyms for claim are thesis, proposition, conclusion and main point.

- Like a thesis, the claim can either be explicit or implicit. Whether it is implied or explicitly stated, the claim organizes the entire argument, and everything else in the argument is related to it. The best way to check your claim during revision is by completing this statement: "I have convinced my audience to think that . . ."

7.2. Grounds/support

- Ground supplies the evidence, opinions, reasoning, examples, and factual information about the claim that make it possible for the reader to accept it.

- Synonyms for ground are support, proof, evidence and reasons.

- To plan ground, ask, "What information do I need to supply to convince my audience of my main point (claim)."

- Common types of ground include:

1. Facts and statistics.

2. Opinions (authorities and personal). When using personal opinion, it should be convincing, original, impressive and interesting and backed by factual knowledge, experience, good reasoning and judgment. Rantings, unfounded personal opinions that no one else accepts, or feeble reasons like "because I said so" or "because everyone does it" are not effective ground.

3. Examples—in the form of anecdotes, scenarios and cases.

- When revising your argument, to help you focus on and recognize the ground, complete this sentence: "I want my audience to believe that . . . [the claim] because . . . [list the ground]."

7.3. Warrants

- Warrants are the assumptions, general principles, the conventions of specific disciplines, widely held values, commonly accepted beliefs,

and appeals to human motives that are an important part of any argument.

- Warrants originate with the arguer, but also exist in the minds of the audience. They can be shared by the arguer and the audience or they can be in conflict.

- Warrants represent the psychology of an argument in that they reveal the unspoken beliefs and values of the author and invite the reader to examine his /her own beliefs and make comparisons.

- Example: I am pro-life. Warrants: Religious: a) abortion is a sin; b) life begins at conception.

7.4. Backings

- Backing is additional evidence provided to support or "back up" a warrant whenever there is a strong possibility that your audience will reject it.

- When reviewing your argument to determine whether backing is needed, identify the warrant and then determine whether or not you accept it. If you do not, try to anticipate additional information that would make it more acceptable.

7.5. Rebuttals

- A rebuttal establishes what is wrong, invalid, or unacceptable about an argument and may also present counterarguments, or new arguments that represent entirely different perspectives or points of view on the issue.

- Plan a rebuttal by asking, "what are the other possible views on this issue?" and "how can I answer them?

- Phrases that introduce refutation include, "some may disagree," "others may think," or "other commonly held opinions are," followed by the opposing ideas.

7.6. Qualifiers

An argument is not expected to demonstrate certainties. Instead, it usually only establishes probabilities. Therefore, avoid presenting information as absolutes or certainties. Qualify what you say with phrases such as "very likely," "probably," "it seems," and "many."

At this level, much on the Toulmin model has been highlighted. This does not mean that the model is free from criticisms. In fact, there is no intellectual work without criticisms. Criticisms are needed for the perfect or to open up the intellectual work for more knowledge. It is for this reason that the discussion below highlights some criticism of the Toulmin approach.

Criticisms against the Toulmin Approach

A sound intellectual work like the Toulmins model to argument cannot be free from short-comings. Some of the main lapses of this model has been highlighted in Rene (2007: 272-275) thus:

However, the Toulmin's model has certain limitations. For instance,

'...it is sometimes of restricted use in discussing specialized forms of argument such as those that occur in certain types of disciplinary writing: commercial, legal, and others' (Werry, Chris, 2001).

The Toulmin's model has also been criticized for being too aggressive to the reader and opposed to other models for argument analysis, e.g. the Rogerian Model (1980), named after the psychologist Carl Rogers, which can be simply defined as an argument that sympathizes with the opponent's view. The Toulmin's model, on the contrary, emphasizes that arguers make their claim, support it with evidence and proof, and conclude it with implications or applications without acknowledging the opponent's argument.

Probably, the form of argument analysis depends on the examiner, or it is just a matter of style and adequacy. Nevertheless, for the purposes of this study, the researcher considers himself to be more familiar with Toulmin's proposal; consequently, he decided to use it in the argumentative essay analysis in the present research work.

The Toulmin's model offers a simple, broad, flexible set of categories, or components, for approaching the study of academic argumentative texts. While the model is simple, each major category can be unpacked and used to discuss arguments in increasing levels of detail.

Conversely, during the last decades, there have appeared other models of analysis, such as the Rogerian Model (1980) and the Swales Model (1990) as tools for analyzing academic arguments, and, probably there will be many others in the years to come. Nevertheless, the main purpose on the part of teachers should be to enhance the improvement of student writing, no matter what model or tool we choose in order to analyze students' academic arguments.

Despite the lapses pin-pointed above, the Toulmin model has been used in many important contexts. Due to the importance of the Toulmin model, the citation below is a good example of a paragraph that constitutes every element identified by Stephen Toulmin. It can be gotten from https://www.youtube.com/watch?v=yZJFDSEBORw It has been presented by the notes-"3 Types of Argument: Classical, Rogerian, Toulmin" and it goes thus:

from John Gage's

The Shape of Reason •

Congress should ban animal research **(Claim #1)** *because animals are tortured in experiments that have no necessary benefit for humans such as the testing of cosmetics* **(Data)**. *The wellbeing of animals is more important than the profits of the cosmetics industry (Warrant). Only congress has the authority to make such a law* **(Warrant)** *because the corporations can simply move from state to state to avoid legal penalties* **(Backing)**. *Of course, this ban should not apply to medical research* **(Qualifier)**. *A law to ban all research would go too far* **(Rebuttal)**. *So, the law would probably* **(qualifier)** *have to be carefully written to define the kinds of research intended* **(claim #2)**.

Based on the citation above, we can observe the manner in which ideas are supposed to be presented in the Toulmin model. In fact, John Gage, the speaker above uses the argument above to put forward his opinion on why and how research based on animals should be banned.

5.5 Logical Patterns of Argument at the level of the whole Body

Everything said and done, a keen reader must have observed that the discussion above in this chapter focus more on the elements that make up a paragraph of an argumentative writing. In fact, we have highlighted elements of pro-paragraphs and those of contra-paragraphs. From the discussion seen so far on the argumentative essay, we observe that the argumentative strategy of writing is very complex. For example, to realize a sound argumentative essay, you must look for a controversial topic, your aims must be clearly known, the elements of your paragraph must be known and how to organize them is also important. Apart from the pattern, we have also observed that the number of paragraphs also varies. Due to its complex nature, the argumentative essay might take various patterns in the body. A summary on some patterns of the argumentative essay has been identified by Maharani (2019: 300) thus:

Argumentative essay can be written by applying several patterns. The first is one sided style: the essay only talks about one point of view (pro side),the second is clustering style:in one essay, there is one body paragraph talks about the opponent argument (contra side), and the other three body paragraphs talk about the pro side, the third is alternating style: each body paragraph in one essay contains one contra argument and it is rebutted by pro argument, and the last is combination style.

The way paragraphs are arranged in an argumentative writing is complex. So there is no fixed pattern that can be used for all contexts. As you might have realized above, there are contexts that may need just one paragraph which handles points-by-points, others demand two paragraphs with con and pro approaches and so on. It is because this complex arrangement of paragraphs in the argumentative genre that we dedicate the section below and some appendices to illustrate some patterns of argumentative writing. The section below handles some common patterns highlighted in Maharani (2019: 300) thus:

One Pattern

Persuasive style (only pro side)

Two Patterns

Under the block pattern, we will highlight three sub patterns

-two or more pro sides and one contra side,

-one contra side and two or more pro side, and

- one pro side and one contra side

A) Cluster style (two or more pro sides and one contra side)
adapted from Tahnda Hawkins/South HS

1)Introduction/Claim (One paragraph)
• Start with a hook or attention getting sentence.
  • Briefly summarize the texts

- State your claim. Make sure you are restating the prompt.

2) Body Paragraph: Evidence/Support/Warrant

- Include a topic sentence that restates your claim and your reason.

o **Example: Video games are harmful because_____.**

- Include text evidence that supports your reason.

o **Example: The author shows that video games are harmful because in paragraph 2 it states_____**

- Include an explanation (warrant) that shows how your text evidence proved your claim.

o **Example: The author uses this evidence to show how/that_____.**

3) Body Paragraph: Evidence/Support/Warrant

- Include a topic sentence that restates your claim and your reason.

o **Example: Video games are harmful because_____.**

- Include text evidence that supports your reason.

o **Example: The author shows that video games are harmful because in paragraph 2 it states_____**

- Include an explanation (warrant) that shows how your text evidence proved your claim.

O **Example: The author uses this evidence to show how/that_____**

4) Counterclaim Paragraph:

- Explain what others who don't agree with your claim might say.

o **Example: Some people might disagree. They may believe_____ because_____.**

5) Conclusion (One paragraph)

- Restate your claim and summarize your reasoning. o Example: In conclusion, the text shows that videogames are harmful by pointing out that

Pattern Two

B) BLOCK PATTERN (one contra side and three pro sides)

By Alexander College: Writing and Learning Centre at https://alexander.mywconline.com

Tentative Essay Title:

Your title should capture the essence of the essay

Part I. Introduction

Introduce your Topic:

Provide background information regarding your topic

Thesis Statement:

A thesis statement clearly articulates your position/argument

Part II. Possible Objections (contra paragraph)

Body Paragraph 1 Topic Sentence:

Present positions that do NOT align with your thesis statement

Body Paragraph 1 Supporting Points:

1.

2.

3.

Body Paragraph 1 Concluding Sentence:

Part III. Responding to the Objections & Building your Argument (pro paragraph)

Response #1 in support of your thesis

-Body Paragraph 2 Topic Sentence:

Body Paragraph 2 Supporting Points:

1

2.

3.

Body Paragraph 2 Concluding Sentence:

Response #2 in support of your thesis

-Body Paragraph 3 Topic Sentence:
Body Paragraph 3 Supporting Points:
1.
2.
3.
Body Paragraph 3 Concluding Sentence:
Response #3 in support of your thesis
-Body Paragraph 4 Topic Sentence:
Body Paragraph 4 Supporting Points:
1.
2.
3.
Body Paragraph 4 Concluding Sentence:

Part IV. Conclusion

Restate your Thesis:

Larger Implications of your Argument:

B) Block Pattern II. (one contra side then one pro side) Summarised by

Please note that all the data and most part of the discussions provided in the following PPT slides are drawn from Oshima and Hogue (2006) Writing Academic English (4th ed.).

Block Pattern I.

Introduction

• Explanation of the issue

Thesis statement II. Body

• Block 1

A. Summary of other side's arguments

B. Rebuttal to the first argument

C. Rebuttal to the second argument

D. Rebuttal to the third argument

- **Block 2**

E. Your first argument

F. Your second argument

G. Your third argument

III. Conclusion:

may include a summary of your point of view.

Pattern Three

Point-by-Point Pattern

A (one contra side follow by one pro side then the conclusion)

I Introduction

- Explanation of the issue, including a summary of the other side's argument.
- Thesis statement

II. Body

A. Statement of the other side's first argument and rebuttal with your own counterargument

B. Statement of the other side's second argument and rebuttal with your own counterargument

C. Statement of the other side's third argument and rebuttal with your own counterargument.

III. Conclusion:

may include a summary of your point of view.

As already highlighted above, the body of the argumentative writing is unique in that there is always a paragraph or more for pro and con. Due to the nature of the body of an argumentative writing and for your exercises, the appendices below offer some more patterns of the bodies of argumentative essays. Below are some suggested summaries of the bodies of writings

A) Persuasive body
-Only pro side
B) Classical argument body
-Block pattern (Pro sides and one contra side)
C) Rogerian argumentative body
-Block pattern (Contra side and pro sides)
D) Toulmin argumentative body
Point-by-point pattern

5.6 Conclusion

This chapter has examined logical patterns in the body section of an essay. Some of them include: chronological, spatial, order of importance, compare and contrast, cause and effects, problem and solution, process order, classification order, listing order and the argumentative order. Within the argumentative order, the chapter has highlighted elements such as claim, reason, evidence, acknowledgement, rebut, warrant and qualifier. Possible sources of questions such as irrelevant, insufficient and incorrect have also been treated. Besides the qualities identified above, the chapter too has highlighted some argumentative questions and patterns that may be of great importance to students. Everything said and done, it should be noted that a work of this magnitude cannot handle everything of the argumentative writing at the level of the body section. However, much time and effort has been used to highlight nearly every important concept related to the body of an argument for a beginner like you. All what we have done in this chapter is aimed at arousing your curiosity for further findings because knowledge is never absolute. As you may have realized, there are certain elements that are not common in other arguments, such as acknowledgement in the Toulmin model but has been treated in this study. This may be so because we intend to arouse your curiosity toward this genre of essay because it is very important for knowledge construction. We pray that this chapter serves as a source of inspiration for further findings in the body part of any argumentative writing.

Chapter Six - The Conclusion Of The Long Essay

6.0 Introduction

From the structure of an essay above, it should be noted that the conclusion part is the last paragraph of an essay. Despite the important function of the conclusion of an essay, many students do no handle it well and some often end up not writing the conclusions to their essays. As we know, a well framed conclusion should leave your reader with an urge to read over your essay again. This section of this book focuses on the conclusion section of an essay. It examines the structure of the conclusion, its functions. Its Moves, and the logical ordering of ideas in it.

6.1 The Structure of the Conclusion Section

Unlike the introduction section, the conclusion part of an essay has the shape of a pyramid. This implies that ideas or knowledge flow from the specific to the general perspective. In terms of space, scholars such as Rao et al (2007) suggest that the conclusion part of an essay occupies 5-10% of the total space of an essay.

Your conclusion ties your essay together. It should normally:

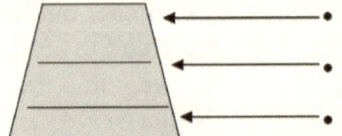

- Begin with a link to the preceding paragraph.
- Restate your thesis and summarise your principal points.
- End with a broad statement relating to the significance of your argument.

THE CONCLUSION SHAPE OF AN ESSAY

SOURCE: Essay writing from the English for Uni website

6.2 Functions of the Conclusion Section

As to how it functions, many scholars such as Afful (2005) and Rao et al, (2007) comment that the conclusion part of an essay usually points backward to the body of the essay. This is achieved through the summarization of the main discussion in the body of the essay. Apart from pointing backward to the body of the essay, the conclusion part of an essay signals the **closure** of the essay. The conclusion part of an essay also provides a strong convincing message, which leaves the reader a longing to read over the essay again. In a more detailed explanation of how the conclusion paragraph functions, Essay writing from the English for Uni website () narrates:

The conclusion should not just repeat the ideas from the introduction. The introduction includes the background to the essay, the important issues and a thesis statement. The introduction leads your reader into the essay. The conclusion reminds your reader of the main points made in your essay and leaves your reader with a final impression and ideas to think about later.

Besides the citation above, other researchers have shed abundant light on the functions of the conclusion section of an essay. For example, Whitaker (2009) states:

The conclusion may be the shortest paragraph, but it's also the most important because this is what the reader will remember. A conclusion usually does these things:

Connect to the last sentence of the previous paragraph

Use an advanced style. In conclusion, to summarize, at the end are rather boring and

16 typical although they will work. Try to be more sophisticated by repeating or connecting ideas in another way.

Summarize the findings of your paper

Remind the readers of the paper's main ideas and wrap up your argument.

o Restate the thesis in different words/phrases.

o Briefly summarize the main points of your paper. Again, say these in a different way, so readers are not bored by repetition of the same sentences and phrases.

o Use your own thoughts, not your sources'. The place for source support was in the body paragraphs, not the conclusion.

o Do NOT *write any new information, points, or support in the conclusion.*

Show the significance of your findings

Explain why your paper is important – What does it mean? What does it solve? What does it say about your topic? What does it show about the future of your topic? What should the readers take away from your paper?

End with a strong, memorable concluding statement(s)

Also known as the "Wow statement," the last sentence(s) of your paper should make your readers say, "Wow! I'm glad I read this paper." There are several ways to do this:

o *End with the significance of your paper, as described above.*

o *Relate your conclusion to the hook sentence(s) from your introduction. This can be a very effective way of wrapping up your paper.*

o *End with an idea for the reader to think about – a prediction or recommendation perhaps.*

Do NOT ask a question that leaves the reader uncertain. The purpose of academic writing is not to confuse the reader, but to enlighten the reader.

Do NOT be too general. Stay focused on your specific topic.

DO NOT be too shocking, unbelievable, sweet, or obvious.

From the quotations above, we realize that the conclusion section of our writings has many functions. It is therefore of prime importance to handle the conclusion section of any academic writing with care and logic. As already mentioned above, you should end your writing in a way that your reader may be aroused to read over the essay once more.

6.3 Analysis of the Conclusion Section

Like the introduction section, the conclusion part of an essay is made up of Moves and even Steps. Depending on the type of essay, the number of Moves in the conclusion part of an essay varies in number. There are essays with two Moves, essays with three Moves and so on. The table below shows the differences in the number of Moves in essays' conclusions from different scholars.

lynch (2014)	Afful (2005)	Hewing's (1993)	Rao et als (2007)
1 Summarize your argument	Summarizing through listing or/ and evaluating	summarizing	findings
2 Reflect on the Implications	Expanding summarized points through recommending action/highlighting significance of Issue/s in prompt	evaluating	Overall conclusion
		recommending	Relation to other problem

From the table above, we observe that many findings have been done on the conclusion section of essays. We can observe essays with two Moves and those with three Moves in the conclusion. As we highlighted above all these Moves are found in the single paragraph which occupies the last position of our essays. However, essays with two moves might have the following moves as Described by Lynch (2014: 33) thus:

Conclusion – has two requirements:

*i.summarise your argument. This is your opportunity to draw together the threads of your argument and tell the reader what conclusions they should take away from your treatment of the literature. Don't simply tell us that you looked at **x**, **y** and **z** topics. Never introduce new substantive material in a conclusion.*

ii. reflect on the implications of your case, returning explicitly to the aims of your paper and the reasons for your interest in the theme. At this stage you are allowed to 'take off the blinkers' and comment on related but wider themes – be they practical or theoretical. Where appropriate you may finish a paper by pointing to areas which, on the basis of your paper, warrant future research.

The citation above serves to illustrate how moves are arranged in the conclusion section according to Lynch. However, based on the table above, we can observe that all the first Moves of the conclusions bear the word summarize. This therefore suggests that the first Move in the conclusion section of our writing should begin with a summary of the entire work before any personal words. However, talking about the possible Steps in the conclusion section, Lynch (2014: 34) contends:

In their analysis of Conclusion sections of empirical papers, Weissberg and Buker (1990) suggest there may be up to six elements:

A. Restatement of purpose *(or hypothesis)*

B. Summary *of main points / findings; whether they support the hypothesis; whether they agree with other researchers' findings*

C. *Possible* **explanations** *for the findings; and/or* **speculations** *about them*

D. Limitations *of the study*

E. Implications *(generalizations from the findings)*

F. **Recommendations** *for future research and* **practical applications**

Since the conclusion section of essays varies depending on the thesis statement in the introduction and the logical ordering of ideas in the body of the essay, it is of paramount importance to know the various steps suggested above and to use them in the Moves that need them. From the reading of Lynch (2014:), we can analyse the two moves in the conclusion section thus:

Move 1: Summarise Your Argument

The most important thing to know here is that you must not introduce a new idea or material in this move. In fact, the first move of the conclusion should summarise only the main points or ideas that are found in your essay. Lynch (2014) gives us two steps that can be used in this Move. However, we know that our five paragraph essay might demand us to use on most parts step 2: summary of the main points. Below are the two steps common in Move 1 of the conclusion section.

Step 1 **Restatement of purpose** *(or hypothesis)*

Step 2 **Summary** *of main points / findings*

Now that we have highlighted Move1 and its two steps of the conclusion section, the discussion below focuses on the explanation of each step of Move 1 of the conclusion section and the phrases that are common in each of the them.

Step 1 **Restatement of Purpose**

In some advanced writings, you may begin your conclusion by restating your hypothesis of your study. The phrases that are common in this strategy according to Lynch (2014:) are:

-The Aim /purpose/objective of these studies was to....

-This study was intended/designed to ....

-Among the aims of this study was the (investigation) of ...

-Our research investigated/examined/explored whether...

Step 2 **Summary of Main Points / Findings;**

In this step, you are expected to make a summary of what you have discussed in your essay. In fact, many five paragraph essays begin their conclusions with the summary of the essay. Common phrases in this strategy according to Lynch (2014:) include:

- The results showed/were that...

-We found that...(x) increased/decreased significantly when...

-We found that the majority of British parents are in favour of ...

-The findings (do not) support the hypotheses that ...

-These findings are (in) consistent with previous research

-The findings run contrary to the conventional view that

Move 2: Reflect on the Implication of Your Case

Considering the fact that you have summarised the main points of your essay in Move1, this move demands you to bring in your personal opinion in relation to your main points. Your opinion may be to agree or disagree or to bring in a neutral point of view. This should be done in a way that your reader feels very happy and might want to read over your essay again. This last move according to Lynch (2014) might have four strategies:

Step1: *Possible* **explanations** *for the findings; and/or* **speculations** *about them*

Step2: Limitations *of the study*

Step 3: Implications *(generalizations from the findings)*

Step 4: Recommendations *for future research and* **practical applications**

Like Move1 above, the rest of the discussion below focuses on the explanation of each of the four steps in Move 2 of the conclusion section and some common phrases of each Step

Step1: Possible Explanations for the Findings; and/or Speculations about them

This step deals with the explanations you give following the summary of the essay you have made in step 2 of Move 1 of the conclusion section. In this step, you should use your personal opinion to explain convincingly how you feel or think the situation should be or should look like. Possible phrases are:

-It may be that the findings were affected/influenced by...

(x) may be due to ...

It could be that...

If these results are confirmed by other studies, we may have to...

Step2: Limitations *of the study*

In this Step, you have to explain some of the weak points of your findings, which you think can help any future work on your domain to add or to subtract anything. Some of these limitation can be low population in the findings, limited time, hash topography and so on. Some phrases in this step include:

-We need to be cautious about these findings, because...

.... there was no control group

..... the study was based on a limited number of ...

.... The survey was conducted only among inexperienced lawyers

-It has to be emphasized/ acknowledged that the study was exploratory

Step 3: Implications

If you choose this Step in Move 2, then you have to state why you think that people should believe in the cause of something, why you agree or disagree or some evidence to support your summary or your findings. Some common phrases in this step include:

-The present study offers clear evidence for

-The study supports the view or claim that...

-There is therefore some evidence that...

-This leads us to believe that...

-This suggest that (x) may be an important factor in (y)

-Our research investigated, examined, explored whether..

Step 4: **Recommendations** *for Future Research and* **Practical Applications**

In many advanced writings, this step is very important because it is based on the results of the findings. This suggests that based on the findings, we have observed x so other works should focus on y so as to give the domain under study a concrete and complete knowledge. Phrases common in this step are:

-Likely areas for further research, work are...

-Future research should focus on..

One avenue for further study would be to..

-Future investigation will no doubt reveal whether...

Future research is needed into...

-It is important or relevant to investigate whether..

We conclude the analyses of the conclusion section of the five paragraph essay with a good example of conclusion from Lynch (2014: 32). Move 1 is normal size, and Move 2 is underlined.

It can be seen, then, that road building mostly directly benefits the rich in the Third World, while it is the poor that pay the costs. <u>With this in mind, it seems that "the construction of motorways is a modern parable, using public funds to make life easier for the rich and harder for the poor"</u> (Ether 1995: 171). <u>These policies carry a serious risk: the differences in effect on the better-off and worse-off in a developing economy could become a cause of dispute and conflict. It is vital that the interests of the majority are not ignored.</u>

Irrespective of the topic, we observe that our writer above concludes the essay by making a summary of the main point which is not underlined in the conclusion above. The scholar then expands on the main point and ends up stating his own point of view (<u>It is vital that the interests of the majority are not ignored.</u>)

5.4 Types of Conclusions

In the course of our research, we came across a work entitled "Types of Conclusions". The unknown author or authors suggested that there are four kinds of conclusions:

-The Embedded Conclusion

-The Retrospective Conclusion

-The Reflective Conclusion

-The Projective Conclusion

In a way to shed more light on the various conclusions above, the unknown author or authors narrate:

The Embedded Conclusion

In some cases, especially with a narrative essay that tells a personal story in

chronological order, the conclusion can be the last paragraph of the body. For instance,

if you are telling the story of how you learned the English language, and the last

paragraph brings us to your current state of increased confidence mixed with lingering

cautiousness, then that last paragraph gives us a solid place to part company.

Example:

I am now studying English in an ESL class at Cabrillo College. I know this is not the last leg of my journey, for I have a lot more to learn about American idioms and phrasing. However, even as I struggle, I feel more confidence than ever before. I am so far getting "A" grades on all my written assignments. Still, I will always feel cautious, like I am walking on egg shells, as I try to use a language that is so different from the one I was born into in a land faraway.

The Retrospective Conclusion

For a narrative essay, or for any essay that uses chronology or traces an historic movement, you may want to consider the retrospective conclusion. This concluding paragraph uses "hindsight" to consider what came before with new insight gained from experience.

Example:

Ten years ago, I would never have believed that I would be living in the United States and using English to buy groceries and make new friends. I would have fainted at the thought of writing professional documents in the English language. Nonetheless, here I am, writing an English essay in my first college English class and expecting to receive an "A." Time will tell how far my English studies will take me.

The Reflective Conclusion

The reflective conclusion is similar to the retrospective kind, but it allows a broader train of thought as one considers the various themes, lessons, or insights that have emerged from the essay writing experience.

Example:

In choosing to approach life's challenges from a passive position, many teens see their bad choices as a result of their circumstances. Whether it's an unwanted pregnancy, a drug addiction, or an abusive relationship, girls especially can make excuses so that they don't have to change. I wish I could tell them that they don't have to be imprisoned by their past choices—it's never too late to take charge of your destiny.

The Projective Conclusion

This type of conclusion works especially well for research papers but can be used for most expository essays and some narrative ones as well. It involves projecting a future outcome of the circumstances you describe. It may project the negative results of a social issue if it remains unresolved or a threat to humanity. In other contexts, this conclusion can state a need for further research in an area to enhance our understanding, or it could predict an interesting, unexpected outcome based on current trends.

Example:

A crisis continues to brew in our school systems where it is no longer the case of just bullies turning to serial violence. As we saw in the Columbine shootings, even victims of chronic bullying, in an attempt to fight back and regain some power or dignity, are taking up arms and gunning down their classmates. Case after case shows us that criminal violence amongst school-aged children in America is not limited to just males or pinned to any one ethnicity or socioeconomic class. It is a crisis of the generation gap increased by rapidly changing technology and a lack of real communication. Unless we start talking to each other, more of our youth will die, and children will be safer on the streets than they are in the schoolyard.

A summary of the various types of conclusion above might go thus: An embedded conclusion reveals your present state, the retrospective conclusion talks about a brief history, your present state, and even your future state. A reflective conclusion is wider and demands the work of the brain based on the issue under discussion. A projective conclusion demands a critical mind based on analyses, evaluations and so on. Conclusions of our Five Paragraph Essay might fall under the embedded, retrospective and reflective conclusions. However, talking of advanced types of conclusions, Wang defines a conclusion thus:

A conclusion is the final piece of writing in a research paper, essay, or article that summarizes the entire work. A good conclusion will wrap up your final thoughts and main points, combining all pertinent information with an emotional appeal for an ending statement that resonates with your reader.

Besides the definition above, Wang highlights three important types of conclusions- Summarization, Editorialization and Externalization. Since conclusions are very important to any writing, the discussion below explains them.

A Summarization Conclusion

Many of the conclusion types highlighted above fall under the summarization types. Talking about summarization conclusions, Wang notes:

Summarization: often used when writing about technical subjects with a more clinical tone, such as surveys, definitions and reports. Because it paraphrases the major ideas of the essay, it is most often used in longer pieces where readers will need a reminder of the essay's main points. As such, it should avoid reflexive

The citation above suggests that summarization conclusions give a summary of what has been discussed in many essays that write about knowledge. These types of essays are often long and you should summarize the main content before you put up your on points of view.

Editorialization

As the name suggests, editorial conclusions are more advanced than the summarized conclusions. Talking about these types, Wang further explains:

Editorialization: primarily used in essays where there is a controversial topic, a personal connection or an appeal to persuade the reader. This type of conclusion will use an anecdote and a conversational tone to draw attention to concerns, interpretations, personal beliefs, politics or feelings.

According to the citation above, editorial conclusion are used when the topic of an essay is controversial and demands your personal judgment to opinions or facts. Some writers may use warrants or evidence to make this type of conclusion very strong or stronger. Students should read many argumentative essays written by experts to identify how an editorial conclusion is written in their various fields. The last type of conclusion is Externalization.

Externalization

Unlike the two types of conclusions highlighted above, the Externalization is different in that it often projects into the future. Wang explains Externalization conclusions thus:

Externalization: frequently used in essays that approach a particular issue that is a part of a much more complex subject, an externalized conclusion provides a transition into a related but separate topic that leads readers to further develop the discussion. It makes your readers think about the future

Most research genres such as dissertations, theses, conference papers often have externalization conclusions. They always highlights further findings in many field.

6.5 Errors to be avoided in conclusions

All throughout this chapter, we have been emphasizing that the conclusion part of an essay is very important to the essay in that it is at the level of the conclusion that the desire to read over the essay once more is aroused. This therefore suggests that the conclusion part of an essay should be handled with care and logic. In a move to reduce the rate of uninciteful conclusions, many scholars have given their directives. The errors that are commonly observed in students' essays have been highlighted by Jean Wyrick below:

Try to omit the following common errors in your concluding paragraphs:

Avoid a mechanical ending. *One of the most frequent weaknesses in student essays is the conclusion that merely restates the thesis, word for word. A brief essay of five hundred to seven hundred and fifty words rarely requires a flat, point-by-point conclusion—in fact, such an ending often insults the readers 'intelligence by implying that their attention spans are extremely short. Only after reading long essays do most readers need a precise recap of all the writer's main ideas. Instead of recopying your thesis and essay map, try finding an original, emphatic way to conclude your essay—or as a well-known newspaper columnist described it, a good ending should snap with grace and authority, like the close of an expensive sports car door.*

Don't introduce new points. *Treat the major points of your essay in separate body paragraphs rather than in your exit.*

Don't tack on a conclusion. *There should be a smooth flow from your last body paragraph into your concluding statements.*

Don't change your stance. *Sometimes writers who have been critical of something throughout their essays will soften their stance or offer apologies in their last paragraph. For instance, someone complaining about the poor quality of a particular college course might abruptly conclude with statements that declare the class wasn't so bad after all, maybe she should have worked harder, or maybe she really did learn something after all. Such reneging may seem polite, but in actuality it undercuts the thesis and confuses the reader who has taken the writer's criticisms seriously. Instead of contradicting themselves, writers should stand their ground, forget about puffy clichés or "niceties," and find an emphatic way to conclude that is consistent with their thesis.*

Avoid trite expressions. *Don't begin your conclusions by declaring, "in conclusion," "in summary," or "as you can see, this essay proves my thesis that . . . ." End your essay so that the reader clearly senses completion; don't merely announce that you're finished.*

6.6 The Order of Ideas in the Conclusion Section (specific to general order).

All through this chapter, it has been highlighted that the shape of the conclusion section of an essay is like a pyramid. This shape means that ideas in the conclusion section of an essay should flow from the specific to the general perspective. It is for this reason that you must start your conclusion with a summary of your discussion from the thesis statement to the ideas in the body of the essay before you tell the reader your own opinion or suggestion which ties with the topic under discussion. The ideas in the last move of your conclusion should be very convincing because these are the words or ideas that will stay longer in your readers' minds, and there are these ideas that will push your reader to re-read your essay

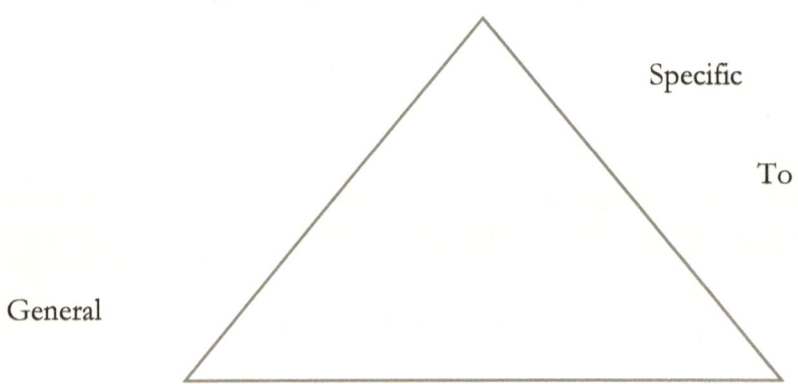

Conclusion

1	**Summarise main ideas**– highlight key topics discussed in main body.
2	**Thesis**– remind the reader of your stance (yes or no).
3	**Recommendation / suggestion / prediction** – finish off your conclusion with general summary on what needs to be done.
Important - no new ideas	

Inter-changeable

Source: Academic English

Below is a summary of the conclusion of an essay, it is drawn from Clive James

Conclusion–Last Paragraph of the Essay

• The following outline may help you conclude your paper:

• Rephrased Thesis: • Restate your topic and why it is important

• Summary: • Summarize your essay's three supporting points

• Clincher: • Tie back to your introduction; give a prediction, suggestion, quotation, or call to action

The Restated Thesis

• How to restate your thesis:

• The restated thesis is the first sentence of the conclusion.

• It re-wordsj(not repeats) the thesis idea.

The Summary

• How to summarize the ideas in the concluding paragraph:

- Briefly summarize the ideas discussed in the body paragraphs (usually 3)
- The summary may be included as part of the restated thesis, or it may be in a separate sentence
- The summary should not sound word-for-word like the plan of development that appears in the introduction
- The summary of the main points should be listed in the same order as they appear in the essay

The Clincher

- How to write the clincher:
- The clincher is the last sentence of the conclusion.
- The clincher is a statement that makes one final observation on the topic and leaves a lasting impression on the reader.
- The clincher may also tie back to the "hook" of the introduction—this is called framing the essay.

6.7 CONCLUSION

In this chapter, we have learned that unlike the introduction section of an essay whose ideas run from the general to the specific perspective, ideas in the conclusion part of an essay whether a Five Paragraph Essay or the Long Essay or argumentative essay flow from the specific to the general perspective. Unlike the Five Paragraph Essay which has two moves, the Long Essay or any argumentative essay might have two or three Moves. The first Move is that of summarizing ideas in the essay, the second Move focuses on evaluation based on the thesis statement and the last Move is that of recommendation or expansion to other general ideas that relate to the essay topic. The recommendation or the extension of the scope to other ideas should be done in a way that any keen reader should be aroused to read over the essay again. Like the introduction paragraph, the concluding paragraph of the Long Essay or argumentative essay also has steps or strategies that should be used in order to identify or write each Move. While the introduction section attracts a reader to read our essay, the conclusion part of our essay urges a reader to read the essay again. The introduction and the conclusion parts are very important because they have fixed logical patterns irrespective of the essay type. For example, the introduction is from general to specific and the conclusion is from specific to general. We urge you to read many conclusion sections of argumentative writings for a better understanding.

References

Abrami, P. C., Bernard, R. M., Borokhovski, E., Waddington, D. I.,Wade, C. A. & Persson, T, (2015). Strategies for Teaching Students to Think Critically: In *A Meta-Analysis Review of Educational Research*, Vol. 85, No. 2, pp. 275 –314. Concordia University, Canada

Academic Centers for Enrichment (2011). Argumentative vs. Persuasive Writing: Subtle, but Significant, Differences. Middlesex Community College

Academic English UK () Conclusion. unpublished

Afful, J.B. (2005). A Rhetorical Analysis of Examination Essays in Three Disciplines : The case of Ghanaian Undergraduate Students.Unpublised PhD thesis, National University of Singapore.

Alamo Colleges Districts Writing Center San Antonio College (2012). Argumentative and Persuasive Essay .Taken from Teaching the Argumentative Standard, 2012 Smekens Education Solutions, INC. unpublished

Alexander College Writing and Learning Center()Block Pattern Argumentative Essay Outline University Transfer Courses. unpublished

Azariadis, M. (2018). Principles of Academic Writing 1: Paragraphs and Sentences://Uniwa.edu.au/ Userhome/ staff/ 00044525/ my picture / UWA/ P 1014475jpg.The University of Western Australia.

Ball, C. E. & Loewe, D. M. (ed.). (2017). *Bad Ideas about Writing*. United States of America. West Virginia University Libraries Digital Publishing Institute Morgantown, wv..

Bazerman, C., Bonini. A., Figueiredo, D.(eds.). (2009). *Genre in a Changing World*. Indiana.

The WAC clearinghouse wac. Colostate.edu. Fort Collins, Colorado. Parlor Press www. Parlor press. Com West Lafayette,

Bineth A. (2020) Towards a Sociology of Curiosity Theoretical and Empirical Consideration of the Epistemic Drive Notion. Master of Arts dissertation. Budapest, Hungary.

Blinn College – Bryan Writing Center Spring (2023). Thesis Statement Types & Models. Unpublished.

Blau, S., Elbow, P., & Killgallow, D. (eds.). (1998). *The Writer's Craft*. Evanston, Illinois. Boston. Dallas: McDougal Little A HOGHTON MIFFLIN COMPANY.

Booth, W. C., Colomb, G. G., & Williams, J. M. (eds.). (2003). *The Craft of Research*. Chicago & London: The University of Chicago Press

Boston Architectural College()LEARNING RESOURCE CENTER 6th Floor Room 605, 320 Newbury Street, 617-585-0174, writingcenter@the-bac.edu

Boyer, E. (1995) The Educated Person - 1995 ASCD Yearbook p.16- at www.ascd.org/

Brown, G. & Yule, G. (1983*). Discourse Analysis*. Aron Cambridge University Press.

Clive James () Thesis-Support Essay Structure & Tips for Introduction and Conclusion Unpublished

Courtesy the Odegaard writing & Research Center (). Developing Your Thesis. http:// www.dept.Washington.edu/ owre. Adapted from www. Dartmouth. Edu/writing / materials/student/ac-paper/develop. Shtm/.

Donald Latumahina, Four Reasons Why Curiosity Is Important and How to Develop It http://www.lifehack.org/articles/productivity/4---reasons---why---curiosity---is---important---and---how---to---develop---it.html

Dubey, R & Griffiths, (). Reconciling Novelty and Complexity through a Rational Analysis of Curiosity. In Psychological Review

English for Uni website. (). Essay Writing from the English for Uni website.

Fahy,(2008). Writing for publication: Argument and evidence. In *ELSEVIER* at www Elsevier.com/locate/wombi

Farah, M.A. & Karls, A. B. (ED.) (1997). *World History*. McGraw-Hill. New York. New York Columbus, Ohio Mission Hill, California Peoria, Illinois: National Geography Society; Glencoe.

Foundation Programme. (2009).*English and Business Communication*. The Institute of Company secretaries of India.

Franklin, A.P., Lavennier, J.& Master, I.(1986). *From Paragraph to Essay: A guide to effective writing*. New York : St Martin"s Press, Inc.

Gündüz, M. (2016). Classifying Values by Categories. In *Journal of Education and Training Studies* vol. 4, n°10, October 2016, 2324-8068.

Ho, T. (2008). The Academic Essays. Unpublished work, accessed at:htt/www sinte.es.

Holy Bible, (2011). New International Version. NIV. Nairobi, Kenya. Www biblicaafrica.com

Hugo Mercier, Dan Sperber. Why do humans reason? Arguments for an argumentative theory.. Behavioral and Brain Sciences, 2011, 34 (2), pp.57-74; discussion 74-111. 10.1017/S0140525X10000968. hal-00904097

Indriani, K. S.(2019) The Effect of outline Planning in Argumentative Essay Writing of Fourth Semester Students of English Department, Faculty of Arts, Udayana University.in *Lingual* (Vol. 8, No.2, 2019)

Institute for the Professional Development of Adult Education ipdae() Strategies for Teaching Argumentative Writing

International Labour Organisation (2012). International Standard Classification of Occupations ISCO-08: Structure, group definitions and Correspondence tables. Vol.1. www. Ifrro.org

International Reading Association NCIE Macopolo. () read.write.think. unpublished

Kum, J. N. (2016). A Discourse Analysis of Students' Essays in Cameroon English. PhD Thesis, University of Yaounde 1. unpublished

Kum, J. N. (2023). *A Rhetorical Analysis of the Five Paragraph Essay. A Discourse on Writing Skills*. Ukiyoto publisher. www.ukiyoto.com

'Writing Essays', Learning Development, Plymouth University (2011). Writing essays. at http://www.plymouth.ac.uk/learn

Loewenstein, G. (1994).The Psychology of Curiosity: A Review and Reinterpretation, in *Psychology Bulletin* vol.116, no 1.75-98

Lynch, T. (2014). Academic Essay Writing for Postgraduates; Independent Study Version; English Language Teaching Centre.2014.

Lynch, T. & Anderson, k. (2013). Grammar for Academic Writing. English Language Teaching Centre University of Edinburgh.

Macgibbon, L. (). Academic Essay Writing. Charles Darwin University Australian Centre for Indigenous Knowledges and Education.

Maggio, R. (2001). *How To Say It: Choice words, Phrases, Sentences, and Paragraphs for Every Situation.* New York. Prentice Hall Press.

Mary Bywater () The Impact of Writing: Ancient and Modern Views on the Role of Early Writing Systems Within Society and as a Part of 'Civilisation' Master of Philosophy (Mphil) Dissertation

McKay, J. P., Hill. D., & Buckler, J. (EDS.). (1983). *A History of Western Society.* University of Illinois, Urbana Houghton Mifflin Company Boston Dallas Geneva, Illinois Lawrenceville, New Jersey Palo Alto.

Messenger, P., Sallee, M., Sullivan, K. & Walker, C. (2013-2014). Guide to High School Writing and Analysis, BHS English Department 2013-2014.

Moorhouse, P.() Curiosity – A strong desire to inquire and understand

National Geography Learning. (). Narrative Essay. NGL. Cengage. Com /ELT.

Naija Book Club (2023) Abraham Lincoln one time speech. Social Medial

Ncheafor, E. A. (2006). *Progress in English Grammar.* Limbe- Cameroon: Vision Educational Publications.

Notes (). 3 Types of Argument: Classical, Rogerian, Toulmin. Unpublished

Oshima, A. And Hogue, A. (2006). 4th ed. Writing academic English. NY: Pearson Education.

Ozagac, O. (2004) Argumentative Essay. Copyright @ 2006 Bogazici University SFL

Prananda, Y. A.() Students' Ability in Writing Paragraphs Using Structure of The Paragraph in Argumentative Essay By The Sixth

Semester of English Study Program of Muhammadiyah University of Bengkulu: thepranandas@gmail.com

Pellegrino, J.W. & Hilton, M.L. (eds.) (2012). Education for Life and Work: Developing Transferable Knowledge and Skills in the 21st century. Washington Dc. The National Academies Press.

Rao, V., Chanock, K., & Krishnan L. (2007). *A Visual Guide to Essay Writing*. Association for Academic Language & Learning (AALL) Sydney.

RedRocks Community College Writing Center (2019) Writing a Strong Thesis Statement.at Writing Center @ CCD.

ResearchLEAP.() Useful Tips for Academic Writing.www.researchleap. com.

René, D. H, (2007). Argumentative writing strategies and perceptions of writing in academia by EFL college students *Literatura y Lingüística*, núm. 18, 2007, pp. 253-282 Universidad Católica Silva Henríquez Santiago, Chile

Available in: http://www.redalyc.org/articulo.oa?id=35201815

Rsa Social Brain Centre June (2012).The Power of Curiosity: How linking Inquisitiveness to Innovation could help to Address our Energy Challenges. www.thersa.org

Sarukkai, S. (2009) Science and the ethics of curiosity in *Current Science*, vol. 97, no. 6, 25

Shuster, k. (2009). Civil Discourse in the Classroom, www.middleschooldebate.com.

Simon & Schuster Handbook for Writers. Ed. Lynn Quitman Troyka, 6th ed. Upper Saddle River, NJ: Prentice Hall, 2002.

The Writer's Workplace. Ed. Sandra Scarry and John Scarry. 6th ed. Boston: Thomson Wadsworth, 2008.

Stab, C. & Gurevych I (2015) Parsing Argumentation Structures in Persuasive Essays.* Technische Universit¨at Darmstadt

Strong, W., Lester, M. & Inc, L.(1993). *Writer's Choice Composition and Grammar*. New York, New York, Columbus, Ohio woodland Hills, California, Peoria, Illinois: Glencoe, McGraw-Hill,

Surdzial, J. (2019) Different Types of Thesis Statements. UCR, Academic Resource Center

Tahnda Hawkins/South HS () Argumentative Essay Outline (Claim). Unpublished

Tasya, M. A. (2022) Students' Difficulties in Writing an Argumentative Essay. Degree of s.pd. (Strata-1). Syarif hidayatullah State Islamic University Jakarta

The College Board AP. (2014). English Language and Composition; Course Description Effective Fall2014. New York, NY.

The Positivity Project (2016). *Curiosity, Open-mindedness, Kindness, Fairness Perspective, Creativity, Teamwork/Citizenship, Bravery, Gratitude, Humility/modesty, Appreciation of beauty & excellence, Self-control, Perseverance..* www.posproject.org

The Ontario Curriculum Grades 11 and 12 (2018). Cooperative Education at www.ontario.ca/edu.

To,A., Ali,S., Kaufman,G. & HammerJ()Integrating Curiosity and Uncertainty in Game Design Carnegie Mellon University 5000 Forbes Ave. Pittsburgh, PA, USA aato@cs.cmu.edu, safinaha@cs.cmu.edu, gfk@cs.cmu.edu, hammerj@cs.cmu.edu

Torbjörn Gustafsson Chorell (2021) Modes of historical attention: wonder, curiosity, fascination, Rethinking History, 25:2, 242-257, DOI: 10.1080/13642529.2020.1847896

TutoringandLearningCentre,GeorgeBrownCollege(2014)ArgumentativeEssays www.georgebrown.ca/tlc

Whitcomb, D. (2010). Curiosity was framed in *Philosophy and Phenomenological Research* 81(2): 664-687

Union University Writing Center(). Writing a Strong Thesis Statement. unpublished

Vu Le Ho (2011) non-native argumentative writing by vietnamese learners of english: a contrastive study . Doctor of Philosophy in Linguistics. Washington, DC

Wang, E () Cuyamaca Writing Center. Unpublished

Whitaker, A. (2009) Academic Writing Guide 2010. A Step-by – Step Guide to writing Academic Papers. City University of Seattle.

Writing Center English 800 Center () Essay and Paragraph Development Tutorial: Tutorial #26: Thesis Statements and Topic Sentences. Unpublished

Wyrick, J. (). Step-to-Writing- Well.

Xin Tang et al () The Differences and Similarities between Curiosity and Interest: Meta-analysis and Network Analyses. Faculty of Educational Sciences, PL 9 (Siltavuorenpenger 5A), 00014, University of Helsinki, Finland; xin.tang@helsinki.fi

Yang, H.S. (2009). Rhetorical patterns in L2 writers argumentative essays. 2009 Fall

TESOL conference. San Francisco state university hsnature@gmail.com.

Appendix 1

Body Patterns

Example 1

Classic Model for an Argument

No one structure fits all written arguments. However, most college courses require arguments that consist of the following elements. Below is a basic outline for an argumentative or persuasive essay. This is only one possible outline or organization. Always refer to your handbook for specifics.

1 Introductory Paragraph

o Your introductory paragraph sets the stage or the context for the position you are arguing for.

o This introduction should end with a thesis statement that provides your claim (what you are arguing for) and the reasons for your position on an issue.

A. Your thesis:

o states what your position on an issue is

o usually appears at the end of the introduction in a short essay

o should be clearly stated and often contains emphatic language (should, ought, must)

B. Sample Argumentative Thesis

o The production, sale, and possession of assault weapons for private citizens should be banned in the U.S.

II Body of your Argument

A. Background Information

o This section of your paper gives the reader the basic information he or she needs to understand your position. This could be part of the introduction, but may work as its own section.

B. Reasons or Evidence to Support your Claim

o All evidence you present in this section should support your position. This is the heart of your essay. Generally, you begin with a general statement that you back up with specific details or examples. Depending on how long your argument is, you will need to devote one to two well-developed paragraphs to each reason/claim or type of evidence.

o Types of evidence include:

- first-hand examples and experiential knowledge on your topic (specific examples help your readers connect to your topic in a way they cannot with abstract ideas)

- Opinions from recognized authorities

- The tipsheet on the three logical appeals covers the types of evidence you can use in argumentation.

1.Claim: Keeping assault weapons out of private citizens' hands can lower the increasing occurrences of barbaric public slayings

- Evidence:

o Jul 93 Law firm murders

o Columbine School Shootings

o University of Virginia incident

o How did these individuals gain access to weapons?

2.Claim: The ban on assault weapons is backed heavily by public opinion, major organizations, and even law enforcement.

- Evidence:

o 12% favor ban (Much 92 Timetable News)

o Organizational endorsements

o Nat'l Sherriff's Assoc./Intn'l Assoc. of Police Chiefs

3.Claim: The monetary and human costs incurred by crimes committed with assault weapons are too great to ignore.

- Evidence:

o 10,561 murders in 1990 by handguns

o Study of 131 injured patients' medical expenses paid by public funds

III. Addressing the Opposite Side

o Any well-written argument must anticipate and address positions in opposition to the one being argued.

o Pointing out what your opposition is likely to say in response to your argument shows that you have thought critically about your topic. Addressing the opposite side actually makes your argument stronger!

o Generally, this takes the form of a paragraph that can be placed either after the introduction or before the conclusion.

A. 1st Opposing View: Strict gun control laws won't affect crime rate

• Refutation: Low murder rate in Britain, Australia (etc., where strict controls are in force.

B. 2nd Opposing View: Outlaws would still own guns

• Refutation: Any effort to move trend in opposite direction would benefit future generations

IV. Conclusion

o The conclusion should bring the essay to a logical end. It should explain what the importance of your issue is in a larger context. Your conclusion should also reiterate why your topic is worth caring about.

o Some arguments propose solutions or make prediction on the future of the topic.

o Show your reader what would happen if your argument is or is not believed or acted upon as you believe it should be.

Adapted from: Simon & Schuster Handbook for Writers. Ed. Lynn Quitman Troyka, 6th ed. Upper Saddle River, NJ: Prentice Hall, 2002. The Writer's Workplace. Ed. Sandra Scarry and John S

Example 2

Here are several different outlines you can use to help organize your argumentative essay. These models can and should be adapted to suit the writer's needs and number of claims.

Outline I - standard format for an argumentative essay

Introduction/Thesis-Claim

Body Paragraph 1: Present your 1st point and supporting evidence.

Body Paragraph 2: Present your 2nd point and it's supporting evidence.

Body Paragraph 3: Refute your opposition's first point.

Body Paragraph 4: Refute your opposition's second point.

Outline II - format that presents the opposition first as a means to demonstrate the significance of your solution (debate)

Introduction/Thesis-Claim

Body Paragraph 1: Refute your opposition's first point.

Body Paragraph 2: Refute your opposition's second point.

Body Paragraph 3: Present your first point and supporting evidence.

Body Paragraph 4: Present your second point and supporting evidence.

Conclusion/Restate Thesis

Outline III - introduce the problem and present your solution format

Introduction/Thesis-Claim

Body Paragraph 1: Present your first point and it's supporting evidence, which also refutes one of your opposition's claims.

Body Paragraph 2: Present your second point and it's supporting evidence, which also refutes a second opposition claim.

Body Paragraph 3: Present your third point and it's supporting evidence, which also refutes a third opposition claim.

Conclusion/Restate Thesis

Further Assistance: For more detailed help or if you have questions, visit the Writing Center located in the Lewis University Library, or call 815-836-5427

Consulted: Owl.english.purdue.edu, Kibin.com, Mesacc.edu, Roanestate.edu

Example 3

Argumentative Essay Outline (Claim)
adapted from Talinda Hawkins South HS

Directions: Use this outline as a "road map" to write your essay. If you need more examples or sentence starters, use page 2 to help you!

1) Introduction/Claim (One paragraph)
- Start with a hook or attention getting sentence.
- Briefly summarize the texts
- State your claim. Make sure you are restating the prompt.

2) Body Paragraph: Evidence/Support/Warrant
- Include a topic sentence that restates your claim and your reason.
  - *Example: Video games are harmful because_____.*
- Include text evidence that supports your reason.
  - *Example: The author shows that video games are harmful because in paragraph 2 it states_____*
- Include an explanation (warrant) that shows how your text evidence proved your claim.
  - *Example: The author uses this evidence to show how/that_____.*

3) Body Paragraph: Evidence/Support/Warrant
- Include a topic sentence that restates your claim and your reason.
  - *Example: Video games are harmful because_____.*
- Include text evidence that supports your reason.
  - *Example: The author shows that video games are harmful because in paragraph 2 it states_____*
- Include an explanation (warrant) that shows how your text evidence proved your claim.
  - *Example: The author uses this evidence to show how/that_____*

4) Counterclaim Paragraph:
- Explain what others who don't agree with your claim might say.
  - *Example: Some people might disagree. They may believe____ because____.*

5) Conclusion (One paragraph)
- Restate your claim and summarize your reasoning.
  - *Example: In conclusion, the text shows that videogames are harmful by pointing out that_____*

Example 4

Sample Outline for an Argumentative Writing

Beginning (Introduction)	Hook – Explanation of Issue – Thesis/Position –
Argument 1	State argument – Explanation – Evidence/Analysis –
Argument 2	State argument – Explanation – Evidence/Analysis –
Argument 3 (optional)	State argument – Explanation – Evidence/Analysis –
Argument 4 (optional)	State argument – Explanation – Evidence/Analysis –
Refutation	State opposing argument – Explanation – Refutation –
Ending (Conclusion)	Restate thesis in a new way – Bring things to a solid close/Give your reader something to think about –

Source: Institute for the Professional Development of Adult Education

Example 5

Dr Julius Nang Kum   245

Argumentative Essays

There are many ways you could organize your argumentative essay. The one thing you need to keep in mind is that you **must show both sides of the argument.**

Here are a few basic possibilities for organizing an argumentative essay:

1.

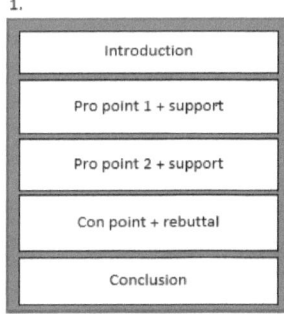

2.

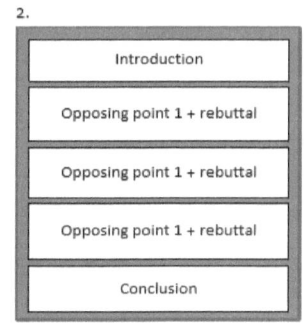

3.

Introduction
Pro point 1 + support
Con point + rebuttal
Pro point 2 + support
Con point + rebuttal
Pro point 3 + support
Con point + rebuttal
Conclusion

4.

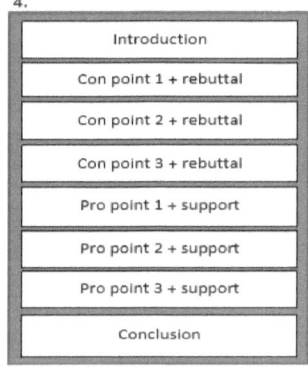

©Tutoring and Learning Centre, George Brown College   2014   www.georgebrown.ca/tlc

Example 6

There are some outline models that can be used in organizing argumentative writing. Those models can be seen in the diagram bellow.

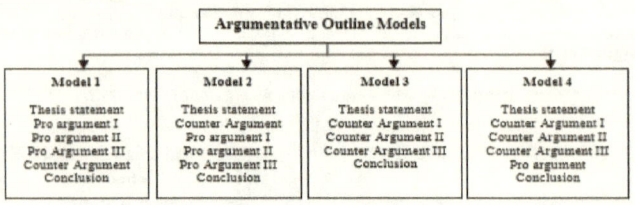

Diagram 1. Argumentative Outline Models

SOURCE ;Indriani, K. S.(2019)

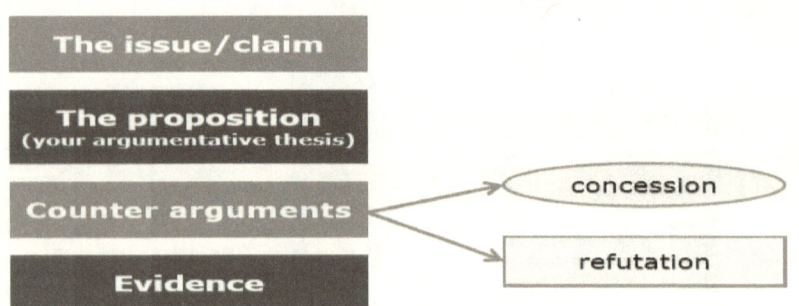

SOURCE : Oshima, A. And Hogue, A. (2006). 4th ed. Writing academic English. NY: Pearson Education, Inc. p. 143.

Example 7

Organization: All argumentative topics have PROs and CONs. Before starting writing, it is imperative to make a list of these ideas and choose the most suitable ones among them for supporting and refuting.

There are three possible organization patterns:
<u>Pattern 1</u>:
    Thesis statement:

    PRO idea 1
    PRO idea 2
    CON(s) + Refutation(s)

    Conclusion

<u>Pattern 2</u>:
    Thesis statement:

    CON(s) + Refutation(s)
    PRO idea 1
    PRO idea 2

    Conclusion

<u>Pattern 3</u>:
    Thesis statement:

    CON idea 1   ----->   Refutation
    CON idea 2   ----->   Refutation
    CON idea 3   ----->   Refutation

    Conclusion

Source : Oya Ozagac, September 2004

Appendix 2
STRUCTURE OF QUESTION

Step 1: Interpret the question and identify the key topics

The first crucial step is to interpret the question; essays questions use specific terms and which reveal how the question might be answered. Question analysis is a crucial part of the essay writing process; the most common reason why students fail assignments is because they do not read or analyse the question correctly.

One method of question analysis is the 'T.A.P. model'. First identify the **Topic** - what the main theme is; then the **Action**(s), i.e. what you have got to do; and finally the **Parameters** – the scope or confines of the task. It is worth spending a bit of time on this, making sure you are clear on what is being asked of you. If are still not clear, contact your tutor **BEFORE** you start work on the assignment.

Figure 1. Question analysis using the T.A.P. model

The 'TAP' model 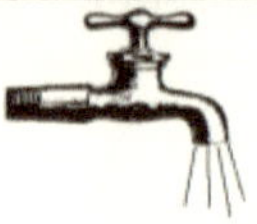
- Topics - the central or key theme
- Actions - what you need to do
- Parameters - what limitations

Sample essay title:
Discuss the impacts of a recent Government initiative on a specific area of care, with reference to a relevant case study.

Topics	Action	Parameters
'Government initiative' - UK context	'Discuss' - analyse, evaluate and put forward your findings or argument	'impacts' - how did it change? 'recent' - last 5-10 yrs! 'specific area of care' - stay focused on this
'specific area of care' - the initiative must be discussed in relation to the effects / impacts on the area of care chosen	'with reference' - your argument must be supported by (in this case the chosen case study)	'relevant case study' - include a case study to support your discussion

'Writing Essays', Learning Development, Plymouth University (2011)

Appendix 3

Arrangement of Ideas in the Three Approaches to an Argument

The examples below illustrate three paragraphs from the classical argument, the Rogerian argument, and the Toulmin structure as demonstrated in "3 Types of Argument: Classical, Rogerian, Toulmin"

Classical Example

Zeke! (yelling) **(Introduction—capture attention)**

2. Stop antagonizing your brother. He had a tough day at school. **(Background –context)**

3. The next time you gloat about beating Luigi's Mansion you are going to be sitting in time out. Proposition **(claim/thesis)**

4. This is the third time that you have brought this up in the past 15 minutes. He is crying on the floor. He knows that you have beat the game; you are just being mean. **Proof**

5. I know that he is a little pipsqueak sometimes, and he gets on your nerves by talking about "Wee-gee's Mansion", but you have to set a good example for him. **Refutation (concession and counterargument)**

6. If you say one more thing about beating Luigi's mansion you will be in time out. I don't care if we are in a grocery store and your friends are watching. **Conclusion (Peroratio)**

Rogerian Example

1. Peanut, you have all of this homework that has to get done. **(Problem)**

2. I know that you really want to beat Luigi's Mansion, and that you are hungry. **(Summary of Opposing Views)**

3. If you had all of your homework done, you could play as much Luigi's Mansion as you want. **(Statement of Understanding)**

4. Right now, I need for you to finish your homework. When your homework is finished, you can have a snack. **(Statement of Your Position)**

5. I am going to put the package of fruit snacks over your place at the table so that you can eat it as soon as you finish. **(Statement of Contexts)**

6. When you finish your homework, you can play Luigi's Mansion until bedtime, and you will have good grades in school. **(Statement of Benefits)**

Toulmin Example

1. Reagan, when was the last time you took a shower?
– Reagan: I don't remember.
– Me: So it has been a while then. **(Data)**

2. You need to take a shower. **(Claim)**

3. You are starting to get stinky. Your hair is looking a little crazy. **(Warrants)**

4. Birds will build a nest in your hair if it isn't clean and brushed. You don't want to be the stinky girl at school. **(Qualifiers)**

5. My Husband yelling from the other room: "She always smells like cinnamon and sugar." – Me: Usually she does, but she is getting a little ripe. **(Rebuttals)**

6. You are a precious girl, but you still have to take a shower. **(Backing)**

About the Author

Dr Julius Nang Kum

Julius Nang Kum was born on the 5th November, 1975 in Zhoa, the Headquarters of Fungom subdivision. He attended Catholic school Mekaf where he obtained his Religious and First school leaving certificates respectively. He pursued his studies in GHS Wum, and graduated with the Ordinary and Advanced level certificates. Admitted into the University of Yaounde 1 in the Department of Linquistics. Kum obtained his Bachelor degree, Master's degree, his DEA and his PhD with distinctions. At the moment, he lectures at the Department of English Modern Letters in the Institution of Higher Teacher Training College of the University of Yaounde 1, Cameroon. He is the author of many books in education, culture and languages.

www.ingramcontent.com/pod-product-compliance
Lightning Source LLC
LaVergne TN
LVHW091634070526
838199LV00044B/1060